Managing the National Curriculum

Some Critical Perspectives

Editors: Tim Brighouse and Bob Moon

Longman

In association with
The British Educational Management and Administration Society

Longman Industry and Public Service Management
Longman Group UK Limited
Westgate House, The High, Harlow, Essex CM20 1YR, UK.
Telephone: (0279) 442601
Fax: (0279) 444501

First Published 1990

Reprinted 1991

A catalogue record for this book is available from the British Library.

ISBN 0-582-05309-9

Printed in Great Britain by Ipswich Book Ltd.

Contents

Preface

This is the second book in the Longman/BEMAS series on the impact of the Education Reform Act 1988. The contributors represent all those who have a part to play in the implementation of the National Curriculum. The range of views they represent mirror the uncertainty and controversy surrounding the changes that are taking place. Indeed, one of the Editors is already leading a move towards the next Education Act which will deal with the issues not addressed by the current legislation! The book is also full of hope however, based on the ability of the education service to reject the dross and build on the opportunities presented to focus attention on pedagogy, to build new and positive partnerships and ensure that the intended beneficiaries of the changes are the children. This book affirms that the National Curriculum strengthens the concept of entitlement, grapples with the problems of continuity and transfer, and focuses on the learning process. Some people welcome the introduction of consumer influence on education, others see the reforms as hasty and muddled. Given the consensus in favour of a National Curriculum the authors conclude that it is here to stay whatever our feelings.

This is a useful source book for everyone involved in the implementation of the National Curriculum. Contributors include head teachers, governors, parents, education officers, teacher educators and (through direct reference to their reactions) the children. One writer observes that the National Curriculum is an attempt to innovate over a very broad front, using people and structures which are still firmly in place 'from the *ancien régime*'. It seems that the problems of educational reform mirror those facing politicians in Eastern Europe. Certainly studies of large scale attempts at school improvement in many countries demonstrate the failure of many large scale reforms. There is hope that this attempt will succeed at least in part. One writer observes that, at least this time, assessment is curriculum led and the tail is not wagging the dog.

The varied contributions to this book reflect the wide range of BEMAS membership which is not confined to paid professional staff but also includes governors, parents, local authority politicians and any individual with a lively interest in education. The first book in the series looked at the local management of schools. This book offers valuable insights to all those whose task it is to deliver the National Curriculum and create the improvements intended by the legislators. Only dedicated and skilled educators can secure improvements. This book will help them to do so with a clear background of information and an incentive to apply a positive and critical eye to all that they are asked to do.

Derek Esp   *January 1990*

Introduction

The National Curriculum represents one of the most distinctive, if not *the* most distinctive features of education reform in the 1980s. Arguably it is the most far-reaching aspect of the Education Reform Act, and likely to endure well into the next century.

During the passage of the legislation, in the latter part of the 1980s, fierce controversies raged. National Curriculum proposals, along with other parts of the 1988 Education Reform Act, were received with considerable hostility by educationalists and the wider community. In the climate of political interventionism that followed closely upon a lengthy period of industrial action, political rhetoric did little to differentiate one part of the legislation from another. Grant-maintained schools, City Technology Colleges, National Curriculum, and testing, merged into one broadswipe against the custom and practice of primary and comprehensive secondary schooling as it had developed in the post-war period.

Some observers saw the legislation as a unified, carefully thought-out policy to inject competition, privatisation and selectivity into the state education system. Others recognised a more complex, even muddled, arrangement of ideas and structures formulated in haste and therefore riddled with inconsistencies.

The National Curriculum, however, whatever the associations made with other aspects of the legislation, is unique in having attracted in principle a measure of cross-party support. The Labour Party was quick to point out similar policy proposals dating back more than a decade. A national framework for the curriculum also appeared to attract a measure of public support. Opinion polls also show a majority in favour of testing – one aspect of the National Curriculum upon which political differences do emerge. The concept of a National Curriculum is likely, therefore, to live on beyond any changes in political control, providing one of the major challenges to school management and organisation for a decade or more.

This volume has been put together as a form of 'source book'

for those with the responsibility and task of implementing National
Curriculum policies. It provides a broad coverage of issues and
contexts, and allows a variety of perspectives and viewpoints to
be explored. Two guiding principles informed the selection of
contributors and the tasks they were set: first the importance of
enlisting teachers, and others, who are actively engaging with the
purposes and form of National Curriculum policies, and secondly,
equally important, the significance of ensuring that this represents
a *critical* engagement with the issues.

The debate about National Curriculum implementation will
extend over many years. The 1988 Act laid down only the barest
of outlines for subjects and assessment policies. Statutory orders
and non-statutory guidance are now appearing on a regular basis,
as are position papers and discussion documents from the new
national councils, LEAs and other organisations. Already it is clear
that a wide diversity of approaches is being adopted. Individual
initiative and distinctive school policies still flourish, as the diversity
of ideas in this volume illustrates.

The National Curriculum has featured prominently in the
burgeoning world of school- and locally-based 'in-service' education.
Teachers, perhaps initially hostile to some of the ideas and
concepts, are displaying great ingenuity in the way, often with
restricted resourcing, that they set about the task of setting up
systems, procedures and consultation mechanisms as well as
National Curriculum schemes of work and teaching plans. Many
of these 'Inset' events have sought to clarify the possible benefits
of a National Curriculum, the growth points for future work, whilst
at the same time pointing out the problems and the pitfalls. In
this introduction a brief summary of the National Curriculum
balance sheet provides a general context for the volume as a whole.

We would suggest five points upon which any school or group
of schools could begin to build a case for the National Curriculum.
First there is the concept of entitlement. In the period after James
Callaghan's Ruskin College speech, an emerging consensus began
to evolve, both at a local level and, for example, through HMI
national conferences and publications, that supported the concept
of a curriculum to which all children, irrespective of their origins
or geographical location could lay claim. It represents, in one form,
the logical extension of the principle of comprehensive primary
and secondary schooling. It would symbolise the end to the highly
divisive curriculum policies, particularly at secondary level, which
have relegated many young people (often including a dis-
proportionate number of girls) to a second class curriculum offering.
Secondly, a national framework does provide a common and public
focus for discourse which opens up curriculum plans and ambitions
to pupils and parents. Along with developments in related fields

such as health, there has been an increasing impetus to give access to the rather closed, even secret, professional practices. This process also has the potential for providing greater clarity about the goals of teaching plans and school policies and, thirdly therefore, it may provide the basis for a renewed interest in pedagogy. There is much to suggest that collective and collaborative planning by teachers yields more imaginative and well thought-out schemes of work. The National Curriculum provides a stimulus and focus for this where the climate for teamwork has been established. The danger, however, probably lies in the period after the National Curriculum has been established, for there will be a temptation to regard the curriculum, then agreed after so much work, as completed, fixed and unchangeable.

Fourthly, there is the issue of transfer and continuity, and here the National Curriculum holds out enormous potential for overcoming the problems faced by many children in transferring between schools in different geographical areas or, the experience of all children, transferring between phases. There is evidence (for example in the later work of the Leicester ORACLE research) that children of all attainment levels regress at the point of transfer, often taking years to catch up in key basic subjects. Transfer can be traumatic, particularly when the environment of learning is markedly different. Curriculum discontinuity exacerbates these divisions. The old but prevalent idea in secondary school of 'starting again' could become a thing of the past if planning, record keeping and liaison across phases is sensitively applied.

Fifthly and finally we see the greatest hope (if also the greatest danger) in the area of expectations and ambitions for what young people can achieve. Although all the evidence points to an across-the-board increase in standards of attainment over the last twenty years, there are still plentiful signs, from the earliest of ages, of under-achievement.

Throughout most of the twentieth century, assumptions have been held about the latent talent available within the population as a whole. The ubiquitous bell curve of ability which, through statistical chicanery, deemed the majority unable to achieve the performance of the few, has, until recently, gone largely unquestioned. Among the public at large, academic talent is seen as a rare quality. This is a peculiarly British phenomenon. The Japanese, despite large class sizes, assume that nearly three-quarters of the population can attain a level that within British schools is expected of less than a fifth. The French have an equally ambitious programme to raise again, nearly three-quarters of the population to *baccalaureat*-level attainment.

If the National Curriculum allows the majority of the population access to the higher levels of performance it will have achieved much – not least in connection with misleading generalisations about ability, and the equally misleading nomenclature of so-called 'high ability', 'average', and 'low ability' children. The second TGAT report put it succinctly in making clear, as Tom Christie points out in his chapter:

> There has been some misunderstanding about the assessment of 'ability', to which our main report may inadvertently have contributed by occasionally using that term. We had intended to confine our proposals to the assessment of 'performance' or 'attainment', and were NOT recommending any attempt to assess separately the problematic notion of underlying 'ability'.

Despite these potential benefits, there are problems with National Curriculum implementation over the coming year. Critical scrutiny by teachers is essential. Most problematic, as it has been since the out-set of National Curriculum deliberations, is the issue of assessment and testing. As we have said, the idea of unlimited access to increasingly improved levels of performance for all children is an attractive one. If, however, the structure of ten levels is allowed to impose ceilings on performance, appropriating some children to levels beyond which it is assumed they will not progress, then all the old problems of stereotypical expectations will extend across the age ranges, with a ferocity never seen before. How the system is managed and used within schools and by teachers will be one of the main determinants of ensuring this is avoided.

There are, of course, technical difficulties of assessments. Teachers will need to be aware of these as the plans unfold. To date, as APU evidence shows, it has been difficult to write assessment tasks that are neutral in terms of gender. However sophisticated the techniques, bias seems to creep in, and usually to the disadvantage of girls. There is also evidence that the more practical the assessment, the more likely the child will display competency. Or do we rely on simpler approaches (much favoured in some political quarters) which reduce performance to a measure of the type of assessment used, rather than the true attainment of the child? There is also the vexed question of aggregation. For assessment to have any meaning, the aggregation of scores should be kept to a minimum. The more detailed the recording, the more we will be able to say something about what the child can do. There is pressure, however, for apparent simplicity. Overall aggregated scores do little for the teaching/learning situation, and give little guidance for future development. They do, however, allow comparisons with other pupils, and therefore rankings of the most invidious and inaccurate kind.

Finally, the emphasis on National Curriculum assessments *could* detract from other means of recording progress and achievement. Schools have a significant level of autonomy beyond the confines of legislated requirements. The extent, regardless of government policies, to which the principles of Records of Achievement (one of the few progressive forces for assessment reform in the 1980s) can be taken up to promote and protect the interests of the child will be an important issue for schools to consider. New assessment systems therefore hold out the possibility of more broadly-based and more accurate means of recording achievement. Equally, however, there are dangers of simplistic and mechanistic approaches which turn the clock back a decade or more on assessment reform. •

The structure and subjects of the National Curriculum also raise difficulties. Significant progress has been made since the publication of the hurriedly assembled, and flawed, DES consultation document of 1987. It is accepted that approaches other than through subjects can fulfil the requirements of the National Curriculum. The subject approach, however, crowds out innovative and imaginative· thinking. This is inevitable, given the way the National Curriculum was established through subject-based working group reports. There are several reasons why this is inadequate. First, it can stifle cross-curricular initiatives, late arriving but now turning out to be one of the most interesting aspects of the National Curriculum. Secondly, it is liable to distort best practice in terms of the integrated primary school day. Thirdly, it makes transfer post-16 into the very different structure of 16–19 education very difficult to establish. Fourthly, it circumscribes assessment at 16 into a rather old fashioned subject-by-subject approach. And fifthly, given the ten subjects in the legislation, it limits for older pupils the range of additional choices and options that have traditionally been available, many of which (second languages for example) are crucial to the new curriculum of the 1990s. In our view, within the legislation there are many different ways to implement imaginative National Curriculum policies. Management of the early years of the National Curriculum (and by this we mean its full implementation – extending over perhaps a decade or more) will be crucial in establishing an exploratory and tentative approach to newly-established structures.

This volume, or source book as we have described it, explores a number of these themes, raising issues for debate and review as management policies emerge. Section One looks at origins and context. To support our view that the most effective curriculum policies are sensitive to an historical and comparative dimension, we have included contributions from Bob Moon and Nick Beattie which explore these themes. Chris Tipple, a participant in the process of establishing the National Curriculum, provides a critical perspective on the national scene as we go into the 1990s. Finally, Tim Brighouse asks 'what does it all mean to the youngsters themselves?' - arguably one of the most neglected but significant questions in the whole process.

In Section Two, three experienced headteachers show how they have grappled with the issues. There is a consistent theme from Michael Duffy, Mark Hewlett and David Winkley, whose initial misgivings are overcome ultimately in their evident optimism and their determination to domesticate and exploit the changes in order to wring every last drop of possible advantage.

In Section Three, which is devoted to certain themes, Sheila Naybour reminds us of the differing expectations and roles of parents. Paradoxically they are simple and complex. Parents are simultaneously consumers, governors, a vested interest group and educators in their own right, but above all, they want what is best for their own children, and will judge any system by that yardstick. Joan Sallis regrets the competitive framework within which the governing bodies created by the 1986 Act will operate. From the vantage point of an Inspector, Mick Molloy points out the implications of the 'exclusive' undertone of the 1988 Act. Just as Sallis sees the Act in conflict with one of its predecessors, namely the 1986 Act, so Molloy sees it sitting unhappily with the thrust of another - the 1981 Act following the Warnock Report. It is scarcely surprising that after a distinguished career training, refreshing and retraining teachers, Len Marsh should find sufficient yarn, as he always has, to assemble a silver lining for teachers to practise their art.

In fact, hope and optimism keep popping up in this volume, nowhere more so than in the offerings of Anne Sofer, faced with the challenging task of providing education in Tower Hamlets; and in the local authority reports as a whole. Christ Saville, now of Avon, wrote his piece when in the metropolitan borough of Wolverhampton, and reflects thoughtfully on the complexities of managing change. The Shropshire duo of Raleigh and Hedger bring us down to earth, both with the cameo of the last national curriculum offering of 1927 in the village of Diddlebury, and with the reality of the everyday habits and experience of today's infants. This section, like much of the book, acts as a snapshot, in this case showing how a sample of LEAs is adapting to a prospective changed role while being saddled, in the meantime, with the task of introducing arrangements which most LEAs opposed during the passage of the Bill through Parliament.

Tom Christie's chapter is intriguing. Here is someone who tracked and chronicled, positively and critically, the Record of Achievement movement, which in many ways is apparently in conflict with the underlying thrust of the Reform Act. After all, those who pioneered Records of Achievement see the best form of competition as relying on the competitive stimulus of one's own previous performance, rather than that of others. Christie moreover wielded a powerfully creative and formative influence as a member of the Task Group on Assessment and Testing, and finally he has led a consortium with a multi-million pound contract to devise a Standard Assessment Task (SAT), which he was reported in the TES as comparable to the search for the Yeti – 'as yet unseen but undoubtedly recognisable on sighting'.

In a sense the chapter stands as proxy for our condition as we attempt to wrestle and ultimately manage the National Curriculum. In a way which is at once persuasive but elusive, Christie examines the argument that the SAT, depending on which model is adopted, could act as a benign aid to teacher moderation. He examines the underlying concerns of many of the other contributors, namely the arrangements for testing, and the impact in particular of trying at the same time to be diagnostic, formative, summative, informative and evaluative. Readers will have to judge for themselves whether Christie manages to square the circle.

However that may be, we hope the book will stand as a source book. People will be able to see how those involved at an important period in the evolution of the English and Welsh education system started to tackle the task of making the best arrangements for children to acquire relevant information and knowledge, develop skills and attitudes, and handle with increasing confidence, diverse concepts and ideas – which, whether nationally prescribed or not, is the rationale of any curriculum.

Bob Moon and Tim Brighouse

Section One: Context and origins

1 The National Curriculum: Origins and context

Bob Moon, Professor of Education, Open University.

The Secretary of State's policies for the range and pattern of the 5 to 16 curriculum will not lead to national syllabuses. Diversity at local education authority and school level is healthy, accords well with the English and Welsh tradition of school education, and makes for liveliness and innovation.[1]

The Government has announced its intention to legislate for a national foundation curriculum for pupils of compulsory school age in England and Wales. . . Within the secular national curriculum, the Government intends to establish essential foundation subjects – maths, English, science, foreign language, history, geography, technology in its various aspects, music, art and physical education . . . the government wishes to establish programmes of study for the subjects, describing the essential content which needs to be covered to enable pupils to reach or surpass the attainment targets.[2]

The English, and the Welsh, now have a National Curriculum. In July 1988 just a year after the publication of a consultation document the Education Reform Bill received Royal Assent and passed onto the statute books. The curriculum clauses survived the Commons committee stages and vigorous, early morning attacks in the House of Lords, to pass unaltered into legislation. The measures represent a remarkable political intervention to change the post-war consensus on curriculum control.

How did a centrally-prescribed National Curriculum come to

11

be established and, moreover, how can the *volte-face* in policy
represented in the change from Better Schools to Baker Bill be
explained? The answer lies partly in the evolution of some recurring,
even predictable, curriculum policies, but arguably more
significantly in the political opportunism of those who achieved
positions of power and influence prior to and shortly after the
1987 Election. This chapter, therefore, will examine these events
and speculate on how the system worked to produce what a few
years ago would have been unthinkable policies. Curriculum
management, to be fully effective, requires a broad understanding
of the policy context within which national policies have evolved.
This is essential if the *critical engagement* with implementation
discussed in the introduction is to be promoted across the school
or local community. It will be equally important in communicating
and debating the issues with parents and others with a legitimate
interest in the working out of the new programmes. Firstly,
however, what form do the measures take?

Ten subjects make up the National Curriculum; English[3],
mathematics and science, defined as *core foundation* subjects,
alongside seven further *foundation* subjects: art, geography,
history, modern languages (11–16 only), music, physical education
and technology[4]. The Secretary of State is required by the 1988
Education Reform Act to establish programmes of study and define
attainment targets for each of the subjects. The attainment targets
provide the basis for national and school reported assessments
at the ages of seven, eleven, fourteen and sixteen.

This simply-stated formulation summarises the English and Welsh
National Curriculum. The Act states that all schools must provide
a balanced and broadly based curriculum which

> promotes the spiritual, moral, cultural, mental and physical development
> of pupils at school and the society
>
> prepares pupils for the opportunities, responsibilities and experiences
> of adult life.

Three new councils, a National Curriculum Council (NCC), a
Curriculum Council for Wales (CCW) and a School Examinations
and Assessment Council (SEAC) are established to provide advice
to government on the implementation of the reforms and to oversee
associated research and development activities.

The Education Reform Act contains little detail on curriculum,
a point not missed in Parliamentary debate, with Lord Grimmond
railing against legislation only being comprehensible when read with
a document that was not part of it[5] and Lord Kilmarnock asking
for some idea of the remit given to each of the subject area working
parties[6] before making decisions about the Bill. These working
parties represent a further innovative feature of the times. The

Secretary of State has set up the National Curriculum through subject working parties independent of the New Councils and reporting direct to government. The reports are published alongside a preliminary ministerial response. The National Curriculum Council then consults on the document and in turn publishes a report. At that point the Secretary of State prepares draft statutory orders and after a brief further phase for comment these are laid before Parliament.

A National Curriculum: the longer view

In many ways the subject basis of National Curriculum is familiar, with origins stretching back at least to the nineteenth century. The historical line is traceable and well documented in general curriculum histories. The Newcastle Report of 1861, for example, led to the 1862 Revised Code of Robert Lowe and a stress on basic subjects, age-related programmes of study, and the notorious 'payments by results' system for teachers. Three years later the Clarendon Commission investigated nine leading public schools and advocated, in addition to the central study of classics, the introduction into the curriculum of mathematics, modern languages and natural sciences. The Commission even made an attempt to assess standards, and proposed examining fifth form boys. The replies from headteachers were terse and to the point[7]:

> Your letter appears to be so seriously objectionable that I must beg to decline to entertain the proposal. The Dean of Westminster concurs with me.

> (Reverend Charles R. Scott, Westminster)

> Objectionable both in principle and detail.

> (Dr. Elwyn, Charterhouse)

More precise objections came from Moberley of Winchester:

> We should be deeply and unnecessarily wounded by having it put on record that we had passed a bad one.

and Balsham of Eton:

> This interference with the authority of the headmaster is calculated to cause evil.

In 1868 the Taunton Commission, after looking at 800 endowed grammar schools, recommended three types of school, serving three classes of society, with leaving ages of 18, 16 and 14. Each school would have a distinctive curriculum. The emphasis of the first grade school would be classics and preparation for university. In grade 2 the requirements of the army, business and the professions required a stronger emphasis on practical rather than abstract activities, whilst the sons of artisans in Grade 3 schools had a less precisely prescribed curriculum, although the basics were essential.

The latter part of the nineteenth century, and the period of this century up to the Second World War, abounds with evidence of curriculum regulations. The Revised Code went through many versions, with Gladstone's fourth administration providing a significantly liberalising influence. The 1904 Regulations for Secondary Schools included detailed syllabuses specifying the amount of time to be allocated to each subject. A senior civil servant, Robert Morant, after a meteoric rise via the Court of Siam and a private secretarial position to Permanent Secretary of the Board of Education in just eight years, drafted the regulations. A workaholic ('the day is never long enough – I must soak all the time in varied educational juices') he is supposed to have recorded in his diary a liking for both centralised administration and for the widespread implementation in secondary schools of the classical curriculum model characteristic of the fee-paying public schools. Morant's political and bureaucratic manoeuvres succeeded on both counts, as well as markedly increasing the powers of Permanent Secretary in the revamped Board of Education. The table below of the subject regulations for 1904 and 1935 show how successful he was and how lasting the early model was to be.

1904	*1935*
English language	English language
English literature	England literature
One language*	One language
Geography	Geography
History	History
Mathematics	Mathematics
Science	Science
Drawing	Drawing
Due provision for manual work and physical exercises	Physical exercises and organised games
(Housewifery in girls' schools)	Singing
	[Manual instruction for boys, dramatic subjects for girls]

* When two languages other than English are taken, and Latin is not one of them, the 'Board' will be required to be satisfied that the omission of Latin is for the advantage of the school.

The 1935 regulations remained in force until the Butler 1944 Education Act. The elementary codes disappeared rather earlier, to be replaced by the Board of Education Blue Book, a *Handbook of Suggestions*, which went through a number of editions again until 1944.

The 1988 specification therefore looked remarkably similar to those of 1935, although planned to cover the whole rather than secondary years of compulsory schooling. What had happened in between? As far as secondary schools were concerned the pattern remained remarkably consistent. Survey after survey, culminating in the 1979 HMI Secondary School Survey, showed how lasting Morant's model was. The subjects of the National Curriculum in 1988 were the subjects of the secondary curriculum in each of the four preceding decades. The grammar school model of the 1940s was copied by the secondary moderns of the 1950s and the newly established comprehensives of the 1960s and 1970s. Some brave attempts to provide otherwise, following the Newsom Report in 1963 on the average and below average attaining child, and the Raising of the School Leaving Age (ROSLA) programme in 1972 were soon reformulated in a subject structure. Even the more recent and prestigious Technical and Vocational Educational Initiative (TVEI), a national project promoting curriculum reform, was almost universally structured within a nine or ten subject pattern.

In primary schooling the picture was more varied. The abolition of the eleven plus examination helped generate a new approach to curriculum organisation. Strong advocates for a more child-centred approach to teaching, such as Alec Clegg in the West Riding of Yorkshire and Edith Moorhouse in Oxfordshire, received wide publicity for the primary school reforms in their local authorities. The Plowden Report, published in 1967, gave warm approval to these new directions, and for a few years English primary schools were inundated with international visitors. More recent evidence, however, suggests that the spread of these ideas was limited. An unpublished survey commissioned for HMI in 1988 showed that in the average primary classroom, over half the week was devoted to studying basic mathematics and English.

The school system therefore resolutely reflected subject traditions across more than a century of compulsory schooling. Government interest in the curriculum waned for only a few brief years following the 1944 Education Act, and up to the point in 1960 when David Eccles made his famous reference to the secret garden of the curriculum. There were then three attempts to provide national institutional structures for the curriculum. A Curriculum Study Group set up by Eccles in 1962 was soon replaced, in 1964, by the Schools Council. The rise, and fall, of this organisation as well as the way it tackled curriculum development has received considerable attention.[8] As an alternative focus of curriculum control, relationships with the DES were frequently strained. The influence of the local education authorities and the teacher unions, represented on the Council as of right, was a source of irritation to some DES officials and the politicians who came to power following the Conservative Party 1979 Election victory. Despite surviving a committee of enquiry chaired by the Principal of an Oxford college, the Council was closed down by Sir Keith Joseph and replaced by two separate organisations, one responsible for secondary examinations, the Secondary Examinations Council (SEC), and a Schools Curriculum Development Committee (SCDC) with the governing bodies of both appointed directly by the Secretary of State.

Red Book to Red Book – A curriculum consensus shattered

The first indication of the form the National Curriculum would take was published within a few months of the 1987 Conservative Election victory. The red consultation document, *The National Curriculum 5–16*, was greeted with forceful criticism. Although the time-scale for consultation was short, two months including the summer holiday period, thousands of responses were received. Comment ranged from the right-wing Institute of Economic Affairs (IEA) arguing that the market, not government, should determine curriculum, to the National Union of Teachers' fear of uniformity and conformity. The tone of the document was strident, and made for more interesting reading than many government publications. A model curriculum was proposed for the secondary school in subject terms. There was no discussion of how the subject curriculum would apply to primary schools. The need for a ten subject school curriculum was boldly asserted without qualification and without reference to the plethora of government and inspectorial publications that had appeared in the decade following James Callaghan's Ruskin College Speech of 1976. Ruskin is referred to in paragraph 4 of the consultation document:

> Since Sir James Callaghan's speech as Prime Minister at Ruskin College in 1976, successive Secretaries of State have aimed to achieve agreement with their partners in the education service on policies for the school curriculum . . .

This pointed political reference, implying a measure of cross party support and concern, is followed by a critical passage:

> . . . progress has been variable, uncertain and often slow. Improvements

have been made, some standards of attainment have risen. But some improvement is not enough . . . the government now wishes to move ahead at a faster pace . . ..

It is interesting to look back to 1976 and trace the curriculum events that led to a National Curriculum proposal. In the mid-1970s the signs of a breakdown in the post-war educational cohabitation between government, local authorities and to a lesser extent the teachers' unions was beginning to show. Political disillusion with the attempts at curriculum reform had surfaced in a confidential DES document prior to Callaghan's Ruskin speech. The widely leaked document (the Yellow Book) caused considerable consternation amongst educationalists. Callaghan commented in the speech on the interest aroused:

> There have been one or two ripples of interest in the educational world in anticipation of this visit. I hope the publicity will do Ruskin some good and I don't think it will do the world of education any harm. I must thank all those who have inundated me with advice: some helpful and others telling me less politely to keep off the grass . . .. It is almost as though some people would wish that the subject matter and purpose of education should not have public attention focused on it nor that profane hands should be allowed to touch it.

and then proceeded, after a brief reference to the dedication of the teaching profession, to comment on:

> the unease felt by parents and others about the new informal methods of teaching . . . the strong case for the so-called 'core curriculum' of basic knowledge . . . the use of resources in order to maintain a proper national standard of performance and the need to improve relations between industry and education.

The outcome from Ruskin was a series of regional meetings (the Great Debate), usually chaired by the new Secretary of State for Education Shirley Williams, and to which a wide range of groups, including industrialists, were invited to send representatives. For a short while the DES was clearly on the offensive in orchestrating national concerns; in policy terms, however, there was little outcome. The Labour government holding power for much of the time, with a small group of Liberals, found the local authority lobby powerful in opposing central government intervention. Attempts to distribute relatively small grants for the in-service education of teachers, for example, were rebuffed and in many LEAs the money was allocated to other, often non-educational, purposes. Any political momentum gained was in any case dissipated by the loss of power in the 1979 election. Ruskin did, however, represent a watershed in the post war history of curriculum reform, and for two reasons. Firstly it brought into the open the ambitions of some DES permanent officials to increase central control over curriculum. In terms of Whitehall politics it heralded a decade of activity that many may see as one of the most significant forces in establishing a national and central curriculum. Secondly Ruskin precipitated a parallel debate amongst prominent interest groups about the way the school curriculum should be structured. Whilst the battles for control remained unresolved, a remarkable degree of unanimity began to emerge on this issue.

The consensus developed around the idea of curriculum entitlement expressed in terms of areas of curriculum experience. The influence of philosophers of education such as Paul Hirst at the London Institute and then Cambridge University, and John White also at the London Institute, were openly acknowledged. HMI were first in the field, publishing in 1977 what became known as the Red Book.

The discussion document focused on the Curriculum 11–16. After making clear that the papers included were not advocating a centrally controlled or directed curriculum, they go on to argue for a common curriculum constructed around eight areas of experience, listed they say in alphabetical order to make clear that none should be weighted more highly than the other:

- the aesthetic and creative
- the ethical
- the linguistic
- the mathematical
- the physical
- the scientific
- the social and political
- the spiritual

This model was soon taken up through the DES documents and, whilst it was still in existence, the publications of the Schools Council, and on the educational conference circuit. Rumours therefore of DES intervention in the late 1970s and early 1980s were associated in most people's minds with a framework based on areas of experience providing coherence and balance across the curriculum. Such a framework, it was assumed, would be interpreted according to school and local circumstances, and the publication of *Better Schools*, quoted in the introduction to this chapter, gave no reason to doubt otherwise.

At first sight therefore the presentation of a model curriculum, complete with possible percentage allocations of time, in the red 1987 consultation was in stark contrast to HMI's Red Book of a decade earlier. In 1977 HMI had asserted that curriculum construction through subjects was only acceptable when everyone was clear what was to be achieved through them (p 6). The disappearance of 'areas of experience' from curriculum debate is one of the significant features of the 1987 consultation document and the debates that preceded and followed publication.

Pressure group politics 1986-7

Behind this change in curriculum policy was a radical shift in the balance of power between government and the interest groups that had been so influential in building educational policy in the post war period. It is now becoming clear that in the months immediately before and after the 1987 general election, a small group of prime ministerial advisors, including or at least influenced by the pamphleteers and polemicists of numerous right-wing 'think tanks', exerted increasing pressure on the Prime Minister. The ideas formulated, first for the Conservative Party Election Manifesto and then the consultation document, bypassed Her Majesty's Inspectorate, the Association of County Councils, the Association of Metropolitan Authorities, the teachers' unions, the Society of Education Officers, and also the Schools Curriculum Development Committee (SCDC) and Secondary Examinations Council (SEC).

Government ministers and DES officials were well aware that none of these groups could subscribe to the form and style of the 1987 Red Book proposals. It was in line with government policy to marginalise the teachers' views and those of the local authorities, but few would have predicted the ruthless exclusion of HMI or SCDC and SEC from policy formulation. This, however, represented pressure group politics of a most active form, sustained over a significant period of time.

The way the National Curriculum finally came to occupy an important niche in the Education Reform Act, and the form in which it was expressed, can be seen to date back to Sir Keith Joseph's final years in office. A more precise understanding of what happened will have to await the publication of personal diaries and testimonies of the sort that are now providing further information on the Ruskin speech. At this stage, however, it appears that there was impatience and disillusion within the Tory party about policy making in the Joseph era. Despite some radical ideas (set out, for example, in his 1982 speech to the North of England Conference) he had prevaricated over many decisions, and in his clumsy handling of the teachers' industrial dispute between 1984 and 1986 he had failed to show the clear and firm resolve expected of ministers in a Thatcher government. There may also have been something of a suspicion that despite the polemic and rhetoric of the times, he had earnt a grudging respect from some parts of the educational establishment. The introduction of the common 16+ GCSE examination was one major source of concern in some quarters. Rumours of his departure circulated for a long period, and the Prime Minister herself was said to be showing an interest in education, particularly as her increasing impatience with local authority levels of expenditure, linked often to policies at variance with those of the government, was most starkly illustrated within the education service. It should also be noted that her own ministerial career, when she presided in 1970–74 over a record number of grammar school closures, was seen as hardly successful against the criteria of Thatcherism in the 1980s. This was a new opportunity to make amends.

The arguments put forward to and by her advisors were opportune and congruent with the way policy was being developed towards other parts of the Welfare State, most notably the Health Service. The polemicist of the New Right had waged a well-publicised campaign for a return to what they saw as traditional values. A number had been leading contributors to the late 1960s Black Papers, an earlier polemic against progressive and egalitarian ideas, and the prospect of a third Thatcher victory and active Prime Ministerial interest offered a unique opportunity to influence policy.

It is now widely accepted that regular informal contact was maintained between the Prime Minister's office and leading members from pressure groups such as the Centre for Policy Studies and the Hillgate Group. In formulating the election manifesto and determining the content and style of the consultation document, this influence was highly significant. A comparison between the Hillgate Group's 1986 pamphlet 'Whose Schools' and the content of the Education Reform Act shows just how significant. In their ideas Margaret Thatcher had detected a populist appeal, in public speeches she was quick to reassert the need for traditional approaches, whilst ridiculing certain attempts to combat some of the enduring curriculum problems. In her address to the 1987 Conservative Party Conference she talked of 'children who need to be able to count and multiply learning anti-racist mathematics – whatever that might be . . .', and promised her audience that the National Curriculum would comprise ' . . . reading, writing, spelling, grammar, arithmetic, basic science and technology.'

The consultation document therefore reasserts the primacy of subjects. Areas of experience smacked of the educational establishment, it allowed flexibility and local interpretation and it hardly made for a rousing address to the party conference. The consensus that had been building around the framework was ignored in the aftermath of a sweeping electoral victory. The symbolic importance of subjects overode all other considerations.

The new curriculum – nationalism, managerialism or the market place?

The National Curriculum in the form presented surprised and offended many in the educational world. It appeared to combine the continental traditions of subject prescription and the North American predilection for testing to create a particularly powerful, and for many threatening, proposal. The level of hostility was fuelled by the scarcity of information, fears about the way the statutory orders would be produced (would the working parties be given over to Hillgate?) and rumours about the form the testing would take. It was also apparent that the measures were to be vigorously pushed through, with compromise in the climate of the late 1980s interpreted as weakness. An ambitious Secretary of State had staked his political future on the passage of the Bill.

It is difficult, close to events, to clarify the way influence was exerted and motivation tapped in establishing such a major reform of curriculum policy. A number of themes, however, in the evolution of policy generally appear to be reflected in ERA and the National Curriculum clauses. A brief review suggests that the events of 1987–8 were less surprising than reactions at the time suggested. Three processes in particular appear to have fused around the National Curriculum: a long term staking-out of bureaucratic control; the drive for efficiency and accountability that had become the characteristic of government attempts to reduce public expenditure; and finally a formulation of policy that brought together competing interests among pressure groups on the right.

John Quicke[9] has explored this final point in an interesting analysis of the politics and ideas of the 'New Right' towards education over the last decade. He points to the differences between neo-conservatives such as Roger Scruton, a member of the Hillgate Group, and neo-liberals such as Stuart Sexton, working within the Institute of Economic Affairs. Neo-conservatives, he suggests, advocate strong government and a hierarchical and disciplined view of society in which a concept of the national is central. Neo-liberals on the other hand emphasise individual freedom of choice through the free workings of the market. In terms of curriculum therefore, the neo-conservatives appeared to have been the most influential. A central, authoritarian prescription seems incompatible with a principle that permits the market (parents) to determine which form of curriculum prospers. The Institute of Economic Affairs in replying to the red consultation paper was clear:

> The most effective national curriculum is that set by the market, by the consumers of the education service. This will be far more responsive to children's needs and society's demands than any centrally imposed curriculum, no matter how well meant. Attempts by Government and

by Parliament to impose a curriculum, no matter how 'generally agreed' they think it to be, are a poor second best in terms of quality, flexibility and responsiveness to needs than allowing the market to decide and setting the system free to respond to the overwhelming demand for higher standards. The Government must trust market forces rather than some committee of the great and good.

And the Institute sees the debate over a government-imposed national curriculum as detracting attention away from what really matters, namely the proposals to devolve management to schools. In establishing the curriculum proposals, these two groups appear to have been in tension. Margaret Thatcher is reported as wavering over the degree of prescription required for the National Curriculum, reaching the view at one stage that English, mathematics and science should comprise the limits of regulation. Kenneth Baker, Secretary of State, is rumoured to have convinced her of the need for more widespread control. If Baker[10] did seek to convince in this way he may have exploited the argument of the neo-conservatives that, uncontrolled, the curriculum serves as a vehicle for the politically motivated, illiberal and indoctrinating tendencies of the left. This is a persistent theme running through both the pamphlets (such as the Hillgate Group's determined attacks on any curriculum activity described as studies – peace studies, multicultural studies) and speeches made by Margaret Thatcher and other ministers in the pre-election period.

For Quicke, therefore, the strategy of the neo-conservatives was to highlight those elements they had in common with all forms of liberal education, and to contrast the values they jointly espoused with those underpinning the radical left-of-centre ideologies said to be dominant in educational bureaucracies, particularly at the local level. Despite the failure to convince market purists at the IEA, the approach was influential with the Prime Minister and with a minister keen to enlarge the role and responsibilities of the DES.

Hargreaves and Reynolds,[11] from a position on the left explicitly opposed to government reforms, provide a further perspective on the apparently contradictory policies of regulation and choice operating within the Act. They see nothing accidental in this juxtaposition, with centralisation and privatisation representing the co-ordinated arms of educational policy making. Centralisation of curriculum and assessment forces competitiveness around the values chosen by government. Ideological control is exerted, because to open up the next generation to socialisation by the free run of market forces runs social and political risks that no government could contemplate, particularly at a time of economic crisis and social uncertainty. For the neo-conservatives, therefore, the form and style of the National Curriculum is paramount and helps explain their interest in the membership of the new national councils and their detailed scrutiny of ministerial and DES statements. It will be interesting to see how this surveillance can be sustained in the implementation of the National Curriculum procedure.

A second influence on policy is the quest for measures that create accountability and efficiency within the education service. From this perspective the National Curriculum 'tidies up' the ground upon which cost and personnel decisions can be made, and testing provides a basis for valid comparative judgements about efficiency of schools and classes. Donald Naismith, formerly Director of Education for Croydon, is one of the few Education Officers to have gained the respect of groups such as Hillgate. He is unequivocal in seeing managerialism and efficiency as at the core of the proposals:

> The way the education service was organised after the war attached greater importance to the separation and distribution of powers and responsibilities between central and local government and schools than to bringing them together in ways which established a direct managerial link between investment in its widest sense and performance. The results were stationary or falling standards and higher costs. By reintroducing objective standards and giving schools and colleges the means to attain them the Government believes it can combine higher standards with better management of resources, particularly as a school's results will be recorded and published in uniform ways, enabling comparisons to be made between schools and local authorities not only in terms of effectiveness but, more important, efficiency, the degree of success with which a school or local authority converts what goes into it and what comes out. We are going to hear a lot about performance indicators in the future.[15]

It is through this perspective that the DES's preference for an objectives-led curriculum, rather than HMI's 'areas of experience', becomes clear. HMI appear to have resisted many aspects of the pressure for comprehensive testing and assessment based on objectives. They would have been aware of the unresolved technical problems and the threat posed to time-honoured styles and inspection. There would also have been concern about a change in the working relationships with teachers and schools.

The curriculum clauses of ERA show, however, the DES in the ascendancy, a quite significant fight-back after years enduring Mrs Thatcher's reported suspicions of obstructionism and inaction, and the more recent activities of Lord Young who, at the Department of Industry and Employment, had launched through the Manpower Services Commission a significant challenge to DES authority over the education service. TVEI, one of the most prestigous of MSC projects, received only the briefest of mentions in the consultative process and represent another group excluded from the process of formulating policy in this period.[12] The ambitions of bureaucrats can develop a momentum of their own. Managerialism promotes bureaucratic activity and the DES prospered, not the least in new departmental structures and an expanded staffing.

The form in which the National Curriculum was laid down represented a victory therefore for those on the right who had seized the political agenda for reform. It also represented a significant increase in the power and importance of the DES and it provided a yardstick against which new and more demanding forms of accountability could be introduced.

A National Curriculum in the 1990s

This chapter has explored the establishment of a National Curriculum, and in particular the political events surrounding the 1987 election. The story insofar as it has been revealed illustrates the potency of pressure group politics if the circumstances are propitious and the players well orchestrated. It is yet more evidence of the shortcomings of understanding educational systems through an analysis of the formal ways in which they are structured. England and Wales, traditionally classified a decentralised system, experienced in this period a process of policy formulation and change of a highly centralised character. In terms of curriculum this new approach seems likely to endure Labour opposition which, whilst opposed to the range of controls and certain forms of testing, accepts the concepts of a nationally prescribed curriculum[13]. What becomes significant therefore is the way that central control operates and the extent to which the influence of those such as the Hillgate Group are sustained. Within a year of the passing of the Act there are signs that the crusading zeal of the polemicists is being eroded through the implementation process. In a number of critical areas the traditionalist model is under pressure. The following three examples may provide touchstones for observing whether some political intentions for a National Curriculum will be realised in practice.

(a) In a number of documents, for example the DES's own 'From Policy to Practice', there is a shift away from stressing the importance of subjects. The 1989 (as opposed to 1988) version raises the Statements of Attainment to pre-eminence. How these are taught, it is made clear, is for schools to decide. Approaches therefore that have been attacked from the right, the primary integrated day, or modular approaches to the curriculum, are seen as compatible with the National Curriculum. One draft of 'from Policy to Practice' even allowed

HMI's listing of 'areas of experience' in an appendix (it was removed in the published version). By focusing on Statements of Attainment rather than subject, a wide variety of curriculum models becomes admissible. It will be interesting to see how far this goes without challenge.

(b) The testing and assessment programme will also be a critical measure of how successful the polemicists of the right will be. Rhodes Boyson has already warned[14]:

> unless we get more testing of facts leaned by heart, then it's all going to be phoney. The educational establishment will have won again and it will be a con trick.

The Task Group on Assessment and Testing report (TGAT) and the brief given to the different consortia preparing standard assessment tasks (SATs) has given considerable emphasis to the formative as well as the summative aspects of assessment. There are inevitably some contradictions between these principles in the different proposals being considered. The importance of the holistic approach to assessment and curriculum, however, appears to command widespread acceptance particularly in the way school based policies for assessment and record keeping are evolving.

(c) Contrary to expectations, the subject working parties so far established have not been packed by those on the right who seemed so influential in 1986 and 1987. The first signs are that policies that would have been clearly associated with the educational establishment in that period are now seeing the light of day through the National Curriculum. The strong advocacy for balanced science as opposed to the traditionalist physics, chemistry and biology, and the reception of the Cox Report, chaired by a former Black Paper contributor, provide two examples, but the reports from further groups in design and technology and history will make clear the extent to which interest groups such as HMI and the subject associations have re-established influence.

The post-war educational consensus may have been broken in formal and organisational terms. This is a significant move setting in motion a host of new relationships and defining the alliances required to question and reformulate policy in totally new ways. Arthur Wise in his study of federal intervention in the educational system of the USA in the 1970s (under the title 'Legislated Learning') came to the conclusion that different parts of the system were nowhere near as closely integrated as the policy makers had anticipated. Local school boards as well as individual schools and teachers rarely responded in the way hoped for. The National Curriculum legislation established in 1988 may have constituted a political victory for those wanting to exert traditionalist values within a differentiated institutional structure. The legislation, however, left much to the ongoing process of both policy formulation and implementation, inevitably drawing back in the interest groups excluded from the limited statements of policy within the Act. The way these groups are reasserting alternative ideas about curriculum purposes and structure suggests that the victory won in establishing a National Curriculum may have to be qualified over time as another story unfolds, not least in the myriad ways in which individual schools set about managing the curriculum process.

References

1   *Better Schools: a summary*, March 1985, p 4.
2   *The National Curriculum 5-16, a consultation document*, July 1987, p 35.
3   In Wales, Welsh can be an additional core or foundation subject.
4   Religious education is also compulsory, but defined by statutory requirements unique to that subject.
5   *Hansard*, House of Lords, May 1988, p 711.
6   Ibid, p 531.
7   Quoted in Sherwood, P (1977), 'Evaluating the English Experience', in Houts, P L (ed) *The Myth of Measurability*, (New York, Hart Publishing Co).
8   See for example Plaskow, M (1985), *The Life and Death of the Schools Council*, (Lewes, Falmer Press).
9   'The 'New Right' and Education', *British Journal of Educational Studies*, February 1988.
10 The rather obscure terminological distinction between core foundation and foundation subjects is said to date from this debate.
11 In *Education Policy: Controversies and Critiques* (1989), (Lewes, Falmer Press).
12 TVEI, or education relevant to working life, was strongly criticised by some traditional neo-conservative writers.
13 See the Labour Party policy review of 1989.
14 *The Sunday Times*, 11 December 1988.
15 Unpublished paper, A.S.C. Conference, Gateshead, April 1988.

2 The wider context: Are curricula manageable?

Nicholas Beattie, Reader, University of Liverpool

Her Majesty's Inspectorate recently published a study of the Danish *folkeskole*[1], one of a series highlighting various aspects of foreign education systems believed to be relevant to British practice[2]. This one focuses particularly on 'the development and implementation of curriculum and assessment policies at national, municipal and school levels and on the degree of professional, parental, pupil and community involvement in decision-making about education'[3]. 'Interesting parallels and differences emerge from the analysis', states the preface, 'and may be of value to those involved in implementing the various elements of the Education Reform Act'.

Encouraged by these words, persons attempting to 'manage the curriculum' within the framework of the Education Reform Act will turn to the body of the text. Headteachers will soon discover that, among their Danish counterparts, 'some see themselves as curriculum leaders, others do not'[4]. Danish schools work to centrally determined guidelines. Locally elected municipalities may modify those guidelines, but 'The vast majority of the municipalities adopt the Ministry guidelines for all or almost all subjects'[5]. Could this be a sign that the Ministry's power is all-pervasive? Not so apparently:

These aims and guidelines were not usually used as working documents in the schools. Their influence was far more diffuse and elusive; as one teacher put it, 'we keep them in the backs of our minds'[6].

Nor does the low profile of central documentation seem to be balanced by particularly energetic assessment procedures at school level:

> [Teachers'] reluctance to categorise children, especially at younger ages, was reflected, in the schools visited, by the low priority given to marking written work, the paucity of written records and the lack of diagnostic testing of ordinary pupils to aid the development of reading and number programmes to meet individual needs[7].

It is perhaps not surprising that when older pupils come to sit their leaving examinations, they generally view the prospect of the examinations without much apprehension; this may be because most decisions about their future are taken on the recommendation of their teachers rather than directly on the basis of examination results[8].

What exactly are 'those involved in implementing the various elements of the Education Reform Act' supposed to make of all this? The 'diffuseness' and 'elusiveness' of central control, the relaxed and constructive atmosphere, the absence of stress and conflict described by HMIs – all these appear to contradict the expectations and experience of the average 'curriculum manager' in England and Wales to the point where he or she must ask: 'Can I learn anything at all either from Denmark or from an international perspective?' Is the HMIs' hope that their study 'may be of value' purely pious? Or is the main value of observing a centralised curriculum in action *reassurance*? Was Denmark chosen specifically to soothe British fears? There are, after all, several senses in which a brief look at the Danish system may bring comfort to a beleaguered 'curriculum manager' in Britain in the early 1990s. Firstly, the system works, and apparently in a generally smooth and humane way. So do most systems, most of the time. If the angle of vision is the classroom, then the basic transaction between teacher and taught produces an inescapable similarity. Introducing an interesting collection of studies of classrooms in different countries, Frankish comments; 'Different as the classrooms described in this issue may appear, it is still surprising that they are so alike'[9]. Administrative and ideological superstructures assume more 'manageable' proportions if they can be seen as subordinate to a more or less universal classroom reality. Osborn notes, for example, of the American classroom:

> . . . while it is a fact that presently desks are usually moveable, thereby permitting various kinds of grouping arrangements, this flexibility is not often required by what actually goes on in the classroom. This

points to a significant disharmony between the rhetoric of schooling and the practice. While the United States is not altogether unique in this regard, it should be noted that the rhetoric of the classroom tends to be 'progressive and liberal' while the practice tends to remain 'traditional and conservative'[10].

Classroom infrastructure tends to appear similar in different societies; what is most various is the bureaucratic superstructure, which attempts to translate rhetoric into regulations and routine procedures for monitoring and controlling what goes on in the classrooms. Yet at this 'superstructural' level too differences may be eroded by classroom realities. As Osborn notes in relation to the USA, 'Individual schools, most often elementary, and determined teachers in the privacy of their own classrooms manage to violate numerous regulations and traditions'[11]. In the highly centralised French system, Puren has recently documented how clear, repeated and detailed instructions on modern language teaching methods have been consistently flouted by teachers over the space of a century[12]. The centrality of such human adjustments and the variability between classrooms even in systems which are ostensibly highly uniform[13] provide a salutary reminder that 'curriculum management' cannot realistically be too ambitious. Problems which loom very large to 'managers' may seem much less important to the 'managed'.

There is another sense in which reading about Denmark, or any other Western Europe system, may be reassuring to British teachers. The National Curriculum in particular brings us into line with our EC partners. 'Many Europeans', writes McLean[14] 'see the 1988 Act as a move towards harmonisation'. For the first time a British government has established a mechanism enabling it to determine the content and purposes of education along broadly similar lines to other Western European democracies. While this instrument is in a way value-neutral and may be used for ends of which different commentators may approve or disapprove, it may turn out to be – is indeed intended to be – a powerful force for overdue change, increased coherence and strengthened accountability. The examples of Denmark or of the other members of the Community may in some respects be encouraging, in others not; but certainly to look into classrooms beyond the Channel, however superficially, is to be reminded that written curricula and centralised administrations do not have to be unwieldy, dictatorial or reactionary. They may indeed be believed by those who operate them to be essentially progressive in character.

A third type of comfort to be drawn from an apparently stable system like Denmark's lies in the reminder of how many of the current fears of British 'curriculum managers' are, precisely, 'current': the transitory outcome of attempting too much too fast, rather than an intrinsic feature of centrally-defined curricula. The ERA represents a major shift of national direction on several fronts: it necessarily runs counter in the short term to structures, procedures and habits of mind which are deeply ingrained. France and Italy have had respectively about two centuries and one to erect and modify their national systems. Politicians, administrators, teachers and parents in those countries know how information moves round the system from centre to periphery and vice versa, and who is responsible for what. Their associations and less formal networks are adjusted to centralisation because that is what they have grown up with. We, by contrast, are at present at the most painful phase of a radical readjustment. Competing bureaucracies carve up a unitary field (DES, NCC, SEAC). Information is still hard to track down and reaches the classroom level in a fragmented and patchy way. Much of the pain centres upon the LEA; a structure which was pivotal and which is rapidly and rather messily ceasing to be so. But we may expect in the long run to become as comfortable in the new clothes as we were in the old. Teachers will wonder how they got on without detailed 'programmes of study', 'Standard Assessment Tasks', etc, and 'curriculum managers', like Danish heads, will perhaps be able to take a more relaxed line on managing the curriculum: 'Some see themselves as curriculum leaders, others do not'. Those who do not can afford to take that line, presumably, because over time the system has built up a stock of people and procedures which allow it to evolve almost under its own momentum.

One finds reassurance in foreign examples if one looks for it: but ought we not to be looking more for stimulus? And for that, we shall need to look rather deeper. For example, in assessing the apparent good order of the Danish *folkeskole* we shall need to consider how much of it flows in fact from deep-rooted cultural factors – and how little those factors are replicated in our own society. A first look at foreign practice may reassure by dispelling myths: a second look may be less encouraging.

Let us turn again to the HMI's comments on Denmark. After describing an examination which is taken at the end of schooling (compulsory schooling ends at 16, but just over half stay at school till 17[15]) and which to British eyes seems remarkably casual, the HMI team observes:

> As with the curriculum generally, there is a readiness on the part of parents, school boards and municipal officials to trust the professionalism of teachers to ensure that the system is consistent and just, in and between schools and municipalities[16].

This is of course directly contrary to the past experience of most British 'curriculum managers', certainly at secondary level. Any

British secondary school head, deputy head or head of department will be acutely conscious that his or her work will ultimately be judged and validated by examination grades. Those grades will be arrived at by a complex and outwardly objective system external to the school. He or she may – and probably will – possess a more subtle view of 'professionalism' than the capacity to deliver examination results, but at the same time it is well known that many parents and politicians see those results as the crucial way by which schools account for their success or failure. If this has been true of the past, it is even more true of the present and seems likely to be truer still of the future. What has always been true of secondary schools is now becoming true of primary schools also, and one of the main vehicles for that change is the Education Reform Act. In Britain, teacher professionalism is not trusted. Whatever the public disclaimers of those in authority, many of the mechanisms set up by the ERA *seem* to teachers to be specifically designed to reduce themselves as professional people to the status of paid servants, to leave them as little margin for discretion as possible and therefore to reduce 'curriculum management' to technical trivia: the drawing up of timetables and the efficient disbursement of limited resources. The question must inevitably arise: 'If Denmark is so different, how has this come about?'

This is, of course, a question which the HMI team, in a brief 17 pages of text and after a seven-day visit, can hardly address; and to do them justice they do not attempt to do so. Nonetheless there are sufficient indications in their study to suggest some interesting and disturbing questions for the United Kingdom – questions which may also help 'curriculum managers' to move beyond their short-term concerns and identify the genuine long-term difficulties of their situation. Perhaps these questions can be usefully grouped under three heads: society, pedagogy and assessment.

Society

Relative to British society, Denmark is small and homogeneous[17]. In such circumstances, it is clearly easier to establish more or less uniform procedures on a more or less informal basis, and to disseminate to the general public the sort of information which will generate trust. Britain, on the other hand – even England – is large, disparate and quarrelsome. It contains many different kinds of groupings (social, political, religious, ethnic) and economic inequalities are pronounced and growing. The pressure to secure a greater measure of uniformity by explicit and formal statement is considerable as is a growing tendency to secure change, or block it, by litigation. In education, the period between the remarkably inexplicit 1944 Education Act (based on the social consensus of wartime) through the closer definitions òf circular 10/65 and subsequent legislation in the 1970s and 80s, to the book-length ERA and its accompanying barrage of programmes of study etc, presents, among other things, an historical progression from implicit to explicit[18]. That progression is not just a matter of fashion: it reflects quite profound movements in society and its values.

Pedagogy

The HMI study indicates, *en passant*, certain features of the Danish *folkeskole* which seem likely to have strengthened public trust in the professional authority of teachers. The *Folkeskole* is a unified ten-year school (ages 7–17): 'Just over half the 1,900 or so *folkeskoler* have 10 forms'[19]. Even in split schools (mainly in rural areas) there are presumably close links between levels, and a high degree of curriculum continuity. This is linked to class sizes which by British standards are small (averaging about 18) and highly stable. They are basically undifferentiated and frequently led by the same class teacher over a 10-year period:

> Most Danish pupils remain in the same class group for all subjects for all nine or 10 years of their primary and lower secondary education . . . . A very important feature of the *folkeskole* is the emphasis placed on the role of the class teacher, who is the major link between the school, pupils and parents. Children often have the same class teacher (usually the teacher of Danish or mathematics) throughout their nine or 10 years in school, and as a result teacher-pupil relationships are close and relaxed[20].

As well as reducing the control problems which beset British secondary schools, and overcoming some of the difficulties of 'secondary transfer', this mode of organisation must also strengthen the relationship between parents and schools. In short, it must extend into the secondary age-range the trust still felt by many parents for the professional judgement of primary teachers. HMIs very properly pass no judgement on whether mixed-ability grouping combined with 'close and relaxed' teacher-pupil relationships produce higher or lower standards of achievement by age 16 or 17. Nonetheless, these circumstances point inexorably to the difficulty of emulating the Danes. In the foreseeable future we are unlikely to achieve an average class size of 18, or a stable class group over the primary/secondary range, or a single class teacher linking both primary and secondary phases, or a more relaxed attitude towards assessment. Much of the virtue of the Danish example lies in the culture of the school and the relationship between school and society. In Britain that culture and that relationship are very different, and there seems no quick and simple way in which Britain can borrow techniques or copy successes.

Assessment

Many of these problems are concentrated upon the area of assessment. To state the dilemma baldly: if you trust teachers as professionals, you will be able to take a correspondingly relaxed view of testing and thus mitigate some of the more interventionist or authoritarian aspects of a defined central curriculum. If you do not so trust them, then correspondingly elaborate testing procedures are required to monitor their impact and effectiveness. This in turn may tend to downgrade the less easily assessable aspects of the educational process.

In the context of Western Europe, Britain is exceptional in two respects. Historically, she has laid much greater stress than her continental neighbours on sophisticated external examinations at the end of compulsory schooling[21]. In England and Wales particularly, the GCSE now dominates the secondary curriculum from 14 to 16 ('Keystage 4') and, many would argue, before that as well. The National Curriculum simply confirms and consolidates this fact. This preoccupation with formal assessment is linked to the unique importance of a highly specialist 18+ examination (A level in England: the Scottish system is less extreme) which is also an instrument of selection for higher education. As a result of the ERA, this tradition has now been supplemented and extended by the statutory introduction of formal assessments at ages 7, 11, 14 and 16. The increased prominence of assessment at all stages of compulsory education is the feature which now most clearly distinguishes the British central curriculum from its continental neighbours. It is perhaps also the feature which from a 'curriculum manager's' viewpoint most restricts his or her professional discretion – all the more so because it is an extension of the existing educational culture: an innovation which to many people seems commonsensical, operating as it were 'with the grain' of the system.

If I wished to be cruel about the discussion this far, I would suggest that it has the evasive character of much comparative writing. The chapter has established, in the words of the HMI study of Denmark, 'interesting parallels and differences'. It has then made two points: (1) that other people manage curricula within centralised systems, which is encouraging; but (2) that other people have cultural backgrounds which make it easier for them to manage curricula within centralised systems, which is discouraging. Curriculum managers reading this discussion may rightly feel that this magisterial balance has rather little to offer to their own pressing concerns. If we are to profit from an international perspective on curriculum management, we have surely to deepen our questions. To move beyond the Cook's tour stage, this chapter must address at least three central questions: What is managing a curriculum? What is particular about the circumstances under which this curriculum has to be managed? Where can management effort be most effectively applied?

What is managing a curriculum?

Like the HMIs, I have more or less avoided this question so far, mainly by talking about 'curriculum managers'. There is, however, a very real difficulty here, and one which curriculum managers in the United Kingdom may not have thought about: that as a concept, 'managing the curriculum' is highly culture-specific. This may be demonstrated by attempting to translate it into French or German. *Gestion du programme? Lehrplan-verwaltung?* What activities could such phrases refer to? The French *programme*, for example, is a list of aims and activities published with authority – the authority, ultimately, of the state. The teacher, too, as a *fonctionnaire* or civil servant, also has authority, which as well as the requirement to deliver to pupils something more or less resembling the words in the *programme*, includes also the authority to interpret, modify, supplement and extend. This teacher normally has no colleague in school with anything like the dominant, even entrepreneurial attributes of 'a good head of department' in a British secondary school; in addition his or her headteacher is in principle *primus inter pares*, with an essentially administrative role: attending to the smooth running of the various councils and committees which since 1968 have clustered round the French school, negotiating with the Ministry usually through its inspectorate, to obtain an adequate supply of teachers, etc. Such a person manages the curriculum in an important but strictly limited way by affecting the conditions within which it is delivered. By personal charisma and/or alliance with other *fonctionnaires* with a more direct professional stake in curriculum content and delivery (especially, inspectors), he or she may *also* and exceptionally become a 'curriculum leader' in the British sense, but that is achieved at the cost of encroaching upon the formal responsibility of other professionals[22].

Thus when the HMI team says of Danish heads that 'some see themselves as curriculum leaders, others do not', they are in reality applying a British idea to a situation which it does not altogether fit. Danish schools whose heads do not see themselves as curriculum leaders are not necessarily sunk in apathy or mechanically carrying out the dictates of a central programme. Managing a curriculum has at least three interlocking components: (a) a formal statement (more or less detailed or precise); (b) those who deliver (teachers), and who enjoy more or less autonomy, responsibility, public confidence, etc; (c) a hierarchy which monitors and supervises delivery, carries varying degrees of 'clout' *vis-à-vis* teachers, and operates at varying degrees of distance from the classroom.

An international perspective should remind British curriculum managers that, because of their present historical circumstances, they are preoccupied with (a) to the exclusion of (b) and (c). It should also remind them that present relationships of power and authority were evolved to reflect a diffused distribution of decision-making and an imprecise definition of curriculum. In such a framework, individuals were often encouraged to take substantial initiatives and carry subordinates with them. If (a) becomes more detailed and precise, then presumably the system as a whole should place more emphasis on each teacher's equal professional responsibility, and less on exceptional charismatic individuals and inspirational management techniques. This is, of course, exactly what some of the rhetoric says. If teachers remain sceptical it is in part because many actors at all levels (including the Secretary of State himself) still think simply in terms of adding (a) to (b) and (c) without modifying the relations between them. They tend also to overlook the fact that changes in these factors are gradual – a matter of small steps rather than sudden leaps or dramatic disjunctions. The establishment of a National Curriculum has certainly been a major historical movement, but it is not the case that nothing was defined prior to 1988 and now everything is defined. That is equally evident in other countries, whether formally centralised or not. It suggests, surely that the job of curriculum management is not simply a matter of trying to insert new ideas into old systems as rapidly and painlessly as possible, but has a number of levels or dimensions, for example:

(a) day-to-day management (eg distributing resources, personnel, organising timetables, etc in ways which enable teachers to 'deliver curriculum' more effectively).
(b) communication: easing the flow of information from centre to periphery and back.
(c) managing structures of relationship so that teacher responsibility is enhanced and top-down direction minimised.
(d) planning: long-term shifts of content and style.

Tasks (a) and (b) are relatively straightforward: for them, examples from other societies may be less useful, more in the nature of 'tips and wrinkles' than of deeper insights. Tasks (c) and (d) are, however, complex and daunting, and easy to neglect in the light of the more clamorous needs of (a) and (b). To say anything sensible about (d) and (c), substantial long-term studies of changes over time as well as in different places are called for.

What is particular about the circumstances under which the curriculum changes of the ERA have to be managed?

A curriculum is such a complex device, and requires the combined contributions, sustained over time, of so many different groups and individuals, that radical curriculum change has often been associated with political upheaval or even war. One thinks, for example, of the Russian Revolution, or the Cultural Revolution in China, or the combined impact upon the Tanzanian curriculum of independence from colonial rule and an undisputed leader with a strong and idealistic interest in education[23]. Political upheaval and war are not necessarily associated with curriculum change; and even when they are, change seems habitually to be followed by a reversion to the *status quo ante*, a tendency to equate change with relabelling, a reassertion of institutional inertia. Hawes, for example, has tellingly demonstrated how the failures of curriculum change in Africa are deeply rooted in structures, resources and attitudes[24].

By contrast, the norm for curriculum change is for it to occur piecemeal and gradually over long periods. Curriculum history (still quite thin on the ground) may stress prominent innovators or pioneering national laws or documents, but many classroom practitioners are usually hardly aware that their practice is being slowly, almost subliminally modified by a variety of external pressures[25].

Current British circumstances are unusual in that the reforms aimed at are highly ambitious, yet lack obvious external impetus of the sort which would clear the way to radical change. It really is rather unusual for a more or less stable democracy to undertake changes of this scope in peacetime. Whatever the reasons for this anomaly, the outcome for curriculum managers is highly contradictory. They must attempt to innovate over a very broad front using people and structures which are still firmly in place from the *ancien régime*. In some ways the parallel is more with Spain after the death of Franco, than with Russia after the death of the Tsar.

Allied to this fundamental oddity is another, built into the provisions of the ERA: a basic confusion between centralism and localism. The National Curriculum sections of the ERA, essentially centralising and directive in character, sit uneasily with a variety of other arrangements which undermine the Local Education Authority as intermediary between centre (DES) and periphery (school): 'opting out', City Technology Colleges (CTCs), open enrolment, local management of schools (LMS). Built into the very heart of the new system is a tension between, on the one hand a central requirement (which is also a local or individual entitlement), and on the other a fragmented delivery system supposedly made dynamic by competition for pupils, parental support, finance and staff.

In an international perspective, what is proposed looks curiously hybrid. It is certainly not a typical European centralised system along the lines of France, Italy or Sweden; nor is it a carefully defined mixed economy like West Germany, where curriculum is centralised, but under the aegis of regional parliaments; nor is it a highly localised system with a multiplicity of small school districts, as in parts of the United States[26]. The post-ERA system has in fact elements of all three patterns. At the time of writing, it is not at all clear how the resultant tensions will in practice be resolved. The impact of LMS has yet to be felt, and attention is still fixated on the flow of central documentation and regulation: curriculum managers' prime concerns remain those of translating words into classroom reality. Before very long, however, the entitlement aspects of ERA will surely lead to conflict and litigation, as parents discover that laboratories and equipment are insufficient to deliver 'science' to their children, or that a guaranteed first foreign language cannot be taught because there are insufficient qualified staff[27]. Britain has a whole new culture of public education to work out: new expectations, customs, relationships and attitudes more profound than the new vocabulary which is at present being learnt. In particular, teachers will somehow have to be 'managed' to participate in change, not just as foot soldiers obedient to curriculum manager 'officers', but as genuine participant professionals[28]. The penalty for not involving them in decisions and discussions beyond their classroom walls is considerable. In the light of the circumstances of change and the inherent contradictions of the legislation, the inertial deadweight of the system must surely be extremely powerful. That could be a recipe for stagnation and frustration; but it could also be another way of emphasising the potential importance of curriculum managers intelligent enough to give scope to individuals and to exploit the coming confusions.

Where can management effort be most effectively applied?

At present (autumn 1989) the British education system resembles an ant-hill to which a boot has just administered an energetic kick. In a frenzy, the ants (teachers, 'management') rush hither and thither. More than anything, they need perspective, a sense of overall direction, or purpose beyond mere busyness.

One way of obtaining that perspective is by looking at the experience of foreign systems. HMIs have clearly sensed that in launching their series of studies, even if their highly focused character may convey the subliminal message that they are interested more in mechanisms and techniques than in broader perspectives.

What I have attempted to argue in this chapter is that to consider our own experience against an international background reminds us of three linked points:

(a) We are all part of an existing culture of education: the ERA aims at a substantial change in that culture.
(b) That change will take a long time, and be accompanied by increasing turbulence.
(c) The turbulence will be all the greater because of the confusions of the underlying thinking as it has emerged from the political process.

If this interpretation is correct, curriculum managers who wish to manage the curriculum in the sense of modifying it so that it is better adapted to the needs of real children and a real society, will be best advised not simply to resist and criticise, but rather to use the power that many people at all levels of the system actually have. As McLean points out, under Mrs Thatcher, 'Legislative proposals tend to reflect undiluted political programmes rather than a compromise between competing interests. Compromise tends to occur at the level of implementation'[29]. No curriculum, new or old, can be implemented or changed without the best efforts of very large numbers of professional people. This process is already evident in the composition of the first programmes of study (science and english). The Secretary of State was able to influence the drafting of the terms of reference and the composition of the working parties; yet the working parties necessarily contained a majority of professionals and in due course reported in ways which again the Secretary of State could only partially modify. Thus the programmes of study represent not tablets of the law handed down by Kenneth Baker, but compromises. This process will inevitably continue down the system to the point where the words are actually translated into teaching acts.

This process will continue whether or not teachers have a broader grasp of their place in the whole process. What an international perspective can add is a sense of the contradictions or points of stress in the new structures: the attempt to shift the whole system by floods of detailed description and prescription and the consequent overloading of channels of communication; the preoccupation with assessment to the point where it may overwhelm the teaching; the ambivalent character of statutory syllabuses as being at once central regulation and individual entitlement; the potentially disruptive and anomalous role of governing bodies which may act simply as local guardians of centrally determined norms, but may also be educated to accept more subtle and flexible views of what schools can and should do, and may develop the political clout to do something about it.

All these contradictions represent opportunities for curriculum managers, who are themselves products of an *ancien régime* which laid greater stress on the teacher as professional leader and entrepreneur than in most other countries. The task is now to create a new 'culture of education' in which curriculum is better supported and understood by the community. What that culture will look like is difficult to predict, but it will certainly not be the same as its Danish equivalent, given the very real historical and cultural differences between our two societies. Nor in my view will it look much like Kenneth Baker's essentially hierarchical or military vision of a chain of command from centre to periphery, because curricula are not ultimately manageable in that way. The new culture will certainly require the forging of new alliances between education professionals and other groups, a redefinition of teacher roles and professional autonomy, a greater willingness to communicate and negotiate. The ERA has not closed the debate; rather, it has started a new one. Until we can understand in what ways it is both new and contradictory, our 'curriculum management' will remain crisis management.

References

1   Her Majesty's Inspectorate (1989), *Education in Denmark: aspects of the work of the folkeskole*, (London, HMSO).
2   *Education in the Federal Republic of Germany: aspects of Curriculum and Assessment*, 1986; *Aspects of primary education in the Netherlands*, 1987; *The Provisional Teacher Program in New Jersey*, 1989; *Aspects of higher education in the United States of America*, 1989; *Initial teacher training of secondary teachers in the Académie*

de Toulouse, 1989. All HMI Reports on education arrangements in countries outside the UK.

3   *Education in Denmark*, p iv.
4   Ibid, p 3.
5   Ibid, p 6.
6   Ibid, p 7.
7   Ibid, p 9.
8   Ibid, p 10.
9   Frankish, A 'Guest editorial', *Aspects of Education*, 14, 1972, p 6.
10   Osborn, R L 'Paradox in the American classroom', *Aspects of Education*, 14, 1972, p 17.
11   Ibid, p 20.
12   Puren, Christian (1988) *Histoire des méthodologies de l'enseignement des langues*, (Paris, Clé International).
13   For example, Italy has a more or less institutionalised but entirely unofficial divide between left and right. For an illustration of how this is reflected in one important feature of curriculum management (use and choice of textbooks), see Beattie, Nicholas 'Sacred monster: textbooks in the Italian educational system' in *British Journal of Educational Studies*, 29/3, 1981, pp 218–35.
14   McLean, Martin, 'The Conservative education policy in comparative perspective: return to an English Golden Age or harbinger of international policy change?', *British Journal of Educational Studies*, 36/3, 1988, p 200.
15   *Education in Denmark*, p 2.
16   Ibid, p 17.
17   'There is not a lot of time and energy devoted to ideology, particularly in Denmark', (Dixon, Willis (1965) *Society, schools and progress in Scandinavia*, (Oxford, Pergamon Press), p 49). For a useful, more recent introduction to the Danish system, see Struwe, Kamma (1981), *Schools and education in Denmark*, (Copenhagen, Det Danske Selskab).
18   See Chitty, Clyde 'Central control of the school curriculum, 1944–87' *History of Education*, 17/4, 1988, pp 321–34.
19   *Education in Denmark*, p 3.
20   Ibid, p 3.
21   Dundas-Grant, Valerie 'Attainment at 16+: the French perspective', *Comparative Education*, 11/1, 1975, pp 13–22.
22   For a slightly different but allied characterisation of the connected roles of headteacher and class-teacher in another continental system, see Her Majesty's Inspectorate (1987), *Aspects of primary education in the Netherlands*, (London, HMSO), pp 7–8.
23   On Russia, see Fitzpatrick, Sheila (1970), *The Commissariat of Enlightenment: Soviet organisation of education and the arts under Lunacharsky, October 1917–1921* (Cambridge, Cambridge University Press), or Shturman, Dora (1988), *The Soviet secondary school* (London, Routledge). Even the prolonged and traumatic upheavals in China seem in the longer term to have left a great deal unchanged: see Gasper, Barbara 'Keypoint secondary schools in China: the persistence of tradition?' *Compare*, 19/1, 1989, pp 5–20.

24   Hawes, Hugh (1979), *Curriculum and reality in African primary achools* (London, Longman).

25   For a summary of curriculum history in Britain, see the introduction to Goodson, Ivor (1983), *School subjects and curriculum change* (London, Croom Helm), pp 3–13. Interesting and contrasting studies of the American scene are Franklin, Barry M (1986), *Building the American community: the school curriculum and the search for social control* (London, Falmer); Kliebard, Herbert M (1986), *The struggle for the American curriculum, 1893–1958* (Boston, Routledge and Kegan Paul); Smith, Louis M *et al* (1986), *Educational innovators: then and now* (New York, Falmer).

26   McLean, *op cit*, comments interestingly on developing similarities and differences between Britain and continental Europe. Cf, also Johnson's historical analysis: 'Educational arrangements are part of a larger pattern of English exceptionalism. The best evidence for this is comparative . . .' (Johnson, Richard, 'Thatcherism and English education: breaking the mould, or confirming the pattern?' *History of Education*, 18/2, 1989, p 96).

27   The blithe unconcern with which central government has manufactured 'a rod for its own back' is one of the more surprising features of the ERA, and may support Weiler's analysis of France and Germany: he suggests that governments value the *initial* policy-making exercise, but not the long-term implementation phase, whose failure is blamed on others (Weiler, Hans N 'Why reforms fail: the politics of education in France and the Federal Republic of Germany', *Journal of Curriculum Studies*, 21/4, 1989, pp 291–305.

28   Conley, Sharon C *et al*, 'Teacher participation in the management of school systems', *Teachers College Record*, 90/2, 1988, pp 259–80. Compare this study of decentralised USA with the rather similar conclusions of a study of decision-making in centralised France: Gaziel, Haim, 'The emergence of the comprehensive middle school in France: educational policy-making in a centralised system'. *Comparative Education*, 25/1, 1989, pp 29–40.

29   McLean, *op cit*, p 214.

3 The national scene

Christopher Tipple, Director of Education, Northumberland CC

There was not much to object to in the bones of the debate. It is much harder to argue for an unclear and complicated arrangement for arriving at what is taught in schools than for the logic of a national curriculum. Once, therefore, a national curriculum for England and Wales appeared on the agenda, the general reaction was to wonder why it had never been seriously considered before. After all, almost everybody else had one. In theoretical terms, too, it is hard to object because, of course, everybody has their own detailed definition of what it might contain. So the almost universal reaction to the proposal was 'yes . . . but'.

The proposals for testing and assessment were more cautiously received. The 'buts' were stronger and more numerous. Again, however, there was little to object to in the broad fundamental. No one would argue that, in principle and in practice, testing should not take place and information be made available to all those who need to know about it. Again all good schools already monitored their pupils' progress, so how could one object?

It is the flesh, not the bones that are potentially a very serious problem. As sound principles come to be reflected in legal phrases and in parliamentary orders, and as good intentions begin to generate a huge superstructure of bureaucracy, there are many causes for concern. Given the detail in which it has been decided the curriculum will be determined and assessed, these problems are inevitable. To expect a national recipe fully to reflect the various needs and circumstances of an advanced industrial nation of over 55 million people and 25,000 schools is not realistic.

This chapter, then, looks at the flesh, at the national machinery for curriculum determination and control in its present state of evolution. Dominating it, of course, is the Secretary of State. Not an individual but, as Sir Keith Joseph used wisely to refer to it, 'the holder of my office'. Immense and quite detailed power now attaches to that office and, to a greater or lesser degree, depending on the actual holder, on the Civil Service and particularly the Department of Education and Science. Indeed their centralising hand is increasingly obvious as more and more of the state machinery appears to public view through what one senior member of the DES himself described as a 'snowstorm of circulars and an avalanche of administrative memoranda'. Let us look at what is being erected.

The foundation is, naturally, the Act itself. It entitles every pupil in maintained schools to a curriculum which is balanced and broadly based and which, as the Act says:

(a) promotes the spiritual, moral, cultural, mental and physical development of pupils at the school and of society and

(b) prepares such pupils for the opportunities, responsibilities and experiences of adult life.

The impact of all this is well summarised in the DES booklet *The National Curriculum, from Policy to Practice*. This makes it clear that each pupil is entitled, as a result of the law, to a broad and balanced curriculum which is relevant to his or her particular needs. It is made clear that this does not simply mean that each school must offer such a curriculum; each individual pupil must take it up. The booklet goes on to make two further fundamental points about the curriculum. Firstly the curriculum 'must promote development in all the main areas of learning and experience which are widely accepted as important'. 'Widely accepted' of course means accepted by the Secretary of State, after an appropriate process of consultation and through a process of parliamentary approval, about which more below. Secondly 'the curriculum must also serve to develop the pupil as an individual, as a member of society and as a future adult member of the community with a range of personal and social opportunities and responsibilities'. Wholly admirable, but perhaps not best expressed in terms of individual academic subjects, nor in a highly complex machinery of published testing and assessment. The philosophy then, is unexceptionable; it is the superstructure designed to achieve it where problems begin. This is not just because giving practical expression to such broad objectives in any meaningful way is inherently very difficult, it is also because the superstructure has to meet demands for close and detached accountability: to parents, to governors, to local education authorities and, of course, to the Secretary of State. The holder of that office must have some way of measuring whether such a huge and expensive change has been successful. The operation of market forces through open enrolment, CTCs and opting out must have something to bite on. But these requirements do not sit easily with the generous philosophy of the DES booklet. They are political requirements, not educational ones.

National Curriculum Council

The first pillar of the new curriculum establishment in England is the National Curriculum Council (NCC). There is also a Curriculum Council for Wales. Each of these bodies is, by statute, comprised of not less than 10 and not more than 15 members appointed by the Secretary of State. The Secretary of State also appoints the chairman and deputy chairman of each body. In practice the membership comprises a range of interests including a Chief Education Officer, adviser, two headteachers and representatives of higher education. Its terms of reference are:

(a) to keep all aspects of the curriculum for maintained schools under review
(b) to advise the Secretary of State on such matters concerned with the curriculum for maintained schools as he may refer to it or as it may see fit
(c) to advise the Secretary of State on, and if so requested by him, assist him to carry out, programmes of research and development for purposes connected with the curriculum for schools
(d) to publish and disseminate information relating to the curriculum for schools
(e) to carry out such ancillary activities as the Secretary of State may direct.

Although they are widely drawn, they have not included the task of producing the attainment targets and programme of study for the foundation subjects. This has been undertaken, to date, for mathematics, science, English, and design and technology by non-statutory working parties also nominated by the Secretary of State. Other subjects followed.

In terms of the law, the Secretary of State is empowered to lay down all aspects of the curriculum, except for the time devoted to each subject and the style in which it shall be taught. Presumably it was both practical and political reasons that led him to the subject working party strategy. To have devised the material 'in house' using DES and HMI would have been and would have been seen to be unhealthily parochial; to have used the National Curriculum Council would have involved too great a delay. Moreover the NCC has its own secretariat whilst subject working parties had, perforce, the DES providing this crucial function.

The size of these working parties has been small, usually between seven and 12, again recruited from the ranks of headteachers, chief education officers, advisers and representatives of higher education. Like the NCC itself they also had an industrialist, a feature which our continental neighbours find curious and which is not generally reflected in their own curriculum working parties. Not even in Japan, where curriculum revision is very much the province of the civil servants, namely the Monbusho or Ministry of Education, and where vocational elements are deliberately left to the post-18 phase of education, is this the case.

These first working parties have had to work very quickly, often moving into uncharted waters as they sought, for example, to make meaningful distinctions between attainment levels 7 and 8 in one aspect of their subject. Speed has been essential because the Secretary of State's timetable is formidable (see below). Their reports have been published and have hitherto formed the basis of the Secretary of State's proposals for the National Curriculum. The National Curriculum Council has consulted all interested parties and published a summary of the results of the process together with its recommendations to the Secretary of State. Should the Secretary of State decide not to give effect to any of the recommendations he has received from the Council, he is required to publish a statement explaining his reasons. The Secretary of State's final proposals are then embodied in orders in Parliament. The draft orders are again the subject of consultation, following which parliamentary approval turns them into legal binding requirements.

It is perhaps too early to make judgements about the meaningfulness of this sequence of events. It promises an openness which is a welcome antidote to the heavy centralisation embodied in the whole process. As a result of this openness it is known that the Secretary of State chose to modify the Mathematics Working Party's recommendations, particularly in the area of 'applied mathematics', that consultation revealed that most of those consulted preferred the stance that the working party had adopted, that the Curriculum Council nevertheless made recommendations which accorded with the Secretary of State's view and that their recommendations were, not surprisingly, accepted. This openness also showed that in relation to science the consultative process revealed massive support for the working party's view on the time to be devoted to science and on the position of balanced science but that the Council, with some reluctance, made recommendations in accordance with the Secretary of State's different view. Again, not surprisingly, these were accepted. In relation to English, however, the Council showed more sympathy for the working party's views in its recommendations to the Secretary of State.

The Secretary of State therefore made some changes which he described as clarifying and amplifying the Council's recommendations. So far then, it is clear that the Secretary of State is going to get his way. This is particularly so when it is remembered that the working parties are serviced by the DES, whose influence on a group of disparate experts meeting only intermittently and working under great pressure, is very considerable indeed. The DES also has high powered assessors on the National Curriculum Council itself. Although, then, the Council has a number of other potentially very useful roles described below, in this key process of getting the main building blocks of the National Curriculum into place, it has not so far provided any really noticeable challenge to the Secretary of State's views. Given its structure and the circumstances of the time, no one should be surprised.

The Council does, however, have other tasks. The Secretary of State has asked it to advise specifically on the whole curriculum context within which work on individual foundation subjects should be carried forward. In particular it is looking at cross-curricular issues, including areas such as the role of careers guidance, health education and other aspects of personal and social education, environmental education and economic awareness and it is considering how these may best be reflected in the curriculum. The Council has to try and ensure that the subject 'bits' of the curriculum form a coherent whole and somehow deliver the broad and balanced curriculum enshrined in the noble opening passages of the Act. A number of working groups have been set up by the Council to look at these matters, but the truth is that the whole curriculum approach is rendered horrendously difficult by the subject structure and by the inevitable fact that the various subject working party reports are coming on stream over a period of at least four to five years. Certainly an observer of the National Curriculum scene in France or West Germany would have to admit that achieving successful cross-curricular approaches is extremely difficult and has not been adequately solved, even with their long experience.

The Council will also have to keep the curriculum under review and promote change where this is felt to be necessary. This is not an immediate problem in the hectic process of establishing the great new structure. But it is going to be necessary because, by the time the later subjects come on stream, there will certainly be a need to look at the first ones again, such as maths and science. There is provision in the Education Act, under special circumstances, for the suspension of all or part of the National Curriculum, so as to allow developmental work to take place. Once, however, the National Curriculum entitlement is in place it does not seem likely that parents will welcome any 'experiment'. Moreover, continental experience of a national curriculum suggests that once it is in place, achieving change is extremely difficult. It becomes part of the establishment. The diffuse, even messy arrangements that characterised the old order did at least encourage change. The new central machinery will not make it easy.

The Council will also be producing in-service materials for teachers to help them cope with the changes and, provided this is prepared and delivered in close collaboration with local education authorities, as is the stated intention, this should be very helpful provided the Council avoids being prescriptive about teaching style.

A cruel analysis of the last 30 years in education might say that the succession of Schools Council, then the Schools Curriculum Development Committee and then the NCC neatly summarises the way that education has been perceived over this period. The Schools Council, with much union and local authority participation would, in this analysis, typify the era of expansion, experimentation and proliferation. Education development for the benefit of the providers, not the consumers. The Schools Curriculum Development Committee, with its modest budget and little union input would, on this model, typify the era of cost cutting in education, of restraint on the professionals without compensating input from elsewhere.

Finally, the NCC would represent the arrival of strong central direction, filling the vacuum never really filled by the SCDC; with much greater powers than any of its predecessors but very much on the Secretary of State's terms. It is ironic that this should have happened under a Government so strongly committed to decentralisation, privatisation and the reduction of the role of the state. It has, however, brought to the surface a dormant temptation evident in even the most illustrious of Mrs Thatcher's predecessors. R A Butler tells a most revealing story in *The Art of the Possible.*

He (Churchill) saw me after his afternoon nap and was purring like a tiger. He began, 'You have been in the House fifteen years and it's time you were promoted . . . and I now want you to go to the Board of Education. I think that you can leave your mark there. You will be independent. Besides', he continued, with rising fervour, 'you will be in the war. You will move poor children from here to there' and he lifted up and evacuated imaginary children from one side of his blotting pad to the other. 'This will be very difficult'. He went on 'I am too old now to think you can improve people's natures. Everyone has to learn to defend himself. I should not object if you could introduce a note of patriotism in the schools'. And then, with a grin . . . 'Tell the children that Wolfe won Quebec'. I said that I would like to influence what was taught in schools but that this was always frowned upon. Here he looked very earnest and commented, 'of course not by instruction or order but by suggestion'. I then said that I had always looked forward to going to the Board of Education if I were given the chance.

Schools Examination and Assessment Council

The second great pillar of the new curriculum arrangements is, of course, the Schools Examination and Assessment Council (SEAC). With much wider powers than its predecessor, the Secondary Examinations Council (SEC), SEAC is also heir to the recommendations of another of the Secretary of State's *ad hoc* working parties, the Task Group on Assessment and Testing (TGAT) which was set up at the same time as the first curriculum working groups and, like them, worked under enormous pressure to produce proposals for the assessment of the National Curriculum. Since the seeds of much of SEAC's work lie in TGAT, it is worth pausing over what this body tried to do.

The size and difficulty of the task facing the 10 members of the Group between September and December 1987 could hardly be exaggerated. It is worth quoting their terms of reference in full.

1 To advise the Secretary of State on the practical considerations which should govern all assessment including testing of attainment at age (approximately) 7, 11, 14 and 16 within a national curriculum, including the marking scale or scales and kinds of assessment including testing to be used, the need to differentiate so that the assessment can promote learning across a range of abilities, the relative roles of informative and of diagnostic assessment, the uses to which the results of assessment should be put, the moderation requirements needed to secure credibility of assessments, and the publication and other services needed to support the system – with a view to securing assessment and testing arrangements which are simple to administer, understandable by all in and outside the education service, cost effective and supportive of learning in schools.
2 In making recommendations, to take into account the need not to increase calls on teachers' and pupils' time for activities which do not directly promote learning, and to limit costs.
3 To advise on the possible staging of the introduction of assessment, including testing to reflect the need for the process to be manageable and for teachers to be adequately trained.

Few, if any, committees can have faced a tougher assignment. Faced with the impossible task of finding something that was cheap, simple and fair, the Group opted, to their credit, for a system that would be as fair as possible in all the circumstances, letting the other criteria take care of themselves. They argued that the basis of the national assessment system should be essentially formative, that is designed to contribute to learning and not simply summative, by which is meant the simple recording of acquired knowledge or skill. They also emphasised that all assessment information about an individual should be treated as confidential, and confined to those with a clear 'need to know'.

They suggested that pupil results should be presented as an attainment profile and that for each subject there should be a very small number of 'profile components' which reflected the variety of knowledge skills and understanding to which a study of the subject gave rise. They went on to urge that the national system should employ tests susceptible to a wide range of mode of presentation, operation and response. These are to be called Standard Assessment Tasks (SATs). The SATs, it was argued, should be integrated into the curriculum as far as possible using a wide variety of practical tasks and observations. Moreover the national system should be based on a combination of SATs and moderated teacher ratings. The Group saw group moderation by teachers as a vital element, as being a process with significant benefit to teachers in itself as well as providing a crucial counterbalance to crudely over-simplified test results.

Subjects were divided into 10 levels of attainment with the average seven-year-old at about level 2, the average 11-year-old at level 4, the average 14-year-old at level 5/6 and the average 16-year-old at level 6/7. However, it was made clear that the assessments were not to be age-related. At any given age a child might be on quite different levels for difference subjects. It was in this way that the Group sought to avoid the creation of a 7+, 11+ and 14+ type of selection examination.

Only on the question of how assessment results should be presented in the light of socio-economic circumstances did the report lack credibility. Resisting the idea that results should somehow be 'doctored' to reflect such circumstances, the Group fell back on the suggestion that LEAs or governors might be expected to issue statements that would put the results of particular schools in the right context. Quite how the governors were to explain to parents that their school's results were poor because of their own poor economic circumstances was not explained. This is, of course, a very difficult area and the Group did not produce a credible response to the problem, because there isn't one, once the crucial decision to publish results at all these ages has been taken.

The Secretary of State accepted the TGAT report as a basis for progress and commissioned further reports from the Group including one on the problems of practical implementation which gave a glimpse of the elaborate machinery that would be necessary.

SEAC is a body similar in size and composition to the NCC. It, too has very wide powers:

(a) to keep all aspects of examinations and assessment under review
(b) to advise the Secretary of State on such matters concerned with examinations and assessment as he may refer to it or as it may see fit
(c) to advise the Secretary of State on, and if so requested by him, assist him to carry out, programmes of research and development for purposes connected with examinations and assessment
(d) to publish and disseminate . . . information relating to examinations and assessment
(e) to make arrangements with appropriate bodies for the moderation of assessments made in pursuance of assessment arrangements
(f) to advise the Secretary of State on the exercise of his powers under Section 5(1) of this Act
(g) to carry out such ancillary activities as the Secretary of State may direct.

The reference to Section 5(1) is to the power which the Act gives the Secretary of State to approve all qualifications granted by outside bodies and arising from courses of study pursued by pupils of compulsory school age in maintained schools. The Secretary of State has appointed SEAC to undertake this approval process on his behalf. As with so many other aspects of the practical implementation of the Act, there is here the real potential for overkill. Clearly it is felt that the Secretary of State has to approve external qualifications taken by pupils in maintained schools. Given his detailed control of programmes of study and attainment targets it is difficult to envisage credible examinations that would not reflect these. However, no loophole must be left, so SEAC is busy drawing up large schedules of such qualifications which catch all sorts of subject competitions as well as mainstream examinations. It is quite likely that the bureaucratic procedure involved in securing the Secretary of State's approval, via SEAC, to these competitions means they may well wither away. That is, assuming there will be room for them once the full panoply of testing and assessment is in place.

As the heir of TGAT, SEAC is now considering appropriate assessment arrangements and has commissioned a number of consortia to produce SATs. As the heir of SEC it is monitoring and controlling the GCSE.

Both NCC and SEAC will be advising the Secretary of State about what information on the curriculum and results of assessment should be required to be made available to parents, or to be published more widely. SEAC will also advise on the form in which teachers' assessments should be recorded, how results should be reported and on the recommendations in the report of the Records of Achievement National Steering Committee, published in January 1989.

The outcome of all this national activity is a formidable timetable in schools, many of which will, over the next few years, also have to face local financial management and the introduction, on a national basis, of teacher appraisal. It is summarised in Table 2.1.

And so the juggernaut rolls on. Inevitably this level of prescription will produce a huge demand for information. The creation, refinement, processing and publishing of this information will produce an industry in itself. Siberian forests will be felled and computer fortunes made. Whether children will get a better education as a result of it all is by no means clear. There is also a grave danger that the essence of education will be forgotten. As a definition for the essence of education I would settle for 'the mastery of the processes by which knowledge can be acquired and a maturity and sympathy gained from exposure to the mainstreams of intellectual thought'. This is not a definition coined by an educationalist. They are is the qualities which Robert Reid, Chief Executive of Shell UK was looking for in new recruits, as he told the North of England Education Conference in the Isle of Man in 1989. Yet, as ever increasing statistical data piles up, these objectives are too easily forgotten. George Canning got it exactly right almost 200 years ago when he addressed the House of Commons:

> Away with the cant of 'measure not men', the idle supposition that it is the harness and not the horses that draw the chariot along. If the comparison must be made, if the distinction must be taken, men are everything, measures comparatively nothing.

The builders of the new machinery, principally the DES, do so with the good intention of putting the law into practice. But good intentions make notoriously treacherous paving stones. And there must be a serious question mark against the massive powers acquired by the holder of the office of Secretary of State, which may be thought less than healthy in a democracy normally dependent on a system of checks and balances. Questions must be levelled too, at a system that requires not only legally prescribed attainment targets and legally prescribed programmes of study, but also standardised national testing. Most other countries have one or two of these ingredients, but not all three. It has been described as the belt, braces and garotte approach.

Yet it would be wrong to end this chapter on a defeatist note. After all, we approach this new machinery from a quite different tradition to our continental neighbours and therefore stand a much better chance of humanising it. Weaknesses in the old order will

Table 2.1: Timetable for implementing foundation subjects 1989/90–1996/97
(Source – The National Curriculum from Policy to Practice – DES 1989)

School Year	Mathematics Science	Design and Technology	English	(Provisional) Geography History	(Provisional) Modern Languages Music Art Physical Education
Autumn 1989	KS_1-AT/PoS KS_3-AT/PoS		KS_1-AT/PoS		
Summer 1990					
Autumn 1990	KS_2-AT/PoS	KS_1-AT/PoS KS_2-AT/PoS KS_3-AT/PoS KS_3-AT/PoS	KS_2-AT/PoS		
Summer 1991	KS_1-SAT^1		KS_1-SAT^1		
Autumn 1991				KS_1-AT/PoS KS_2-AT/PoS KS_3-AT/PoS	
Summer 1992	KS_1-SAT^1 KS_3-SAT^1	KS_1-SAT^1	KS_1-SAT^2		
Autumn 1992	KS_4-AT/PoS		KS_4-AT/PoS		KS_1-AT/PoS KS_2-AT/PoS KS_3-AT/PoS
Summer 1993	KS_3-SAT^2	KS_1-SAT^2 KS_3-SAT^1	KS_3-SAT^1	KS_1-SAT^1	
Autumn 1993		KS_4-AT/PoS			
Summer 1994	KS_2-SAT^1 KS_4-GCSE/SAT	KS_2-SAT^1 KS_3-SAT^2	KS_2-SAT^1 KS_3-SAT^2 KS_4-GCSE/SAT	KS_1-SAT^2 KS_3-SAT^2	KS_1-SAT^1
Autumn 1994				KS_4-AT/PoS	
Summer 1995	KS_2-SAT^2	KS_2-SAT^2 KS_4-GCSE/SAT	KS_2-SAT^2	KS_2-SAT^1 KS_3-SAT^2	KS_1-SAT^2 KS_3-SAT^1
Autumn 1995					KS_4-AT/PoS
Summer 1996				KS_2-SAT^2 KS_4-GCSE/SAT	KS_2-SAT^1 KS_3-SAT^2
Autumn 1996					
Summer 1997					KS_2-SAT^2 KS_4-GCSE/SAT

KS = Keystage   SAT^1 = Unreported assessment   SAT^2 = First reported assessment
AT/PoS = Statutory attainment targets and programmes of study take effect in the **first year** of the keystage shown

KS_1 = Years 1 and 2, ages 5/6–6/7.
KS_2 = Years 3–6, ages 7/8–10/11.
KS_3 = Years 7–9, ages 11/12–13/14.
KS_4 = Years 10 and 11, ages 14/15–15/16

be remedied. Greater precision of objective and firmer guidance is generally being welcomed by teachers and parents alike. The trick will be to distil these desirable attributes from the new arrangements and to discard the harmful elements; once they have been shown to be so. The next few years may be, in some respects, painful, but history suggests that the excesses will be eroded. The pendulum which seems to have swung very far in one direction will either swing back or over in a circle and the extreme position will not be maintained. Perhaps we should concentrate on the potential opportunities and rewards involved in the process of getting there, rather than the doubtful pleasures of its full achievement. There is more than an even chance that the end will, in the end, be changed by a wise deployment of the means. And it's a journey that's been travelled before, even in Ancient Greece:

> When you start on your journey to Ithaca,
> then pray that the road is long,
> full of adventure, full of knowledge.
> Do not fear the Lestrygonians
> and the Cyclopes and the angry Poseidon.
> You will never meet such as these on your path,
> if your thoughts remain lofty, if a fine
> emotion touches your body and your spirit.
> You will never meet the Lestrygonians,
> the Cyclopes and the fierce Poseidon,
> if you do not carry them within your soul,
> if your soul does not raise them up before you.
>
> Then pray that the road is long.
> That the summer mornings are many,
> that you will enter ports seen for the first time
> with such pleasure, with such joy!
> Stop at Phoenician markets,
> and purchase fine merchandise,
> mother-of-pearl and corals, amber and ebony,
> and pleasurable perfumes of all kinds,
> buy as many pleasurable perfumes as you can;
> visit hosts of Egyptian cities,
> to learn and learn from those who have knowledge . . .
>
> Ithaca has given you the beautiful voyage.
> Without her you would never have taken the road.'

C P Cavafy, 'Ithaca', *Complete Poems*, Hogarth Press, London

4 What does it mean to the youngster?

Tim Brighouse,
Professor of Education, Keele
University

There has been much discussion over the last decade about an 'entitlement' curriculum. The idea of entitlement probably represents an attempt, during a much longer debate about the need for a 'national' curriculum, to bring into focus the child's individual needs and rights: it is needed to counterbalance any propensity towards the state's collective needs – totalitarianism if you will – which a move towards a nationally prescribed curriculum might bring with it.

Of course debate about the National Curriculum has been around a lot longer, but its popularisation and public debate is a relatively recent phenomenon. It was a 'secret garden' at least to David Eccles who when Secretary of State for the second time, in 1962, was determined (against the better judgement of many of its guardians) to strip it of its secrecy. Eccles' vehicle for clearing the garden's secrecy was the Schools Council – not a very efficient or fast-moving garden Rotavator. When James Callaghan accelerated the debate in 1976, the quality of discussion was indeed raised, in what turned out to be the Schools Council's declining years, under the combined influence of the Chair, John Tomlinson, and the Secretary, John Mann. Indeed, the midwifery, if not the conception, of the notion of 'entitlement' when applied to the curriculum probably should be credited to those two.

There were, however, other professional and institutional voices

55

apart from the Schools Council. Sometimes, presumably in order
to try to influence the climate, there was even a little skirmishing
at the highest level, about the timing of various publications. *The
Practical Curriculum*, for example, a useful, practical discussion
document for schools from the Schools Council, had to be held
up so that it should not upstage an HMI view of the curriculum.
Such *frissons* of jealousy, petulance and energy-consuming rivalry
in presentation are still not unknown in the School Council's
genetically different grandchild, the National Curriculum Council,
and in its relationship with the DES.

Indeed HMI's influence in the debate has been cumulative,
insistent and strong: it began with a briefing paper from Sheila
Browne, the Senior Chief HMI, at the time of the Callaghan Ruskin
speech, which on a political front launched a debate on education
which seemed to run and run, until it was brought to an unexpected
denouement and an abrupt closure with the Education Reform
Act of 1988[1]. Probably HMI's greatest influence was *Aspects of
Secondary Education* (1978)[2], which first commented so
authoritatively and adversely on the short-changing of youngsters
through the unfettered and badly guided option system at the end
of the third year of secondary education. HMI pointed out that
the arrangements for choice meant that by the mid-point of the
third year, some youngsters had decided to discontinue study of
a particular subject – at a point only three-fifths of the way through
what was presumably a coherently planned five-year course. They
also observed that for some of those youngsters subsequently the
change of direction brought only short-lived renaissance of interest
and motivation before the same boredom and lack of achievement
returned.

From that analysis there emerged a call for a 'broad', 'balanced',
'coherent' 'relevant' and 'differentiated' curriculum, in which there
should be a good match of learning experience and materials of
a particular subject to the child's abilities. HMI lost no opportunity
in ramming the message home, whether in individual school reports,
in the 'Education Observed' and in the 'Curriculum Matters' series,
or in their annual reports on the 'effects of public expenditure
policies on educational provision'. The words 'broad', 'balanced',
'coherent', and 'match' occur with a reverberating insistence –
a kind of 'two-legs good, four-legs bad' propaganda, which in the
end brooked no answer. The discipline and meticulous care in
HMI writing owed a great deal to the changes introduced during
Sheila Browne's tenure as Senior Chief Inspector. It is by no means
an unmixed blessing, for while politicians cannot ignore HMI, their
own common, insistent and unquestioniong advocacy of certain
practices and policies, tends to bind the hands of future HMI

commentaries and to marginalise any substantial, alternative critiques. So it is proving to be with the National Curriculum.

The influence of the notion of *entitlement* when applied to the curriculum is, as we have seen, attractive. Indeed it is so beguiling that it can lead to an accommodation between the educational right and the educational left. The former welcomes the unexpected certainty that at last 'we shall all know what they are all learning in school'[3], while the latter sees entitlement as finally pinning down the right of every child, be their circumstances never so mean or deprived, to access to science, maths, modern languages, and so on. The frequent argument of the left is that a greater clarity on the National Curriculum would provide a lever with which to prise out more resources for the schools. After all, so the argument runs, once there is a legislative requirement, the need for further resource to implement it brooks no further argument. Many LEAs which have considered 'curriculum protection' arguments, during a decade of falling rolls, will bear witness to that thesis, but they will also honestly point out that in the face of budgetary imperatives, the purity of the curriculum protection policies has been compromised, and even whole schemes deferred or abandoned. So of course it is proving already with the National Curriculum.

For example let us consider, not the secondary school, with the oft quoted[4] prospective examples of teacher shortages in science, modern languages and maths which will render nugatory the pious hopes of implementing the National Curriculum in many secondary schools, but the apparently much simpler case of the primary schools. Once again there is a looming shortage, both of experienced leadership to implement the National Curriculum in primary schools, as there is an unprecedented turnover of headteachers, but also a prospective shortage of teachers themselves, especially in the early years. Moreover to implement the change there is no sign of introducing the extra resources which most commentators see as necessary. Norman Thomas, former Senior Chief HMI (Primary) and author of the ILEA review put the case elegantly, recently:

Primary does not mean simple
The 1944 Education Act signalled the end of elementary education for children over 11. The 1988 Education Reform Act ought to mark the end of elementary education for the under-11s.

Elementary education was characterised by the belief that schools needed no more teachers than there were classes. For many years, secondary schools have had about 40 per cent more teachers (including heads) than classes. Primary schools have had less than half that margin.

The danger is that this disparity will be enshrined in the formulas for distributing funds that local authorities are adopting as required by the 1988 Act.

It is time to bring the staff of primary and secondary schools into line to recognise that there is no argument for giving 15-year-olds more teachers than seven-year-olds. Otherwise, the National Curriculum, which promises much, will be a charade.

It is true that primary schools are providing a better educational service (with the possible exceptions of spelling and mental arithmetic) than they were when I began teaching in 1948. The range of work has increased beyond anyone's dreams. The quantity and variety of reading and writing, the mathematical ideas and vocabulary, the competence shown by many children in instrumental music, physical education, art and light crafts would have amazed my first class of children, and their teachers too. A struggling beginning has been made in science, a very modest start in technology and computers. The National Curriculum is rightly demanding much more.

But the service is not yet good enough by a mile. The system is based on the view, dating from the days of elementary schools, that education is simple. More or less any adult can provide the whole curriculum single-handed after being trained to control a class and given an occasional top-up day of in-service training.

Primary education is actually more complex than secondary education. The latter can often be parcelled up into specialist teaching packets.

For their younger pupils, some secondary schools combine two or three subjects in 'humanities' or 'integrated science', putting the emphasis on understanding and application of skills. They do not therefore say that they need fewer teachers. They recognise that teachers from different subject areas must work alongside each other if the work is to have the necessary sharpness.

This is just as vital in primary schools. In each of the National Curriculum foundation subjects, there are primary school teachers with more than ordinary knowledge: out of 160,000 teachers, some 20,000 have qualifications in science, 16,000 in maths, 40,000 in English. These are not enough – but it is absurd that, under present arrangements, they and others with specialisms have almost no chance of using them directly with other teachers or with children.

The large majority of primary school teachers are officially allocated just over 40 minutes a week away from the classes. What good is that to the poor soul who is supposed to take the lead in science teaching, when there are seven colleagues requiring help, two or three with neither O- nor A-level in science, and none with post-initial training of any substance? Or, for that matter, what good is it to the teacher who has to keep up with the ins and outs of teaching reading and who needs to diagnose the difficulties of Jason, Amil and Della and then advise a colleague on how to help them?

There are times, too, when the class teacher should see the school nurse, the social worker, the educational psychologist and, above all, the parent who cannot wait. And, of course, all teachers need to prepare their lessons.

For primary schools, the National Curriculum can only be a success if authorities use the opportunity of the new funding formulas to increase their staffing. Then, at last, elementary education will die[5].

Nor is Norman Thomas alone. Edward Simpson, former Deputy Permanent Secretary at the DES, and ironically in charge of planning for almost a decade, has argued cogently the same case for more resources for primary schools as a result of the introduction of Local Management of Schools[6].

If the unholy alliance in favour of the National Curriculum is likely to come apart at the seams over the issue of resource, so also, given the very different aspirations of those who support its introduction, there is likely to be a parting of the ways over principles. 'Pupils should be entitled to the same opportunities wherever they go to school'[7]. That sentence from the Red Consultative Document provides the clue to the major misunderstanding which so often links those with very different views. Sometimes those who espouse notions of equal opportunity in education confuse that expression of intent with providing the *same* for everyone, which of course is a denial of equal opportunity. Individual children require different treatment. Moreover, even the definition 'equal opportunity' without qualification is insufficient: it could be equal opportunity to fail or succeed according to their innate capacity and backgrounds. Such advocates would say, 'It's a hard old world . . . . the law of the adult world' – from the right, of course. So those who espouse equal opportunity need to elaborate its purpose. For most such an elaboration would be, 'To grow up confident, contributing, competent adult citizens, capable of living harmoniously within our society'. From this elaboration will flow our obligation to help those without favourable backgrounds to have such a chance.

Given the possibility for agreement, albeit confused and for different reasons, from both left and right, legislation to enforce a National Curriculum should have come as no surprise to the educational world.

For the few unreconstructed opponents of any sort of National Curriculum, still less one which is legislated, there have been two principal objections. The first lay in the effect it might have on teaching and learning and the second in too great a concentration of power in the hands of the government of the day and especially with one person, the Secretary of State. It is of course possible to attempt to meet the second objection through the construction of checks and balances, principally through the National Curriculum Council and the Schools Examination and Assessment Council. The fact that the appointments to such councils are in the hands of the Secretary of State advised by civil servants, makes one question those bodies' ability to be very independent. One would have had greater confidence if the selection were from a longer list nominated by other bodies unconnected with the government of the day. It would even have been possible for the

Secretary of State to have a reserve power to insist on ever more
names from which to choose. One's reason for doubt lies not
merely in the way selection is made: it is simply that those selected
have to be very independent indeed to withstand or divert the
direction pushed by permanent staff, all of whom seem already
to be behaving with unwonted circumspection.

Nevertheless it is the other objection, namely the effect on
children's learning and teachers' teaching which is the most serious.
From the child's viewpoint arguments over management are largely
irrelevant. The nearest attempt to a child's entitlement expressed
by adults on their behalf lies in the United Nations Charter. It
has a peculiarly romantic ring about it and refers to 'special
protection, opportunities and facilities to enable them to develop
in a healthy and normal manner in freedom and dignity', to 'special
treatment, education and care' and 'love and understanding and
an atmosphere of affection and security'[8]. In much the same vein,
one LEA considered recently a draft of a newsletter to parents
outlining the implication of those rights so far as a child's education
in their early years was concerned. A sample of the document
runs as follows:

> Each child is entitled: to be loved and to feel loved, to feel secure,
> to be well nourished, to be protected, to be recognised and respected,
> to be praised, to experience responsibility for oneself and for others,
> to have opportunities to explore and be imaginative, time to explore
> their own feelings, space to develop emotionally, physically, spiritually,
> intellectually and socially according to their individual talents.
>
> Each child needs: to be listened to and understood, to be recognised
> and believed, time to laugh and have fun, time to explore and develop
> their own feelings, the opportunity to make choices and decisions, time
> to understand and respect others' cultures: should have the best of
> what Health and Education can provide.

Such approaches probably owe a great deal to consideration of
research by the National Children's Bureau under Dr Mia Pringle
and a consideration of children's needs as well as their rights.
They are very different from the underpinning of the National
Curriculum's framework which, if similarly old-fashioned, is not
so romantic. Indeed the National Curriculum is expressed in terms
of subjects – the same list, technology apart, and in the same
order as that contained in the secondary regulations of 1904. Such
a curriculum had served well, and did so for many years afterwards,
that small percentage (less than 10%) who enjoyed grammar school
education and were marked out to be the leaders of the nation[9].
Nevertheless to consider the National Curriculum as a list of
subjects runs the danger of expressing it in a way which
overemphasises information and a narrow range of skills at the
expense of the development of a full range of socially useful skills,

attitudes and ideas, which is usually the concern of interested parents and can even be seen in a child's view of the purpose of education.

More seriously, a definition of the curriculum in subject terms alone, militates against the guarantee of 'breadth, balance and coherence' which the preceding debate demanded. For in secondary schools, so often organised in this way, a child's experience may not be as 'coherent' 'broad' and 'balanced' as the curriculum planners imagine. To illustrate this one has only to look at the account of a pupil pursuit in a school which had thought through clearly its broad curriculum and made plans accordingly.

Notes of a visit to Abbeydale School
The day started at 8.50 with a tutorial period taken by Mrs Joiner. Susie was my guide. She came from Bagnol and had started her day at 8 o'clock: she would arrive home at 4.0 to 4.15 after her bus journey. Her father and mother, who holiday in France, have organised a job, as a cook, for her when she leaves at sixteen. She is a 'low ability' child in the second year who attended St Mary's School where she remembered the Head playing a guitar. She prefers secondary school because 'there is more on'. 'You meet more people and teachers'. 'You move about during the day'. 'I can learn an instrument here'. 'I can join a club'. 'We do more different things'. School had been tiring at first on transfer but she had soon got used to it: originally she had belonged to a number of clubs in the early day (Thursday) when all such activities take place, but now preferred to go home early. In conversation this appeared to be the pattern of most youngsters and presumably is coinciding with early adolescence.

The day consisted of eight periods of thirty-five minutes each – and one of thirty minutes namely the first, the tutorial period. Mostly lessons were arranged in double periods.

Each day starts with the tutor period: children gained points, minus or plus, which were displayed (mostly pluses) which could lead to detentions or favourable report comments. Soon the tannoy system announced all the lower school messages: Mrs Joiner and I were deafened and it was sufficiently painful for me to feel relief when it stopped. (John Banton confirmed at lunch that the system is only used once a day and I was in a room where he suspects that the volume control may have been defective. He made a note to look into it.)

Otherwise the period was used for pupil chatter apart from the normal chores of reporting absences and dinner money. There were twenty-six pupils in the group. Mrs Joiner was very pleasant to the children in her tone and announced success in work for Amnesty International.

The content of the tannoy message and the tutorial period showed the balance towards positive rather than negative messages to children – indeed there was something almost pythonesque about the one negative comment on the tannoy message when it was said 'You know what we do to transistor radios'. Susie laughed at that.

There was no assembly but there would be on other days for my group. Children talked, read horoscopes, collected dinner money and completed homework. They talked of clothes and friends, of music and what they would do at the weekend . . .

Boys and girls naturally grouped themselves separately.

Lesson 1 OMLAC (French)

Mrs Joiner took what was a bottom set (14 pupils) for French. We had Eclair and the instructions were in English apart from the opening remarks about opening doors and so on. Some of the Eclair exercises were faulty in the sense that the tape support was superfluous to the children who had done it already. By 10.35 am (it was a double lesson) the children were pleased to be on the move. The French Head of Department said later – as did others – the periods were too long for their subject. Certainly with lower ability children doing oral work and class work that was true. Whether it would be so if there had been practical tasks associated with the French language is another question. Mrs Joiner's relationship with the children was very pleasant and she remained remarkably encouraging when they were a little restless. Susie idly jotted names of friends in her rough book when she was lost. I honestly do not believe that the children I saw will take French in year four, nor that any of them will remember much, if anything, when they are twenty or more. They have learnt the skills of listening and answering questions.

Incidentally the lesson would have been better if there had been more tape recorders in the school and if the tape had been ready at the right moment. The time of the children was spent entirely on tape listening (15 minutes) question and answer (25 minutes) and working on their own for the balance. Homework was changed in mid-stream but was definitely expected and would be completed. The teacher spoke to every child during the lesson and when one looked like being missed other children cheerfully pointed out the omission. There was no occasion on which there was any negative or sarcastic comment to any child.

After ten or fifteen minutes break with Susie when she chatted about her social life, I went to the second lesson.

Lesson 2 Science (double period, Mrs Morden)

Friendly babble of noise. The children clearly liked her. Very well prepared and laid out. She went round groups and helped. The children in groups of two, three or four, tackled an experiment of mixing hydrochloric acid and sodium hydroxide and then testing for the result and boiling the outcome to see what was left. It was well tackled by eager students. They discovered the outcome and recorded it very well.

Mrs Morden spent all the time talking to the groups and helping where needed. Questions were open and she often made interesting an unexpected connections which clearly stimulated and reassured the children.

Susie liked Science 'because you do things – and it's a break from normal lessons'. 'Working with Tracey is much easier than a group because you would have to stand around in the group and not get a chance of doing things. Besides I see Tracey at the weekends so we can talk about that'. The bit she did not like was writing it up. She was a bit careless at adding drops – a kind of baker's dozen approach – but she knew the answer would be salt and she identified the right one. She even knew that the indicator caused the discolouration.

She cheered up after writing the experiment because she had obviously done it rather well. The homework was interesting and demanded more investigation and some discussion with parents: she – the teacher – provided some useful clues for those who could not find names in an encyclopaedia.

Lesson 3 English (double period, Mrs Whittle)
Another very interesting lesson with lots of discussion including group work as a class. Open and closed questions with a period of miming thrown in. The actual work was related to scientific observation, enquiry, recording as well as learning how to behave in a group. The subject matter was home economics and meal preparation. All the children enjoyed the lesson. I attach an example of one child's written work of a previous lesson which shows something of her view of education and the teacher's comments.

The teacher's comments to children were always friendly, powerful and positive. As Susie said, 'I like English even though I am not good at it'. In this she was realistic. The reason she liked it was the variety and pace of work and the rapport with the teacher. Fifteen minutes was spent in discussion and ten minutes miming, ten minutes in group activity and twenty-five minutes writing. The lesson concluded with the request that the youngsters should go home and make the 'beans on toast for themselves' and ask their mothers if they had described the process accurately.

Lesson 4 Humanities (Mr Smith – class size 26)
The children settled well into an area which was carpeted. For the first time too, tables were in a random arrangement rather than in rows. The lesson was very strictly controlled although it began with lots of open questioning which stimulated the class to decide where Rome should be founded and some of the reasons for its being in that position. They were then very pleased to read in the book that it had been done for the very same reasons. They then spent the rest of the lesson – the first part had taken twenty minutes – in writing an account of why Rome was settled where it was and comparing it with the legends that they knew concerning Rome.

Susie smiled when I thanked her for putting up with me. I confessed to tiredness and asked if she was tired too. 'I was at first. You get used to it . . . and you can always see your friends if it gets too much'.

Example of a child's work – Abbeydale School

What I would do if school were at home
Eight o'clock – my mother wants me to lay the table and get breakfast ready.

Nine o'clock - we go down to the park and look at the trees and animals which is very interesting.

Ten o'clock - we come in from the park and then write up what we saw and do a project on it.

Eleven o'clock - I get a book to read and then write about it. Sometimes I find the book very interesting which is good because when it comes to writing about it I find it easy.

Twelve o'clock - I then have lunch with my parents and talk about things which have happened in the morning.

One o'clock - after lunch my mother shows me how to make a cake so that I can have it for tea.

Two o'clock - I then sit down in front of the television with a pen and piece of paper and watch the schools programme which I like because you can have a rest from writing and reading.

Three o'clock - I just finish off everything that I did not have time to do.

Then the rest of the day is my own.

The account mainly speaks for itself. Certainly there is little coherence in her timetabled day: indeed perversely its very staccato pattern is a feature Susie quite enjoys. Nor did she see coherence over a longer period partly because her own world was a social one dominated by friends, clothes, music and beckoning adulthood.

Susie had come from a village ten miles from the Oxfordshire market town in which the school was placed: her previous village primary school had had two teachers; her experience in that school at a younger more protected age seemed to her less interesting and more childish. She recognised, as youngsters will, the need for different approaches at different ages. A cursory perusal of my file of pupils' pursuits in both primary and secondary schools shows similar experiences and reflections. Interestingly there is inevitably more coherence in the primary child's day because one or two adults experience the same things - indeed they are the conductors of the total experience which is planned for a day in detail within the week and the year. Those who, with some justification, criticise the lack of continuity within some primary schools, should consider it in comparison with the secondary school when viewed from the child's viewpoint. The coherence, the progression, one can argue, lies in the eye of the curriculum planner rather than that of the individually different children who experience it haphazardly, often guided into a general context by the pastoral strength of their form tutor who may not always see the whole picture themselves. All the experience suggests that their minds are absent on social issues, as Susie confessed hers were during at least part of each day. This is the model on which the National Curriculum is to be created and by degrees imposed on the primary schools.

Sir Peter Newsam was fond of quoting a paper of Sir Alec Clegg, to teachers who were inclined to get over-complicated about the curriculum. He repeated it with some commentary in an issue of the *Times Educational Supplement*[10].

Alec Clegg once wrote a fable. It began: 'About 100 years ago there was a small boy called Fred and he lived on an island with his father and mother and nearby lived his uncle and aunt. His father kept pigeons and bees and a garden of flowers and vegetables. His uncle was a forester and planted acre after acre of trees in rows. The boy did not go to school; there wasn't a school on the island, but his mother taught him to read and write and encouraged him to draw and paint pictures, she also recited poetry to him and sang to him when he was little . . . .'

As the fable continues, it tells of family visits to York and Malham and of how the child grew up in understanding of many things. Came the Fall:

'Then one day a learned educationist visited the island and met the boy and was astonished at his understanding of many things and at the knowledge which he had developed round these things, and the educationist said to himself how wonderful it would be if every child in the land had the learning which this boy had built around the simple experiences which he had had with the bees, pigeons, flowers, vegetables, forestry and visits to York and Malham. And the learned educationist reasoned thus:

'It is impossible for every child to lead the life that this boy has led and to develop the knowledge which this boy's way of life has given him. But what we can do is give the children all the knowledge that this boy has without the experiences.

'First of all we will look at his numerical and mathematical ability which he has gained from reckoning areas from odd shaped bits of land and working out the number of trees they will take, and from his mother's shopping expeditions, and we will reduce these to simple symbolic formulas and tables and make children learn a lot of them very quickly.

'Then we will take the boy's speech and writing which is so good and subject it to careful analysis and if we teach the other boys whose writing and speech is not so good how to subject what they say and write to this kind of analysis they will realise how badly they speak and write and will promptly set about trying to improve the way they speak and write. . . .'

The fable sends the learned educationist home to divide Fred's knowledge into parcels which he hands out to various expert textbook writers. Inexorably the fable continues:

'And so it came about that all over the land children were assembled in groups of 40 and made to learn the facts set out in the books written by Messrs Hall & Stevens, Warner & Martin, Durrell & Palmer, and Potter and Ridout.

'And the learned educationist began to entertain a horrible suspicion that the reverse process didn't work. In other words, whereas Fred grew in understanding because he started with experience and read to feed the interest which derived from it, those who started with the reading failed to develop understanding because the interest was not there.

'But the learned educationist thrust these horrible suspicions aside and said to himself that the facts derived from books are making no impact because they are not properly learned. It is all these inefficient teachers who cannot impart facts that are causing the trouble. What we want is something wherewith to prod the teachers so that they impart more facts more efficiently.

'So he said we will have external examiners who will set tests to the children to find out whether they have learned the facts. Those who have had facts imparted to them effectively will pass the tests and those who have not will fail to pass the tests, and when the lsits are read out on Speech Day the incompetence of the bad fact-imparters will be revealed to the world and this will act as a goad and make them impart their facts better in future . . ..'

'However, in due course a few, a very few indeed, intelligent teachers came to take a cool look at what was happening and they realised that for the vast majority of children the majority of our educational processes add about as much to the mental stature of our children as a diet of sawdust would add to their physical stature . . ..'

Since the fable was written in 1965, ending on a note of hope, the whole prodding apparatus has been formidably increased; so too have the mounds of curricular sawdust. Clever people, with no apparent understanding of how children learn or good teachers teach, have been busy seeing to that. In particular, examination fever is leading to ever more fatuous and expensive efforts to measure the immeasurable. In the 1970s, Sir Alec set us laughing at some of the items in the Educational Assessment Program in the state of Michigan:

'By the end of the pre-kindergarten experience 90 per cent of all children will demonstrate their recognition of at least three of the five basic emotions: fear, anger, sadness, joy and love (in self and others) as measured by a future Michigan Education Assessment Program (MEAP) battery of tests.

The story reminded me of a report I once received from an Advisor about a youngster who was out of school. It was dated 8 June 1982 and read as follows:

I have paid a lengthy visit to John Kingdom and his parents at Westhouney. John is fourteen next term and would normally leave school in a couple of years time.

I am happy that he is receiving education suitable to age, ability and aptitude at home, in fact, between ourselves, it is probably more appropriate and worthwhile than that which he is likely to be receiving at school – not through any fault in the local schools but because schools cannot always provide ideal circumstances for all learning and certainly cannot provide the context in which John is operating.

John is looking after a sizeable vegetable garden single handed and has plans to extend considerably on to other land owned by the family. He has numerous animals to care for, he is playing the organ in the next door church and the piano at home. He also does some composing.

He reads a lot, both for pleasure and factual books about farming and natural studies. He is following a correspondence course in gardening for adults with comparative ease. His written work is average, he entered for O-level English this year and obtained a C grade.

He has a tutor, a retired teacher who visits the house for mathematics and is following a traditional and largely irrelevant course in it (such as he might be following at school) and he is learning quite sufficient about mathematics in context apart from that (shades of Cockcroft!)

His mother takes him to Farendon twice a week for tutoring in English and Roman history which he is keen on. He is studying elementary Latin for pleasure with a local friend.

There are teenage cousins in the local schools and obviously there is plenty of contact and company and they seem close as a family.

He hopes to have a farm of his own as soon as possible. Two uncles own a farm in Weston, North Oxfordshire and Mrs Kingdom tells me that the family have the necessary finance to offer him a job.

Mr Kingdom is a gardener at a local school, so he and John have a common interest and work a lot together. John learned to drive a tractor recently and can already ride a motor bike and drive a car on private land.

He attended a primary school some miles away and tried secondary schools but without a great deal of success.

In a sense John is really too busy to go to school. In my view there is no need to worry about exams. John will get what certificates he wants if and when he wants to I expect: I am only glad that there are so many more opportunities for adults who want to study later in life.

I have told them that I am satisfied that John is having a suitably full and varied programme with plenty of work experience. We all intend to continue the same sort of programme for the next couple of years and I have said I would like to call in next term and on a periodic basis until our responsibility ceases. They seemed to welcome it. Need I say more?

In a sense the Advisor did not need to say more, for both her report and the fable of Fred begin to capture the mood of growing up. Newsam who wrote the piece before the National Curriculum and its assessment procedures were planned ended the piece by remarking with irony 'As with any good joke, a child can understand the fable. The puzzle that has to be solved is why many adults cannot'[11].

Many secondary teachers know that among their most fulfilling experiences with children are the 'residential', whether abroad, on a field trip or to an Outdoor Education Centre, and the extra-curricular events, such as sport, music, theatre visits and drama. Among the reasons for this is the subtle change in relationship which occurs, enabling the teacher to be seen more often alongside the pupil, a person of humour and unexpected worldly interests, taking part in the everyday activities of life, sharing the triumphs and disasters of such occasions and bonded by unexpected confidences. For months after such experiences, the exchanges, both in glance and spoken aside, between teacher and student are redolent with 'in-jokes', half-remembered stories that grow with the telling. Of course there are many factors in the comparative success of these occasions and in the weeks or days when the timetable is 'suspended' in favour of interest-led activity, but among them certainly the opportunity to really 'know' the child, and vice versa, is a powerful ingredient.

This factor is naturally much less pronounced in the primary school where the teacher in any case knows the child in much greater depth by virtue of living and working alongside the youngster on a daily, weekly and sometimes more than yearly basis. Indeed in the primary phase the arrangements for children's learning are founded more securely on a theoretical basis of child development designed to match their different developmental needs at different ages.

It can be argued that children need to be part of a mixed age school community from time to time, for that is the pattern of life. Additionally they need individually different attention, not simply because each child is unique but because the different stages require different interpretations. For example the toddler needs the rhythm and songs of the parents to develop their early language skills, whereas the seven- to eight-year-old finds the joy of escape into the fantasy world of children's fiction, of uninhibited and expressive art, of the beginnings of sharp observation, detailed investigation, hypothesis and study. They even talk aloud to themselves and to adults, who will never betray what they hear of the Walter Mitty dreams of their future lives.

The teenager, especially in those uncomfortable years of compulsion before sixteen, both demands and rejects individual interest and attention. Walter Mitty still inhabits the mind, but so do the shadows of more menacing muses, as they experience the growing pains to adulthood. The educators at home and at school are on their guard, wary of, yet understanding their secrecies and confidences, and in particular the need for such youngsters to take risks as they strike out towards independent adulthood. In those years it is the sudden traumatic experience which may be the spark to engage fierce enthusiasms in their educational development. Hence the importance of the residential and extra-curricular activity – above all occasions and activities in which the teenager can know that someone is unobtrusively and undemandingly interested in them. Of course, as every teacher knows, there are many exceptions – the children who test their skill as diagnosticians and facilitators and push to the limit their cheerful, generous, forgiving brisk optimism about the pupil. I refer to the children closer and closer to the margins of predictable deviation – the hyperactive youngster with emotional problems, which brings autism to the edge of the teacher's diagnosis; the child, otherwise quick-witted, who has massively disabling short-term memory and a confusion in decoding letters: what some would call dyslexia; the child whose spatial intelligence is exceptionally and marvellously out of line with the celebratory rites of the school community, who fails in conventional school work. At every turn the successful teacher strives to capitalise on the child's exceptionality, to turn difficulty into opportunity.

To all this complexity the skilled teacher brings a fine judgement tempered by a generosity of expectation, in the determined hope of 'unlocking the child's mind and the shut chambers of the heart'[12]. To the teacher with a deep knowledge of how children at a particular age and stage develop, the first recipe for success is to vary their style of teaching from time to time, both to suit the circumstances, but also to vary the tempo and engage the child's interest. Such a teacher has two approaches to subject knowledge – the curriculum and culture into whose mysteries the child is to be initiated. On the one hand the successful teacher has an infectious enthusiasm for parts of the information, ideas and skills which continue to underpin their original and continuing role as an artist, an historian, a scientist or whatever. It is from this stance that there has been much recent emphasis on subject depth in the training of teachers, and a virtual embargo on teaching for those with degrees in subjects 'not on the school timetable'. On the other hand too, the successful teacher can sometimes be someone with a very slight grasp of subject, because then they understand more closely the problems of many children. 'The successful scholar is normally the person who has the least difficulty in identifying the route from A to B . . . yet are these always the best people to put in charge of those with the greatest difficulty?'[13]. One personal recollection confirms this point aptly.

On my first administrative promotion in Buckinghamshire I encountered Geoff Link, for me a new colleague, but also a former teacher. I greeted him with the age-old aphorism: 'Those who can, do; those who can't, teach; and those who can't teach become administrators – in your case I know whether that is true'. Geoff looked cheerfully but doubtfully tense, a certain pallor betraying his discomfort as he awaited my verdict on his teaching performance all those years ago in the sleepy three form entry grammar school, in an east coast town.

'Oh you were terrific,' I said. 'You taught me maths in 3B. I know how good you were because I was at that stage in maths where I felt rudderless and becalmed, drifting helplessly as it were, as my peer group – the rest of the fleet – sailed serenely on towards the horizon. Should I give up the unequal struggle and wait until

I reached the age of 16? Then you strode in, as the new maths teacher, and you would set the problems on the board and stride around the class getting us all to co-operate in sharing the problems. Each of us was encouraged to try out solutions on the board and you would ask other class members what they thought and whether they had anything to contribute as an alternative. I learned so much and soon caught up with the fleet'.

As I warmed to my eulogy of his skills, Geoff Link's smile was not quite right, it had a certain relief, of course, but it held the promise of something more. His rejoinder explained it all.

'That's interesting, because I was a history teacher. Yours was the only group I ever taught maths – a stop-gap teacher for a year. As for the problems, I often didn't know the answers myself'.

Now to extrapolate from this example to a general argument that familiarity of a subject is a disadvantage would clearly be absurd. Nevertheless, the example points up the paradox of the advantage to the teacher of having to experience new learning alongside and in co-operation with the children, and yet at the same time having to be an expert in the subject. Geoff Link had a firm grasp of classroom techniques and a deep knowledge of children, so he could cope with a small part of his week in exploration of a subject matter with which he had only a tenuous acquaintance. From a child's viewpoint, his style and his forgiving of mistakes, his ability to explore the origin of false assumption and deduction (doubtless springing from his own learning process), was a powerful illuminator of the path of learning.

Above all, from the child's viewpoint, the teacher needs to be an interesting person, one with whom they can readily identify. In the reception class it can be seen in the first moments of a school day. First one child sidles up to the teacher with some trinket to show in order to allow the warm, cheerful voice of teacher questioning and encouraging to wash over the beginning of their school day; then another, more venturesome, rushes into the teacher's arms, with breathless news to convey; and finally a third arrives preoccupied with the task in hand and refers inadvertently to teacher as 'mum'. At an older age it is perhaps better encapsulated by the following:

> I met a teacher recently, one of our best, the sort of charismatic individual with a ready smile, a mind full of anarchic ideas, a love of literature and an effortless but much practised classroom skill which bounces back from the interested eyes of his students. No bored resignation for his turbulent teenagers. He teaches history, so the timetable says. His pupils will tell you differently – well not tell you exactly but demonstrate it in their changed lifestyle, which even their parents notice. They read books now and sometimes a few of them write poetry. Others love to argue and challenge incessantly the established wisdom of

television, the press and the older generation. They know about the development of science and its effect on their environment: one of them is a radio ham, another an electronics freak. In twenty years' time they will remember their history teacher: his mannerisms, his irony and self-deprecating asides, his friendly interest in each of them. They will remember the school play and the theatre trips he organised: they will remember his interest in sport and music: they will recall how they shared their worries and not so ridiculous hopes with him'[14].

On a wet Wednesday in March 1987, as part of a short survey – not scientifically conducted, but as part of a personal investigation into the cause of alienation among secondary age children – I found myself with a group of seven girls and one boy, between the ages of twelve and fifteen, at the Didcot Health Centre at four o'clock in the afternoon. A couple of hours later, when the awkwardnesses had receded and giggling and fidgeting had given way to my acceptance as part of the furniture, they were engaged in an enthusiastic frank exchange about the qualities of teachers whom they had liked, whose lessons they had enjoyed and for whom they were prepared to concede the comment: 'Mr So and So was decent – yeah, well decent, weren't he Sue?' The consensus that emerged about the teachers who had mattered to them was neither that they were strict nor that they were liberal, but simply that they were interested in them as people. What was fascinating to me at the time, was their naming of teachers whom I also recognised, from familiarity with the five or six schools in that particular area of south Oxfordshire: I could immediately apply a cross-bearing as it were of confirmation that what indeed singled out these teachers was a vividness of personality, a cheerful infectious enthusiasm and an unusual energy and commitment.

The introduction of the National Curriculum from the child's point of view is to be judged against the effect it will have on the world which children and teachers occupy. It will be an 'entitlement' to children only if the teachers' intepretation of it and their teaching style, as it is affected by its requirements, will make them more rather than less likely to be the teachers with the sorts of qualities which are likely to engage their learners' interests. In short it seems unlikely, especially with younger children whose grasp on autonomy in learning and responsibility and social action needs much support, that the National Curriculum framework alone will achieve anything. It is its impact on teachers and their style that is at the heart of the matter. Will it be a useful reference route map and a compass? Or will it be so difficult to interpret, so rigid in its framework that there is no room for the teacher to try interesting diversions and take the opportunity for exploration of unmapped territory – even of contributing to the design of the map itself?

The immediate prospects are not promising for the child, at least in so far as primary schools are concerned. The curriculum description, as we have seen, has a compartmentalism (English, maths, etc) which in its extension through science, technology and the other foundation subjects, is quite incompatible with the daily experience of the teacher of thirty mixed age children in many small schools. Even in the larger schools the curriculum leaders with full teaching commitments will find it difficult to find a way of imparting to their other colleagues a sufficient degree of self-confidence about their particular curriculum responsibility which will avoid the deadening grind of 'something we have to do' – a phrase so reminiscent of teachers of external examination syllabuses in every generation.

It is in the field of assessment that the new arrangements are likely to pose the most difficulties for teachers and distract them from their first task of finding their way into 'the very queer and tortuous passages of children's minds'[15]. There are, for example, so far in maths, science, English and technology alone, no less than 14,910 potential separate considerations of statements of attainment for a group of thirty children from level one to level five. When one hears and sees the grids and axes within which the teachers are being encouraged to monitor the progress of each child, it ought to be sufficient to give any sane person pause for thought! Put another way, each teacher is required to monitor and record for each child, within the primary sector, progress under the attainment targets in maths, science, English and technology alone, no less than 497 separate differentiated statements of attainment for each child. It seems unlikely that such discrete and precise measurement is something which can be effortlessly and efficiently stored away in the teacher's mind in the everyday bustle of school life for subsequent 'after-school' recording. Equally it seems nonsense to anticipate the recording of that volume and complexity of assessment for each child during lesson time. The early experience suggests that for the enthusiast of language, for example, the latter approach and even the former is possible: equally too the science enthusiast in primary schools protests at the ease with which they can familiarise themselves with the process. This, however, is to evade the acid test, as I have already implied, which is the ability even of these talented enthusiasts to perform with similar confidence and panache in the designated area of the curriculum with which they are less familiar. This of course is what will be required of all teachers, and what they will need to coach their colleagues to do in their own particular specialism. When recently I asked an enthusiastic practitioner to test the technique in maths, although they were themselves enthusiastic about language, I received confirmation of insecurity, of a self-confessed distraction from the task of teaching in favour of essentially a technician-type reliance on the scheme, and a domination of the teacher by the process of recording progress.

So, simply in its volume the assessment system itself represents a burden for primary school teachers.

For secondary schools with their singular subject specialisms, it is less of a problem – merely an extension of some of the approaches of GCSE to the assessment for the first three years of secondary work within keystage 3. The warning here, however, is of the difficulty encountered by some enthusiasts for graded assessment tests in persuading other colleagues in their discipline of the practicality and value of the detailed record-keeping of various 'grade related criteria' within the subject area itself. Nor has there been experience yet of the voluminous records for individual children when the same approach is extended from science through maths, English, technology, geography, history and modern languages. The form tutor, even with the best information technology support system, is about to assume the considerable duties of maintaining the total child record. The same form tutor will also be a subject teacher. (As so often happens in secondary schools, the same individual may be enthusiastic in the one capacity for activity which he or she adamantly inveighs against in the other capacity. Shades of disputes about children being released for field trips or school visits).

To these logistical difficulties of recording each child's progress is added the initially difficult task for primary and secondary schools, of mapping their own curriculum against the National Curriculum, the detail of which is emerging only piecemeal. The DES has required (Circular 14/89) a bureaucratic return which embodies an assumption that teachers can plan curriculum time to the hour, even the minute, and that such a detailed record has some worthwhile purpose. In fact it is a classic example of losing sight of the wood for the trees, and in fact it distracts from the process of detailed curriculum design and review which thinking schools embrace as part of the atmosphere of intellectual curiosity which is their hallmark. At the moment, at secondary level any school's review of a National Curriculum plan has two main imponderables – namely how to organise keystage 4 from fourteen to sixteen in a way which accommodates choice and avoids boredom and alienation amongst those with the least attainment in the compulsory core and foundation subjects in the first three keystages. Secondly the 'curriculum auditors' are examining the cross curricular themes so threatened by the separate subject curriculum design approach to the implementation of the National Curriculum. There is an interesting difference here between the approach in England and Wales from that in Northern Ireland where a cross-curricular front has been started before embarking on marching orders for the separate subjects. In England and Wales, cross-curricular analysis started earlier than in Northern Ireland, for example with 'Language Across the Curriculum' after the Bullock Report and in the 11–16 Red Book analysis pioneered by some of the HMI. Nevertheless its roots have evidently been shallower than in Northern Ireland, where the absence of comprehensive schools perhaps made it the more necessary. On both sides of the Irish Sea it has made all practitioners keenly aware of the deep *oubliettes* of the timetable, in short of the incoherence even of the apparently most broad and balanced curriculum. It is an incoherence, as we have seen earlier, not only in design but especially of receipt by the pupil.

Both these points – the cross curricular theme and the overcrowding in keystage 4 – underline the point that, so far as design is concerned, the exercise of planning the National Curriculum has been flawed from the outset. Nobody decided the length of the journey in what is almost an infinite mapping process. The explosion of knowledge, skills and ideas, which has occurred in the last half century makes any mapping to some extent arbitrary. Hence the belated and misguided call from Kenneth Baker for longer school days – again betraying a rather narrow view of the use of time – which has been one of the unremarked and growing features of secondary curriculum development of the last twenty years. Indeed at secondary level the timetable of the week seems to blind one to considerations of the length of a course: the number of periods in a week or six days is debated, rather than the length of a period or the number of hours in a course.

If there is an overcrowding of the scope of the curriculum, however, it is more than matched, as we have seen in the primary illustrations, by the prospective assessment system. The national assessment system will serve several purposes. It will be:

- **Formative**, in providing information which teachers can use in deciding how a pupil's learning should be taken forward and in giving the pupils themselves clear and understandable targets and feedback about their achievement. It will also provide teachers and others with the means of identifying the need for further diagnostic assessments for particular pupils where appropriate to help their educational development;
- **Summative**, in providing overall evidence of the achievements of a pupil and of what he or she knows, understands and can do;
- **Evaluative**, in that comparative aggregated information about pupils' achievements can be used as an indicator of where

there needs to be further effort, resources, changes in the curriculum, etc;

- **Informative**, in helping communication with parents about how their children are doing; and with governing bodies, LEAs in a wider community about the achievements of a school;
- Helpful for **professional development**, in that the process of carrying out systematic assessment, recording attainment and moderating the outcomes and discussion with other teachers will provide a valuable basis for teachers to evaluate their own work and to gain access to new thinking[16].

It is a bold aim, especially if all the purposes are to be kept in balance. One suspects that the other purposes of the 1988 Education Act, in particular the need to emphasise parental choice and to bring the brisk benefits of the winds of market forces to the education system, will mean that the summative, evaluative and informative purposes might squeeze out emphasis on the other two.

Testing of children has always legitimately had separate purposes: diagnostic – to enable the teacher to calibrate their own assessment of a child's difficulty and judge the next best line for development; setting of tests to establish mastery of a particular piece of learning when of concept, skill or information; and standardised to set one's own information against some comparators. It is a personal activity at best, an aid to the individual teacher, the individual child and the parents. To this normal activity of teachers, however, the 1988 Education Act has added the competitive market aspects we have noted, the combination of which threatens to disturb and distort the normal observation and assessment techniques of the successful teacher.

The sheer volume of the many assessments externally required by the Act and now under design by SEAC runs the danger of forcing the less confident teachers – indeed all of them in the first instance, as they ascend the steep learning curve – into 'rote teaching', a much more dangerous activity than rote learning because it tends to shut down that sense of intellectual curiosity without which children are not really being taught.

In America within some states there are many school districts with decades of experience of such externally imposed and grade-related tests to enable teachers to make predictions and check by observation and testing the outcome. What that experience demonstrates is that the teacher very rarely uses the voluminous information, which is nevertheless conscientiously stored and retained. The volume may be judged by an anecdote of a teacher in Massachusetts, a comparatively liberal state, which has come only lately to such activity and to a degree which would be surpassed by many other states. In a visit in the spring of 1987, I met a teacher who confided that the externally-imposed testing system pre-empted the use of 30% of her total professional time, and that her own independent judgements (which she saw as more valuable and inseparable from her natural teaching style) occupied a further 20–25% of the time. The official 'tests' were seen as important from the point of view of accountability, but not of teaching. Indeed it is that aspect of the new arrangements which distorts the previous use of assessment by teachers, parents and children.

The requirements of such a system may lead to a number of outcomes, some of which are unlikely to be beneficial to the child. The first is that enormous amounts of professional time and effort will be absorbed in explaining apparent differences between classes and schools. Another will be that teachers cheat in order that their children perform well in the test. Such cheating may take the form of coaching or practice, but it may also take the subtle form of the chemistry teacher who asked the GCE student, 'are you sure that is what you want?' when she was asking for some particular potion to complete an experiment in a practical examination, or the American teacher on the same 1987 visit who pointed to a particular answer in a workbook and asked the student to 'check that out'. Such actions may be indicative of a climate of fear, or of caution, or of simply teaching to the test. It is hard to see how they benefit the child.

It may be argued that the new designs of the assessments will avoid such obvious pitfalls. Nevertheless the SATS, however elegant the design, will of course be liable to the same dangers. The cause after all lies not in the nature of the test but in the context of its use, and if the pay of the teachers (or more likely the viability of the school) depends on the results, there will be a temptation to massage the outcome. Moreover, the inevitability of pecking orders for children and institutions presupposed by such a market index of comparative performance will render less propitious the circumstances for learning, for those children who, through no fault of their own, are in a school which is perceived by the articulate watchers of the school results index to be failing. For failure will beget failure.

There is one more point which demands notice in the design of assessment – namely its untried novelty. That quality, at least initially when combined with other innovation being imposed on the school system, is likely to lead to a distraction of the teachers' time from the sort of effortless teaching strategies, hard won over decades, as they are drawn into the steep learning curve of the unfamiliar new language of the National Curriculum and its assessment. For a while, every teacher becomes a probationer: indeed visiting headteachers said to the young teachers from university, polytechnic and college courses in September 1989, 'You tell us about it – inevitably you have had more time to learn about it than we have.'

Clearly there will soon come a point where every practising teacher will become familiar with the 'newspeak' of attainment targets, statements of attainment, levels, keystages, programmes of study, standard assessment tasks, and profile components, with none of which any of us was familiar two short years ago[17].

The point is made: there is a disadvantage to children immediately in the learning by teachers of so much that is at least newly described, if not new in reality. The child, of course, needs confident and competent teachers above all else.

If the weight of the assessment detail were to lead to an understandable desire for simplification, there is another awful danger awaiting the child. Will this simplification, especially as the assessment system is to be discussed in terms of levels, lead to the child being labelled and known prematurely as a 'level one child' or a 'level two child' and so on? If that were to be the case it could be a return to the profoundly damaging effects that the daily streaming, even in primary and elementary schools, produced in an earlier age. We have never quite shaken off its effects. Its persistence is evident in *Gentleman Jim*, one of Raymond Briggs' classic cartoon books written in 1980. It depicts the sad tale of a lavatory attendant, Jim, who reads newspapers to seek a new career. At every turn he is confronted with the need for O-levels, A-levels, etc and reflects and wonders 'what the levels can be all about?' He guesses that it is something to do with education and reflects wryly that 'all we got was a bible and a thick ear'. The story becomes an enactment of his fantasies, with predictable tragi-comic side-effects, such as the failure to apply for planning permission when establishing some new profitable activities in his garden, or committing driving offences, even some petty crimes. When he is sentenced to gaol he pleads in mitigation that he 'might have been a better citizen if I'd had the levels', to a Judge who didn't understand what he was saying, and of course the last page sees him studying for 'the levels' in prison.

It is remarkable that the language of Briggs' book, a sad commentary on the preoccupation up to now with examinations in England and Wales, should be so accurate in its awful warning of the new system. Clearly neither Paul Black himself nor his committee could have read the book: otherwise they would surely have paused for thought before designing a system with such awful possibilities.

If there were a wish to record 'the levels' on a precise and continuous basis, differences between children will be considerable and the change the greater for youngsters who might, in a less overtly labelled system, be confident late developers. Worse still, of course, is the prospect of recording progress within 'the Record of Achievement' which all schools, at least at the secondary level, are likely to have by the early 1990s as a result of government policy and local initiative.

The Records of Achievement, however, are a move from an earlier, more romantic and generous age. The following source represents the beginning of the movement:

An Oxford Certificate
(The end of the 16+ energy trap)

1. For twenty years the 16+ has been to educationalists what the Irish Question has been to politicians for somewhat longer: it has consumed enormous energy, made and destroyed reputations, absorbed and dissipated creativity and made most men and women with common sense as well as intelligence adopt the stance of peripheral critics.

2. There are two reasons why common sense and intelligence now demand one more effort in Oxfordshire:

    (i) the very existence of any examination at 16+ (whether GCE, CSE or a unified examination or examination system) as opposed to a series of assessments at the right stage of development for the individual pupil is questionable because firstly sixteen has already ceased to be the date for leaving education for the majority of pupils, secondly employers look increasingly to school recommendations, college course experience, and examination *expectations* rather than evidence of 'O' Level/CSE *achievements*, and thirdly the Universities and Higher Education look for and stipulate 'A' Level achievements rather than 'O' Level evidence.

    (ii) the possibility of removing the 16+ as a series of examinations to be taken after a one/two year course for 14–16 year olds at the age of sixteen would remove a constraint which has a distorting effect on the pattern of the curriculum of schools. That is to say it would remove the overemphasis on a simultaneous and over-rich diet of information gathering and testing.

3. So the aim should be to create an Oxford Certificate/Portfolio/ Diploma for all students, moving into the world of work or higher education. It would be taken with them at any age and would contain:

    (i) cumulative certificates of achievement awarded by GCE examination boards at Ordinary and Advanced Level, certificates awarded by City and Guilds, BEC, TEC, etc.

    (ii) results of graded objective tests and profiles of skills and information for all pupils, devised by a partnership of Oxfordshire teachers, industrialists, the University, the Southern Regional CSE Board and the Oxford Delegacy in at least Science, Mathematics, English, a modern language and Aesthetics*.

Validation by the Boards, marking by the schools, moderation
by the partnership.
(iii) self-chosen evidence of pupils' thought and action in written,
visual and taped form designed to be a self-selected commentary
on the pupils' character.
(iv) such other evidence to be decided by the partners in (ii) above
(eg work experience, community service)[18].

What followed is well chronicled elsewhere[19]. In practice,
Oxfordshire, Somerset, Leicestershire and Coventry set out on
an ambitious exercise simultaneously with the development of the
Northern Record of Achievement and the London Record of
Achievement. The three groups co-operated loosely so that none
could be isolated and stopped. Government policy statements grew
out of their involvement in the movement and the intention of
it subtly changed.

The document is especially interesting in retrospect because
it can be seen to be a fairly crude thought about the need to
escape the deadening effects of 16+ examining. (Earlier publicly
recorded testing was eschewed as too damaging to youngsters'
morale.) It envisages graded tests with levels between the ages
of 14 and 16. In practice, the enormous investment in design that
followed – £250,000 a year in the Oxford Certificate scheme for
four years – revealed the potential impracticality of the graded
test part of the design between the ages of 14 and 16. While in
isolation and in the hands of enthusiasts, each subject had merit
(although there was great concern about premature labelling), in
total it was unmanageable. It may be significant that Paul Black
was involved heavily at the London end in the design of such
schemes, but again not from the total viewpoint which in any case
would probably be regarded as one of the weaknesses of the London
development where there was less overview than obtained in
Oxford.

The merit of the Record of Achievement movement lay not in
the graded test profile therefore, which proved impractical. It lay
in the changed stance between teacher and learner and in the
modification of techniques and strategies of the former, and
increased motivation and precision of objectives in the latter –
in short in the formative rather than summative stance of
assessment and learning.

The child at whatever age needs stimulation and assessment,
competition against self and against others in a carefully constructed
and sensitively handled framework. What the Record of
Achievement has provided is a context for positive discussion and
a location for each child to record success.

The Secretary of State has in mind using the Records of
Achievement as the repository of pupil achievements in the tests

and assessments at age 7, 11, 14 and 16 – at least so far as the sole mandatory requirements are concerned. The implicit dangers of this are too obvious to need much elaboration. Put simply, the Record of Achievement could become a Record of Failure, at least for the child who makes a slow start to achievement within the prescribed National Curriculum.

The challenge to the teacher is how to avoid that happening: it will test the ingenuity of the most imaginative, but of all the challenges, it is surely the most important.

References

[1] *The National Curriculum 5–16 – a consultative document* (DES) July 1987 p 2 acknowledges origin to 'Sir James Callaghan's speech as Prime Minister at Ruskin College in 1976'.

[2] *Aspects of Secondary Education in England* – a survey by HM Inspector of Schools (DES) December 1979. Other influential HMI and DES documents have been:
      Education in Schools: a consultative document 1977; *A Framework for the School Curriculum*, 1979; *The School Curriculum*, 1981; *Better Schools* 1985; *Curriculum 11–16*, 1977.

[3] Extracts of speech from Prime Minister Margaret Thatcher at Conservative Local Government Conference, Torquay 1987.

[4] See, for example, *TES* issues: 6 July 1988, p 1, 22 July 1988, pp 1, 8 and 9; 19 Aug 1988, p 3; 9 Sept 1989, p 23; 30 Sept 1989, p 8; 4 Nov 1989, pp 1 and 3; 11 Nov 1988, pp 14 and 15.

[5] *The Independent*, 29 June 1989.

[6] *Education*, 21 April 1989, pp 377 and 378.

[7] *The National Curriculum 5–16: a consultative document* (DES), July 1987.

[8] United Nations Declaration of Rights of the Child.

[9] The phrase comes from Robert Lowe, the architect of the Revised Code in the 19th century. He saw 'the education of the poorer classes as just sufficient to give them that sense of awe and respect for higher education, which the leaders of the poor demand'. In that sentiment he echoed the comments of the Bishop of London who in 1803 declared, 'Men of considerable ability say that it is safer for both the Government and the religion of the country to let the lower classes remain in that state of ignorance in which nature has originally placed them'.

[10] *TES*, 7 June 1986, p 84.

[11] Ibid.

[12] *Life and Letters of Edward Thring*, Parkin.

[13] *The Times*, Dec 1886: Letter to same from E Thring.

[14] *The Guardian*, 23 July 1987.

[15] *Life and Letters of Edward Thing*, Parkin.

[16] *National Curriculum: from policy to practice* (DES) 1989, 6.2.

[17] An illustration of how far we have come in 'newspeak' and the difficulty

it presents even for the most eminent in its initial stages, was experienced by 700 teachers in Portsmouth Guildhall in November 1988 which, it should be noted, is less than a year before the introduction of the new arrangement. I was following Eric Bolton, Senior Chief HMI, who persistently referred in his address to standard *attainment* tasks instead of standard *assessment* tasks. At that stage I believe I was the only person in the room to spot a mistake which, with greater familiarity, a few months later would have caused anyone to blush and which now seems incredible in the telling.

18 Internal Memo, Oxfordshire Education Department – CEO/PJF, 4 April 1982.

19 See for example *Records of Achievement – Report of the National Evaluation of Pilot Schemes*, P Broadfoot *et al* (DES) 1988 on 'Records of Achievement – Report of the Records of Achievement National Steering Committee' (DES) January 1989.

Section Two: Implications for primary and secondary schooling

5 A View from a secondary school

Michael Duffy, Headteacher, King Edward VI School, Morpeth

The 'Polo Syndrome'

When the National Curriculum was first unveiled, in the shape of Mr Baker's celebrated 'Little Red Book', I wrote a piece which began: 'If this were genuinely a consultative document, I should reply to its chief begetter that 20 per cent of it is potentially helpful, 20 per cent unexceptionable, and 60 per cent either foolish or dangerous or both'.

Within that first fraction of potential benefit, I classified the endorsement of 'science' in place of the separate sciences that have for so long unbalanced or distorted the secondary curriculum; the opportunity to rethink the nature and role of technology; and the challenge to begin planning, for all secondary students, a foundation course in a foreign language.

About much of the rest, I was hostile or pessimistic. The curriculum that was sketched out seemed ludicrously inadequate. It was a production-line model, stereotyped by an obsession with quality control – as though education were just another product on the market, and teachers merely the operatives who delivered it. The great danger of the proposals, I said, was not that they would fail to improve our schools, but that they would make them worse. 'What we need, if we are to achieve better schools, is better teachers: teachers with a sense of vocation, a sense of responsibility and a sense of esteem; teachers who feel, in the fashionable jargon of management, that they "own the job". Without such teachers,

85

the best possible curriculum is no more than one lesson after
another.'

Two years later, a great deal has changed, but some of the
danger still persists. It is still true that the political drive towards
the National Curriculum is towards uniformity, so that the
consumer – still seen as the parent, not the student – can more
easily discern the quality. There is still, therefore, a tension between
the idea of the National Curriculum as an *entitlement* for all
students, and the idea of education as a product in the market
place, where the thickness of your wallet counts. There is still
a strong political pressure towards the Gradgrind model of
curriculum design, as though education were just a game of 'Trivial
Pursuit'. There is still real concern about the nature of the
assessment process, though now it has to do more with its extreme
complexity than with the simplistic *naïveté* of the earlier proposals,
and with the fundamental differences of approach that are emerging
between the examiners and the curriculum planners. There is still,
too, about the whole exercise, something of the 'Polo Syndrome':
a sense that, for all the subject reports, and statutory orders, and
non-statutory guidance, there is nothing at the centre: no clear
vision of the values that should lie at the heart of a national system
of education. And there is still huge concern about the resources
available. Partly, this is a matter of teacher supply: in certain areas
of the country it is not just the National Curriculum that is at
risk – it is *any* curriculum. Partly, it is about the funding of change.
The government has allocated, for the introduction of the National
Curriculum into 24,000 schools, the sum of £30 million. In the
context of the £33 million earmarked for 20 City Technology
Colleges, that figure makes interesting reading. Which of these
changes, one wonders, is the more important for our national
education?

It is clear, nevertheless, that there is room for optimism. The
grosser absurdities of the consultative document have disappeared,
and it is now apparent that the cross-curricular elements (those
aspects of learning that will not slot into the conventional 'subject'
boxes yet are still too important to be left to chance) are going
(somehow) to be retained. The subject working parties have proved
more independent of mind and judgement than critics had expected:
less like Rosencrantz and Guildenstern ('You were sent for: and
there is a kind of confession in your looks which your modesties
have not craft enough to colour'); more, perhaps, like Polonius,
given to worthy but occasionally tedious advice. Professor Black's
TGAT report, for all its expensive complexity, has saved us from
the test-led teaching that seemed at one time inevitable. Most
important of all, it is now possible to discern in the structure that
is emerging from the subject reports and the National Curriculum

Council some windows of opportunity for good teachers and thinking schools.

Windows of opportunity

The statutory framework of the National Curriculum is contained in sections 1 to 25 of the 1988 Act. Here, in primary legislation, the essentials are prescribed: the three core subjects of mathematics, English and science; the seven foundation subjects (history, geography, technology, music, art, physical education and – in secondary schools – a modern foreign language); the 'basic' subject, religious education; the mechanisms of programmes of study, attainment targets and keystage assessment by means of which the objectives of breadth, balance and quality were to be achieved.

It was widely felt, while the Bill was passing into law, that the programmes of study were going to be inflexibly prescriptive. In the event, wiser counsels prevailed; the proposals that had emerged by the summer of 1989 from the subject working parties and the National Curriculum Council were far from being the national syllabuses that had at first seemed likely. For all their detail, they still require subject departments and faculties to plan and develop their own approaches. They put the emphasis where the emphasis ought to be: not on 'the syllabus' (which in the upper secondary years has often deadened and stereotyped the teaching process) but on the scheme of work. The syllabus, after all, is no more than a sketch of the terrain; the scheme of work is a strategic plan which identifies objectives and tactics, and which allows for review and reinforcement. The need to think in these terms, and to build in systematic and continuous assessment of progress, is an unexpected by-product of the legislation, and probably a bonus.

So is the need to make provision for progression. Progression has been one of the keystones of the TVEI extension, and there are few secondary schools which are not committed to the concept that a student's learning should grow out of, and build upon, what has been learned before. In practice, however, progression has been difficult to achieve, and the rites of passage that have been such a feature of our educational organisation – at 11 plus, at the options stage at 14, and again at 16 – have compounded the problem. Quite rightly, we have put considerable stress in recent years on 'liaison' with contributory schools – not always with conspicuous success. We have not stressed so frequently the importance of liaison with our own colleagues, arguing (with sometimes dubious validity) that because it 'happens all the time' it does not need to be explicitly provided. Now, however, the assessment provisions of the 1988 Act (turned by TGAT into a model for curriculum construction) actually demand that it takes place. By definition, many nine-year-olds in junior schools will be achieving at the level of many thirteen-year-olds in secondary schools. By definition, many thirteen-year-olds in secondary schools will be achieving at the level of many sixteen-year-olds. In theory, we have always known that. In practice, it has been extraordinarily difficult to recognise – and it fits uncomfortably, of course, into the framework of the legislation. Nevertheless, schools are going to have to come to terms with it – and nothing but good can come of that.

By the same token, we can at last begin to see an effective mechanism for identifying special learning needs, at either end of the educational spectrum. Hitherto, our provision here has been at best haphazard, and at worst deplorable. It has depended (in spite of the excellent intentions of the Warnock Report) on the ability of individual schools to identify, without specific criteria, children who are 'under-performing', and to make (largely without professional advice) appropriate provision for them. Too often, such provision tended to focus exclusively on slow learners, and took the form of 'remedial' provision which tended not to remedy and which sometimes created, in the return to the 'normal' curriculum, extra problems for the child. We do not as yet have full details of the standard assessment tasks which will be used at the ages of seven and eleven and subsequently; if they do not provide a means of screening for learning difficulty, and identifying the nature of the difficulty, a significant opportunity will have been missed.

One of the most valuable outcomes of this intially prescriptive and limiting legislation is the opportunity to take a whole school view of curriculum planning and delivery. Again, we have paid lip-service to this for a long time, but it has not been an easy ideal to achieve. Too many factors out of our control have militated against it. The traditional subject structure of the curriculum tended to lock curriculum planning into a matrix of departmental responsibilities, and departmental responsibilities were locked, in their turn, into the salary structure, and were reflected in staffroom perceptions about status and value. There was a certain strength in this; for good teachers, that sense of professional independence was challenging and exhilarating, and there was a sort of pride in the assertion of ownership. For less good teachers, 'my subject, my classroom, my class' could too easily become 'my territory, my problems'. Whole curricular thinking was inhibited by the need to preserve the first; the breaking down of professional isolation by the need to conceal the latter. Under the National Curriculum, there is no room for either.

In part, this is because of the shortcomings of that highly specific subject framework. The barrage of criticism that greeted the consultative paper persuaded both Ministers and mandarins of something that schools and parents had known experientially all along; that the problem of curriculum planning is not deciding what to put in, but what to leave out.

Faced with the outcry of the excluded subjects and the discreet protests of Her Majesty's Inspectorate, the DES retreated. The National Curriculum is certainly *not* a complete curriculum, it stated: the whole curriculum must include for all pupils (and in some cases at all stages) areas of learning which, though not separately identified, are nonetheless 'clearly required'. For most schools, there is nothing new about this thinking: TVEI has already made them familiar with the concepts of cross-curricular dimensions (such as equal opportunities, independent learning) skills and competences (such as literacy, oracy, numeracy, computer literacy, and the less obvious visual literacy) and themes (such as health education, careers education and guidance, environmental and economic education and – increasingly – citizenship). What *is* new, however, as the National Curriculum comes into effect, is the impossibility of providing for these areas of learning within discrete subject entitlements. This, of course, is what schools have tended to do in the past; they have created new 'options' on the over-crowded curriculum shelves. Now, the government has shifted the focus of curriculum planning from availability (the options system) to entitlement, and has unwittingly ensured (by filling most of the time available with the statutory curriculum) that the dimensions, skills and themes of this entitlement can be met most easily *inside* the foundation subjects, and not *outside* them.

The second reason for this impetus to cross-curricularity lies in the not unexpected discovery of the subject working parties that 'subjects' are not the most appropriate descriptors of the learning process. Each working party has surveyed its territory, so to speak, and found significant areas where the boundaries are unclear. In science, for example, the earth science component (attainment targets 9 and 16, with aspects of attainment targets 5, 6, 7 and 8) includes much that has in the past been described as geography, while the materials component (ATs 6–8) includes a great deal that has conventionally been regarded as technology. As if to underline the shifting boundaries of our assumptions, the working group on design and technology has challenged its 'subject' status, preferring to describe it as a 'capability' that will be developed not only through design technology, business studies, information technology and home economics, but through most other subjects as well.

All of this is both sensible and encouraging. It is a belated recognition that good learning is as much about knowing *how* and *why* as about knowing *what* – as much about process as about product. It is clearly absurd to try to restrict the teaching of measurement to mathematics, and the teaching of good, clear writing to English. It is equally absurd, once the working parties have consulted on content and won substantial professional support for their proposals, for subject departments to claim that content as their own. There is simply too much of it. Schools will have to learn to look across the whole curriculum, to identify where and by what means an individual attainment target can best be taught and assessed. Otherwise, both they and their students will be seriously overloaded.

That imperative itself is an opportunity, and an important one. It is the opportunity to reconsider two of the taken-for-granted assumptions that hitherto have shaped so much of our curriculum planning. The first is the assumption that the basis of our timetabling is the year group; that, however we group pupils for teaching purposes, those pupils will all be of an age. It is true that the initial rhetoric of the statutory curriculum, with its emphasis on keystages and age-related testing, appeared to confirm the traditional belief that pupils have of necessity to be taken through their learning like an army in the field, moving in step through the year group fronts. The logic of TGAT, however, and its ten levels of attainment, suggests that alternative strategies are open to us if we care to use them; and this is borne out by the small print of Circular 5/89, which stresses that the keystages themselves are to be understood with reference to the pupils' average ages, so that a pupil may 'be taught with another age group for one or more subject areas where appropriate . . . while remaining with his or her peer group for other subjects.' Particularly in the upper reaches of the secondary school, this could be a useful means to flexibility.

The other great assumption, of course, is that the framework for timetabling has to be the 40 period week. It is probably time that this was reconsidered; in secondary schools it has led to absurdities like the daily dose, the thirty-five minute lesson, and the conviction that, though all subjects are theoretically equal (hence the standard four period per week allocation) some (English and maths) are more equal than others, and need a longer allocation. It is difficult to see the National Curriculum requirements fitting into this sort of timetabling pattern. Given the substantial experience that many schools have built up of alternative timetabling structures – through the provision of BTEC courses, for instance, or CPVE, or through modular and cyclical courses under TVEI – it is hard to believe that schools will not take the opportunity of reviewing present practice to reflect more closely what we know about effective learning. The Chairman of the National Curriculum Council apparently agrees: 'The National Curriculum,' he has said, 'is leaving us free to question custom and precedent and to be imaginative in finding new solutions. The NCC will not allow the ghost of precedent and the *status quo* to prevent changes which are shown to be necessary.' Or, more succinctly: 'The 40 period week is dead.'

Imperatives for change

It might be objected that these are not opportunities at all, except in the sense that a life-raft is an opportunity to sailors shipwrecked by their captain's folly. The government has waved the magic wand of legislation over longstanding curriculum problems: overload, differentiation, progression, examination domination. But it has passed the actual resolution of those problems back to the schools, and has charged schools and LEAs together with the task of reviewing how the curriculum *as a whole* can best secure the aims of the Act. The italicised words take us back to the 'Polo Syndrome', and remind us that the fundamental difficulty of all curriculum planning – how to get a quart into a pint pot – still remains to be addressed. Making sense of the National Curriculum, at the moment of its introduction, is rather like making sense of a jigsaw with no picture on the box and half of the pieces missing. New pieces continue to arrive, as subject working parties report and orders are made: but there is a strong sense that the master picture is being made up as we go along. The same is true of the all-important assessment arrangements, where secondary schools must wait to see how the tensions between TGAT and the GCSE boards (and between Standard Assessment Tasks and school-based assessment) will finally be resolved. All of this creates genuine difficulties for schools, not lessened by the fact that curriculum and timetable changes (and all the other changes that the Act demands) have to be resourced within the limitations of a formula-funded school budget and an LEA budget effectively determined (because of the way the community tax will work) by central government.

So the difficulties are real. Nonetheless, they have to be negotiated; and the schools that do this best are likely to be the ones that anticipate most realistically and plan most effectively.

Anticipating the detail of the National Curriculum and assessment arrangements is unlikely to be helpful, as Circular 5/89 revealingly points out. Work here, we are told, should proceed 'on the basis of the information currently available, with modifications being

D

made as necessary, as further details emerge.' Anticipating the inevitable, though, is a different matter. There has been no shortage of pointers; the NCC and DES have been bombarding schools with advice, and there is a danger of overkill. The trend, however, is clear:

1.   Schools will need a mechanism for whole-curriculum planning. In most secondary schools, TVEI has laid the necessary foundations; but TVEI criteria are (sensibly) less specific than the statutory requirements of the National Curriculum, and planning for the latter will need to be sharper.

2.   They will need, too, a mechanism for turning planning into policy, and for identifying and allocating the resources needed to put policy into effect. Curriculum planning will become strategic planning. It will involve prioritising and costing, consultation within the school and with governors and parents, and the taking and implementing of hard and often unpalatable decisions. The framework will be important.

3.   It will be essential to establish whole-school assessment and recording procedures. Hitherto, few secondary schools have been able to do this consistently. The emphasis on terminal public examination tended, before the arrival of GCSE, to turn internal assessment into something of an interim process. External assessment against defined attainment targets at 7, 11, 14 and 16 (and, inevitably, internal assessment between those ages) will demand a systematised approach. The challenge for secondary schools in particular will be to ensure that the system reflects the learning, and does not dictate it. It will be important to incorporate into it from the beginning an agreed policy for the recording of achievement, along the lines of the national steering group report. There is some indication that the Government would like to put this on to the back burner, in order to concentrate the minds of schools on reportable results and market performance. Broad-brush recording of achievement, however, is essential if the formative potential of effective assessment is to be realised. Schools will need to recruit support for this aspect of their reporting procedures, as a counterbalance to the more limited (and more educationally-damaging) reporting that might otherwise ensue.

4.   Effective guidance will be crucial. Students will need to be piloted through the maze of attainment targets, and in the fourth and fifth years particularly they will need advice on which core and foundation subjects to follow to GCSE and which to follow for what the Act coyly describes as 'a reasonable time'. If, as

ministerial pronouncements have indicated, additional subjects will also (somehow) be available, (such as a second foreign language) the need for guidance will be greater still. In any case, the traditional distinction between the 'pastoral' and 'academic' roles of the school may become increasingly unhelpful. Guidance is primarily about maximising learning capacity, and many of the conventional 'pastoral' assumptions – about the role of the daily form period, for example – will need to be reviewed.

5. It follows that schools will need to re-think their allocation and use of teacher time. On any reading of the proposals for key stage 4 (and on any rational curriculum planning model) different courses will require different time allocations. In all courses, teacher-time – the most expensive, and increasingly the scarcest, resource we have – will be in short supply. Many secondary schools will look to a rationalisation of the timetable on a three-block model, providing in a 25-hour week something like: 11 hours for the core subjects, 10 hours for the foundation subjects, on a modular basis, and 4 hours for guidance, RE, physical education, and extension learning.

6. All schools will have to learn how to review their performance. Ministers speak of the 'delivery' of the National Curriculum as though it were a manufactured product, just needing to be packaged in the schools. The reality is very different. Teaching is about making learning happen, and that is a profoundly complex process. Schools are going to have to think hard about that process. They are going to have to learn how to monitor it: how to concentrate their professional expertise on what happens in the classroom, in the interaction of teacher and taught, and how to improve it. Appraisal will be fundamental to this process. There is a growing fund of goodwill in schools towards this end, reflected in the report to the Government of the national steering group in July 1989. It is to be hoped that the Secretary of State, when he sets up the national appraisal arrangements to which he is committed, will build on this goodwill.

7. In all of this there is a huge (and widely recognised) need for training. There will be no shortage of training opportunities: INSET has become one of the growth industries of the new service economy. But schools, which will have to pay for their training needs from delegated budgets, will have to prioritise those needs and devise means of ensuring that they are properly met. They will also need to remember that *development* – and particularly the development of attitudinal change – is more important than the acquisition of skills. Staff development will be a major task.

8.   The last imperative, however, is the most important. All of these needs, additional to the demands which confront individual teachers in their subject and departmental roles, have to met at a time when the morale of teachers is dangerously low, and the supply of teachers in some subjects and localities is breaking down. Many, if not most, good teachers are suffering from fatigue and innovation stress; almost all teachers in state schools are profoundly resentful at the way that they and their schools have been made the scapegoats for the ills of society. Now, in every staffroom, the talk is overload, and of diminished esteem and status. This is the context in which schools, and secondary schools in particular, have to respond to the demand for change. It is going to be a difficult task.

Managing the response

Motivation, leadership, team-building

In the first instance it is headteachers and their deputies who will have the task of meeting this challenge, and making reformation work. This has become part of the rhetoric of reform. 'Management' (which is relatively cheap) is seen as the key to change: so education support grants are made available for management training, management consultants proliferate, and the Secretary of State sets up a high-powered task force to investigate the management training and development needs of heads and senior staff.

That is all as it should be: but there are some dangers in conventional wisdom. Put too much stress on 'management', and you are risking creating a sterile managerialism, which reduces management to 'the right to manage'. There are powerful undercurrents in the 1988 Education Act which pull in this direction. So it is important to remember that schools are not factories – however frequently we are told that they have to 'deliver' the curriculum, and however deliberately we are exposed to the pressures of competition and market forces. Education is not a production line, teachers are not operatives, and assessment is more than quality control. Good heads and deputies know that the management of their school begins with their colleagues' management of their classrooms. All teachers are managers, for they have to manage the learning process. That is where the simplistic industrial analogy breaks down.

It is therefore important, when we look at the problem of making the National Curriculum work to the benefit of the children in our schools, to recognise that effective management is as much a matter of attitude as of technique. The really crucial skills, to the headteacher charged with the responsibility of taking a school into this new territory, will be those of motivation, leadership and team-building. The management style that such a head must at all costs avoid is the style of the legislation itself. Spurious consultation, a patronising attitude to teachers, and a tendency to regard all criticism as captious and ill-formed, are – while not unknown among headteachers – unlikely to win the hearts and minds of those who actually have to make things happen.

Participation

Management is about making things happen. There is a substantial body of evidence to indicate that the most effective schools – the schools that are high-achieving, highly regarded and adaptable – are those which have found ways of involving teachers in decisions, and hence in the ownership of them. It is not easy to do this: the tensions between control and autonomy, accountability and delegation, or action and consultation, are real and unavoidable. Nonetheless, many heads resolve them too conservatively. Even the now-conventional senior management team can be counter-productive, for it can be seen by those outside it as remote, exclusive and authoritarian.

The management of the National Curriculum is going to demand participation. By virtue both of the imperatives already identified, and their financial overtones, every decision taken will have budget implications, the onus of which can no longer be passed to the policies of the LEA, safely remote from the staff-room. A decision, for example, to make separate provision for slow-learning students will mean less provision for all the rest. A decision to make a marginal increase in the school's contact ratio, in order, say, to purchase administrative and clerical assistance in the recording of assessments (probably a sensible response to the demands of the new curriculum) will affect the conditions of service of every teacher. There is no doubt at all that heads have the power, in managerial terms, to make such decisions; but it would be a foolish head who put them to the governors without first winning staff support. Schools will need mechanisms for doing this; and the level of professional understanding of the issues and the imperatives underlying them can only improve thereby. In terms of both sharing the problem, and sharing the solution, there is likely to be a case for the establishment, in secondary schools at any rate, of consultative committees – with governor and parent representation – on curriculum and resources.

The management structure

That is not to say that day-to-day management can be accomplished by committee. That is both wasteful, and ineffective. But schools often under-use the talents and energies of their teachers, or fail to develop them in any consistent and systematic way. That is true, I suspect, at every level: a recent survey of the responsibilities of secondary deputies shows a disturbing tendency to use them as administrators, and not as managers at all.

The impact of the National Curriculum and all the changes it brings with it gives heads a pressing reason – just as Mr Baker's off-the-peg allocation of incentive allowances gives them an opportunity – to review the structures and responsibilities of management in their schools.

The new 'E' allowance posts are likely to be particularly important. In so far as they have a derivation, it is from the post of Senior Teacher established at the time of the Houghton Review – but seniority, *per se*, is not a management function. Curriculum co-ordination, however, certainly is. So is the co-ordination and management of the school's policies on assessment and achievement recording; or the management of information technology in the curriculum and in administration; or the co-ordination and management of staff training and development. All these responsibilities are implied in the National Curriculum proposals, and it is important to schools at any rate (the DES Teacher Supply Branch seems to have different ideas) that the salary and allowance structure should be used as a means of identifying and defining the whole-school curriculum imperatives with which they are faced.

On this basis, 'D' allowances would identify team leaders, charged with major responsibility in particular sectors of curriculum and guidance, and 'C' allowances would reflect subject responsibility, within the framework of school and LEA policy, at foundation subject level. 'B' and 'A' allowances would be available for specific responsibilities within teams, often temporary, and always with implications for professional development. Deputies would be free to deal with day-to-day management on an institutional level, and with long-term management in areas such as staffing and staff review, budget and resource control, and community liaison and provision.

Vision and values

And what of the head? Traditionally, the head has played the central role; the tip of the pyramid, the centre of the web. In a literal sense, the management of the school has depended on him or her. That sort of centrality, and the dependence that it can entail, may be unhelpful in the secondary school of 1990 and beyond.

A powerful head can sometimes disempower the teaching staff, and create among them a sort of passivity that is close to inertia. In any case, no head is powerful enough to carry effectively the sort of responsibility that the management of the National Curriculum, in the context of the rest of the Act, will bring.

So heads are going to have to reassess their role. I think there will be three areas, each crucial to the successful introduction and adaptation of the National Curriculum, that only heads can manage.

The first is external, and is concerned with managing the boundaries of the school. This has always been part of the role, but it has not often been done well. The ability of the school to enlist – and respond to – parental involvement, will be crucial. So will its ability to generate support, including financial support, from community and commercial organisations, so, most of all, will be its relationship with its governing body. The wise head will make this a priority call upon his or her time.

The second is internal. The commitment of teachers is the most valuable resource that a school can have. It is also the most vulnerable. In 1989, at the moment that the National Curriculum begins to take effect, that commitment is evaporating. The morale of teachers generally is desperately low. That has something to do with the stress of constant innovation, and rather more with the fact that they and their work have been systematically devalued by a government determined to bring schools under political control. Whatever the reason, however, the result is clear. Heads now have the task of leading tired and disenchanted teachers through the greatest innovation of all. Maintaining teacher morale will be crucial. Paradoxically, the management implications of the changes may prove to be, as this chapter has suggested, a means of restoring professional self-esteem. Praise will be important, too, however; and a sense of humour will help.

And the third? That comes back to centrality – the centrality, at the heart of education, of a sense of values. A school that loses sight of its values runs the risk that it ceases to be a school at all, and becomes instead just a learning centre, the sort of educational service station that the sub-text of the 1988 Act seems to envisage. Perhaps the most important task of all, for the head leading a school into the still uncertain territory of Mr Baker's Brave New World, is to make sure that the school fills that vacuum at the centre of the legislation. The ability to do that – to create and articulate and constantly reinforce an awareness of the values that drive the learning process and bond together the learning community – is the ability to turn a curriculum into education. That takes more than management expertise: it takes a sort of vision, too.

6 A view from a primary school

David Winkley, Headteacher, Grove Primary School, Handsworth

The National Curriculum represents a major intellectual challenge for teachers in the coming years. How schools set about developing the statutory orders in the context of whole – curriculum policies represents a significant challenge for leadership and, not the least in primary schools, the strategies adopted by headteachers. Key decisions, for example, are required from the first as to whether the best approach is:

- to develop thinking alongside colleagues in other schools
- to bring all staff together for discussions
- to develop small working groups
- to have one or two teachers undertake the development of working papers, guidelines, materials
- for heads to take on tasks themselves
- to bring in outsiders (consultants or advisors) to develop the work.

Such questions are strategic ones, of a kind which have not often been successfully accomplished in the past.

Decisions about the nature of planning will of course vary greatly from school to school, but it's important for the head to remember that we accomplish most when the staff and children are working *together*. There is no strong co-operative tradition anywhere in our educational system, and the National Curriculum above all offers an opportunity for groups of teachers, parents and schools to think together about the nature and delivery of curriculum.

The head needs then to be very conscious of the use of time. It might be argued that the National Curriculum is more of a challenge to thinking about time than about anything else. It is, after all, about sequence, pattern, linear movement and periodic assessment. All along it has been concerned with schedules and deadlines. Consciousness of time is clearly in the forefront of the government's concerns, both for teachers and pupils. And key questions emerge here:

•   how do we deliver a linear curriculum without undermining the cyclical nature of the learning experience[1]?

By this I mean how do we prevent the curriculum experience of the children being continually teacher-directed forward, moving without time for reflection, reinforcement, space to breathe? How do we prevent learning becoming the educational equivalent of driving up a motorway?

•   how do we get it all in?

The curriculum requirements are extensive and there will be expectations that children 'get through it all'. This presents an immediate challenge. Teachers will need to think of new ways to plan timetables. The overall design of the National Curriculum is not planned. It is for schools to work out balanced programmes for themselves, and the pressure is on to find ways of convincingly managing ever-increasing demands. Certainly if the school can come to terms with the planning of time, it is likely to be well on the way to implementing the programme. To do this the head needs to lead the staff to address four issues in practical, original ways: 'continuity', 'balance', 'subject specialism or integration', and 'assessment'.

Continuity

The National Curriculum does not require schools to stop teaching the 'old way' on Friday and begin anew on Monday. There needs to be continuity not only internally in the relationship between the elements of the curriculum, but between existing and new practices. We begin therefore by considering our current practice, and then looking at how the National Curriculum fits in. What are we already achieving? What adjustments will need to be made?

What do we already do well that the National Curriculum planners have neglected – remembering that if we think we do something well we need to be able to look closely, give reasons, describe in detail.

There are obviously many questions to ask in matching current practice with the new programmes. At the simplest level we can ask whether we 'cover' the content. Many schools find, on investigation, that much of the maths or English currently in the curriculum (for example) fits fairly into the programmes of study. Equally, many schools have problems in putting hand on heart and admitting they cover the science or history or design and technology courses; and new problems will lie ahead as further subject programmes evolve.

On close investigation, we often find a surprising number of elements in different subject courses that interrelate. The school may find components of science in existing health (say) or English or music programmes. The question for many primary schools may be not so much one of content-coverage, as of ordering and sequencing events so that they are appropriately arranged across the child's school year. The programmes of the future need closer preparation in detail in order to ensure both sequencing and comprehensiveness of delivery. The problem in part is (or ought to be) one of generalising successful practice, shaping it up so that it encompasses the whole school and motivates all the teachers, not just those who are keen, or authoritatively skilled, in transacting bits and pieces.

Balancing the pieces

I always find 'balance' a curiously bloodless word, extraordinarily difficult to hold on to in practice in the heat of the classroom. Nonetheless, a feeling for continuity will need to address the sticky issue of curriculum balance – balance between elements in each individual class, and balance between curriculum arrangements across the school as a whole.

It is not difficult to find examples of the kinds of problems arising in practice:

Mrs X encompasses science at the moment entirely in her interdisciplinary topic work. There's a strong and well delivered geographical link (she uses the excellent Central Television series 'Going Places' as a starting point for her second-year juniors), but she doesn't allow her topics to develop systematically into related areas of the curriculum. Her art is a bit *ad hoc* (lots of free painting, little three-dimensional work). Only a few of the science attainment targets are covered. There is no systematic attention to history. And there's not a lot of co-ordination between what she's currently doing and what the children did last year, or what they will do with another teacher next.

* * *

Mr Y teaches maths entirely from textbooks and hasn't addressed the potential of maths for sustained practical work. He hasn't explored the potential relationship of maths with design, some science and language components. He clearly hasn't achieved the right balance between 'mental skills' and exploratory delivery of those skills into meaningful situations.

* * *

Miss Z works through sustained projects on an integrated day programme, allowing a lot of 'choice' between activities. These projects are of considerable interest and lead to a lot of activity work but much of the work is done in groups, and the issues of the individual skills and abilities of children aren't addressed much at all. There is little focus in this arrangement on the teaching of appropriate skills in systematic ways. As a matter of fact she finds it quite hard to teach more than one group at a time, and many children spend part of the day on low-supervision activities or 'busy-work', which doesn't really move their thinking on. Moreover some individuals don't actually contribute a lot to the groups and only seem to be working. The real thinking and activity is being done by only a proportion of the children.

These are the kinds of issues which an analysis of curriculum balance needs to address, and the head will need to be clear that the heart of the matter is the question of the deployment of time in ways which allow adequate attention to all parts of a curriculum. Here, above, we have teachers who in their different ways are having partial, and perhaps important successes, without offering their pupils a complete diet.

It is very evident that 'balance' is a complex matter in practice. Some teachers interpret balance as a signal to piece together the school week into boxed timetables that have the solidarity of tablets of stone. Others take 'child-centred' – a sniper's victim of a concept if ever there was one – to mean that there should be no necessary variety in the diet. The National Curriculum has the virtue of concentrating the mind on the requirement of variety, but we must recognise that adequate provision of variety is in practice very difficult to achieve, calling for intense and careful planning. It is worth noting that the ever-increasing complexity of curriculum in contemporary schooling – and the growing problems of delivery teachers have to face – is now becoming a major international concern, especially in the countries of the Council of Europe[2].

Subject specialism or integration?

Choice

One of the crucial decisions, now, is whether to teach a subject discretely, or to integrate. Choice will have implications both for the timetable and for teaching styles. Our first thought might be that the easy way out is to develop a subject-orientated curriculum. The pressure is, perhaps, to think unilaterally of transacting one subject after another in routines of set timetabled periods. One infant school I know has opted for selecting three core subject specialists and moving the children around part of the day to work with their specialist teacher. And for some schools, this may be an interesting option, though if carried to extremes, it has serious limitations.

In fact the closer the content of the programmes of study are analysed, the more apparent potential relationships between different subject disciplines become. So the second thought might be: why not integrate fully? There's a great deal of language, for example, which can be transacted in science and maths. Many aspects of science could be drawn into a variety of project/topic work arrangements, and some of the maths and science items could also be delivered in tandem.

There are, however, constraints on creating a fully-integrated curriculum. The two main ones are:

(i) subjects, whilst cross referencing, also have their own internal logic. There are discrete as well as generalisable elements, both in content and in the network of knowledge and skills underpinning the subject matrix;

(ii) the principles of sequencing. It is possible to sequence learning in interdisciplinary contexts, but for some kinds of content-sequence it is undoubtedly much easier to keep a steady eye on the subject. It would be interesting and potentially lively to engage in maths or history or music in the midst of a project on 'Warwick Castle' (say), or 'Myself', or 'Transport', but projects tend to contain inherent biases to one subject area or another. Moreover, subject areas contain discrete skills and make particular content demands. It is extremely difficult to maintain a full interdisciplinary focus whilst at the same time maintaining equitable balance between subjects, and also planning the internal subject inputs in a meaningful patterned way. There's always the danger of the learner's experience looking more like a patchwork quilt than an ordered and informative sequence of events that builds knowledge on knowledge, experience on experience. All this presents a problem, even before we consider issues of differing attainments.

The evidence is, in fact, that currently most schools teach some curriculum areas discretely, particularly maths, music, and PE, whilst delivering others in a 'project format', particularly in the humanities. There is also some evidence that 'projects', whilst aspiring to be interdisciplinary, often consist of subject-orientated segments, usually with a strong bias to one subject.

Above all it is important for the staff planning groups to decide what 'interdisciplinary' work or topic work will actually mean for the learner in practice, and choice will depend in part on the school's view of the 'whole picture' spread across quite long periods of time, with the teachers planning carefully how they intend to create a balanced curriculum over weeks and months.

Patterns of timing

It is useful, as a guide, for the staff to decide how much time it intends overall to devote to different subject areas, and what the pattern of delivery will look like for the learner. One of the key questions is how much time can be spent on any particular curriculum area. And this is not merely a bureaucratic exercise. It is important in thinking about time, for teachers to have some sense of the moment-to-moment experiences of the children. I once followed a pupil around for a whole day, and was impressed by the peculiar mixture she experienced of dislocated bits and pieces, and longer sessions where there were 'spaces' for her to enjoy and explore learning or – occasionally – to waste time in.

There are different ways of dealing with the timing of 'learning experiences'. Patterns of timing can be planned across weeks, months, or longer. One of the strengths of an analysis of timing is being able to distinguish between curriculum elements that are likely to require frequent input (eg items in mathematics) and items that might be effectively delivered at least in part in an interdisciplinary 'project' format, (eg perhaps history or geography or RE).

Example: the timing of music

Let us imagine that a school is planning a music curriculum programme. The first question to ask is how much time does it want to spend on music overall? The school might, for example, recommend that musical activity takes place on a weekly basis. There are certainly virtues in regularity, but the 'weekly session' procedure is not necessarily the best way to proceed. Studies of children who learn music successfully suggest that whilst routines are important, there is also a case for 'focused periods' during which music might occupy longer and more sustained periods of attention – as part of a project, for example, or in preparation for a performance. Quality teaching often leads to striking conclusions that call for what might be best described as an 'intensification of activity' at crucial periods.

This can present problems for teachers. How do they find ways of maintaining routines and sequences whilst also retaining flexibility to develop these intensifying periods or activity which can be the hallmark of achievement? And if subjects or parts of subjects are to be taught discretely, they must dovetail with other aspects of the curriculum, avoiding a piecemeal and bitty example. If the children learn a music activity (eg exploring performance in tuned percussion, or singing) it may be important to link the activity and the performance with other arts activities, or even to explore its relationship with (say) science or maths or language.

There are clearly – even just for music – a variety of options, and the school must eventually come down for one pattern of timing rather than another[3]. The head, in promoting the discussion and holding the 'overview' of developments across the school as a whole, will be aware that there are many different possible patterns, ranging from a simple 'lesson-a-week' pattern to a more complex planned programme which might (for example) integrate music into a thematic project or topic, and allow for an 'intensification period' at the end of term (say for the children to build up to a performance).

Here are three examples of different planned programmes spread over twelve weeks, based on the assumption that (i) the school has agreed to allocate a basic six hours per term to music and (ii) the school spends a proportion of its time on an integrated project. Projects in this imaginary school change each half term (Figure 6.1).

Example A is a simple sequence of subject-based lessons. Example B builds a three-hour music component into an integrated project each half term. Example C combines a sequence of four planned 30-minute music lessons with two longer music inputs in the integrated project. Project 1 contains 1½ hours' music. Project 2 contains 2½ hours' music. The content of the different lengths of music inputs would be planned in sequence – more time being given to music activity as the music programme evolves. The 2½ hours in the second half of the term (plus one hour of subject-based lessons) would lead to a 'musical event' – a finished performance.

It seems very likely that the most effective curriculum design is likely to show evidence of use of all three models, for different purposes. This will be adapted for children of different ages. Young children probably work best to a more 'integrated model'; older children may get something from some more sustained subject

Figure 6.1 Music

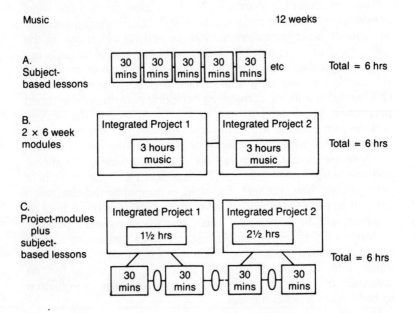

focus. But even within an integrated model there will be clear 'subject elements' built into the theme. And in 'subject specialist' delivery there will be sensitivity to the fact that subjects are never watertight and there are considerable attractions in bringing interdisciplinary elements even into subject teaching.

Heads will need to exercise skills in working through the stages of this analysis and encouraging teachers to sharpen their awareness of timing, without discouraging timetabling flexibility. The last thing we want is teaching by numbers, reducing learning to a series of mechanistic measured units. On the other hand, a mastery of timing is one of the keys to successful teaching and learning – and always has been.

We have now some thought-out sense of a general plan of campaign based on decisions about whether (and how much) we stick to subjects, and to what extent we integrate. We've also developed some sense of patterns of timing – a sense of what a typical week and a typical term might look like for the learner. And we've agreed the key point that the teacher and the learner must have the opportunity to 'bring things together' in meaningful and productive ways.

Transacting the plans

The further question arises now of how the teacher brings together (say) history and art (or mathematics, or music, or science) in practical ways which really help the learner to achieve a genuine sense of coherence across the subjects. We need to address Eric Bolton's blistering criticism about interdisciplinary work in primary schools:

> more often than not it lacks continuity and progression or any serious attempt to ensure that adequate time and attention are given to the elements said to comprise the topic.

I have never been convinced that HMI realise the extreme difficulties of managing interdisciplinary work in sustained ways in primary classes. It seems to me interesting and useful here to engage in a more detailed breakdown of the curriculum, and to look more closely at the 'components' or 'activities' that, when added together, make up the 'curriculum course' or topic.

Example

One school decided to implement a half-term topic on the Victorians for term three. This is a history topic or module which specifically drew in:

- elements of art and drama
- some science work, looking at the evolution of electricity, and at the discoveries of James Watt and the impact of steam
- language work of various kinds, involving the drawing together of evidence, descriptions of artefacts, writing stories, recording observations based on trips to museums and local environment
- some maths, based on looking at simple statistics
- some geography, focused on mapping
- some work on health, looking at epidemiological questions of disease and its prevention, with discussion of vaccination.

When they came to plan the project in detail, the teachers (planning together in this school in year groups) worked together to construct a series of carefully designed 'activities' – a total of six in all.

Key to this stage of planning is the acceptance (once again) that there must be some time limits given to each 'activity', or the whole project will become lopsided and won't be completed in time.

Important also is the planning at this stage of resources needed, and of staffing deployment. For one of the activities there will be a change-round of teachers who will be engaging in a semi-specialist role. Five activities will be delivered, mostly by the class teacher, then. One will be with a specialist teacher.

The general point is that primary schools might be more imaginative and flexible in their deployment of staff: there is no law that says that there should be one teacher to one class for all of the time, and that this is the best possible arrangement in all circumstances.

Each activity is broadly timed, and space is allowed for each activity to be taken further by the children, so that they can develop ideas for themselves, and pursue the possibilities of the activity both at school and at home. An 'activity' might last any length of time from one and a half hours to (say) a sustained activity lasting, over a period, as much as ten hours. The total of the six activities will be comfortably encompassed in six weeks, with an approximate total of 72 hours in all.

Each activity has a main subject focus, though (i) it is held together by the history theme of the project, and (ii) it will not be exclusively mono-subject based. The health activity, for example, will look closely at health issues and progress since the Victorian age – but it will involve writing, talking, and some art work with graphic illustration.

Each activity looks specifically at the delivery of a number of national curriculum elements in the different subject areas, though the activity is planned to make sure that it is not too didactic, and not too heavily content-orientated. Throughout the activities, the children will be expected to develop both general skills in (say) researching material, working in groups, managing their own learning, and specific skills in understanding history – this being primarily a history-focused topic.

Wider aspects of the 'activity' are also considered very carefully. When we look closely at 'activities' we realise what a range of choices we have at our disposal. The 'activity' needs to consider such critical questions as:

- How precisely does the main focus (eg art) interlink with the secondary focuses (eg here, history)?
- Is the activity closely determined by teacher selected content? Or does the child have a role to play?
- Does the child have choice? And space to work at his/her own level of interest?
- Does the activity require co-operative group work of one kind or another?
- Does the activity take into account a range of attainments?
- How are cross–curriculum themes such as equal opportunities and multicultural issues built in?
- What outcomes are expected? Written, dramatic, group folders, individual work, etc?
- How is the child's performance on the activity assessed?

• How is the activity itself recorded and evaluated[4]?

There is, of course, a number of other questions to be asked. The important thing is that the teachers have a clear sense of the relation between the content chosen (from whatever subject areas) and the way in which the whole activity is delivered. All the six activities (in this case) can then be carefully balanced, one against another to achieve an overall picture of the topic. If one activity needs to be very closely content-focused (maybe, for example, at the opening of the topic where the children are put clearly in the picture as to what the topic is to be about), another needs to be constructed to allow pupil exploratory work. If one is inclined to the didactic another might be the reverse. If one encourages independent individual learning, the next might be a group activity. The important thing is that the whole programme is planned in a way that brings out learning in depth, allowing for sustained involvement with the children, and has clear developing purposes.

I would argue that this careful planning of activities is already the current practice of many teachers. There is evidence to show that effective practice uses a variety of approaches to teaching style appropriate to the particular task in hand. No single activity, of course, will be able to address all the issues. Human affairs, and especially matters involving learning, are on the whole a lot neater and easier to understand on paper than they are in reality. Indeed there is a naïve assumption underlying the national curriculum that there is 'out there' a cohort of super teachers who can ensure an undiminished progress of perfectly intricately balanced tasks all day long, according to lists of criteria[5].

The criteria, however, and the precision of planning do, I think, help. Some of the reference points are critical. If they were taken seriously we would have all children going through our schools with no experience of group work, of confident oral discussion, of knowing how to make choices, of being asked to produce demanding individual work of high quality and developing key research and technical skills. A very strong impression, even now, is of a lack of diversity in the planning and delivery of activities in ways that may not be in the best interests of the children. It is particularly useful to look at overall patterns which emerge from a sequence of activities and (maybe) to discover obvious gaps in the child's experience. And the head – above all – needs to take responsibility for the whole programme.

We can, of course, go further still in trying to analyse the transactions of learning. We can, if we want to, move into the somewhat esoteric but extremely interesting area of micro-analysis of teaching. We can show that within an 'activity' there will be numerous various smaller engagements between teacher and children. An activity could be analysed into quite short sections, each of which might be described (using traditional language) as a 'lesson', or for the learner, 'task'. A successful activity will consist of a series of varied lessons and tasks. And it is the moment-to-moment tasks children engage in, that will be the focus for much of the observational assessment we shall need to look at next.

Assessment and evaluation

There is already an ever-increasing variety of suggestions and recommendations emerging as to how best to assess and record this whole process of transaction of subjects, topics and activities. As with the general delivery of curriculum, there is unlikely to be one single effective model. But certainly we need to try to develop (i) a recording system for the transaction of curriculum activities and (ii) ways of recording and assessing the child's progress.

A recording system for classroom transaction

Example
One school is currently developing an activity recording system. The idea is to note the activity (which is planned by the classteacher alongside other teachers) very briefly, to describe whether it was for a whole class, a group, or perhaps an individual. The attainment targets, if any, are recorded. And there is a column for timing and for a brief evaluative comment. What's good about this is that it doesn't take too much time. Five minutes ought to be an outside target for recording (Figure 6.2).

This brief recording is not, of course, the only record the teacher keeps. Activities are planned in groups, and a more detailed description of them is put together in the planning process. So, for example for our six activities above there would be a description put together for each activity in planning meetings. This would be kept as a record. It would also be evaluated by the staff group, and the information passed on to colleagues who may be taking up similar activities the following year.

Recording and assessing the child's progress

Already many schools are working on various ways of recording attainment targets for individual children. There obviously needs to be a simple, convenient way of assessing children in the process of one or more activities. And at the end of the day these will

Figure 6.2

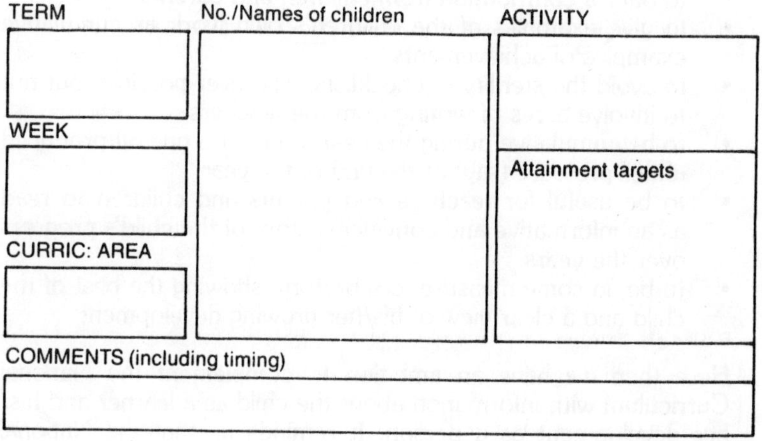

TERM	No./Names of children	ACTIVITY
WEEK		
		Attainment targets
CURRIC: AREA		
COMMENTS (including timing)		

need summation in a single document. Again the key factor is time. It has been clear from the beginning that there are problems here for teachers having to assess a whole range of attainment targets across the curriculum. There is a real danger that the language of the assessment process is too vague. Teachers need to retain intellectual honesty. If the recording process lacks substance, is grossly time-consuming, or meaningless, then there must be major modifications. But they must first study a variety of assessment procedures, try them out, and research the outcomes rigorously.

The children themselves must not be forgotten in the headlong race to reach attainment targets. Many schools are now looking at the whole issue of profiling and records of achievement. There needs to be some procedure for describing the child's wider development, as a person, as a learner. We have a lot to learn here, both about the most effective and workable formats for such a document, about the way in which we can most usefully and perceptively make comments and in ways which (again) fit practically into time demands. The most effective profile is likely:

• to make reference to broad achievements across the attainment targets

- to describe the child's personal emotional and behavioural development
- to describe abilities at general achievements in the process of learning
- to offer a contribution from children and parents
- to give examples of the children's own work as cumulative examples of achievements
- to avoid the sterility of checklists, wherever possible, but not to involve acres of writing from the teachers
- to be cumulative during the year, and not a one-off produced under pressure (say) at the end of the year
- to be useful for teachers and parents and children to read as an informative and convincing story of the child's progress over the years
- to be, in some measure, celebratory, showing the best of the child and a clear view of his/her growing development

Here then we have an ambition to complement the National Curriculum with information about the child as a learner and his/her development as a person. It reminds us that the National Curriculum is not the whole educational experience of a child.

Some reflections

We now have a general strategic plan, which represents the outline of this analysis (Figure 6.3). All this, of course, could well be seen as an excessively constraining interpretation, smacking of a kind of behaviourist structure analysis common to well-developed traditions of curriculum development in the USA. Certainly the programme potentially creates a way for the teacher to describe practice in a new kind of detail. It will (at best) clarify the intentions behind the choice of tasks and activities, and will give a sharper sense of timing and may offer more variety for the children. The National Curriculum can certainly be used imaginatively to explore improved learning.

The role of the head in leading the school's interpretation will be critical. If teachers can be encouraged to clarify their thinking and make learning more varied and fun for the children – sharpening and deepening thinking, then this will be because the head has taken the staff along an analytical path that actually raises the level of efficiency and excitement in the classroom. It is equally possible for the National Curriculum to be used as an instrument for managerial convenience and prejudice. Quality of activities could be short circuited by a pressure to 'get through' programmes of content. Instead of developing careful analytical thinking, the staff

Figure 6.3

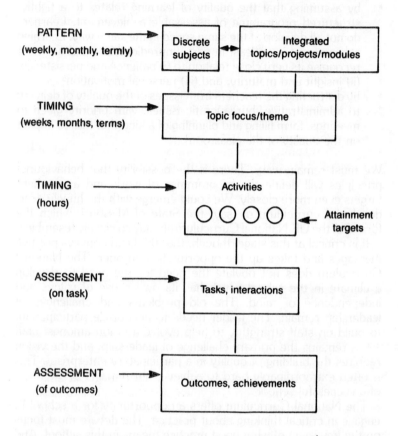

could be instructed to introduce closed didactic procedures that are heavily information-driven. There is no learning without content, and the National Curriculum helps formulate thinking about content choice, something the post-Plowden primary tradition has fought shy of. But content-driven curriculum is conversely always in danger of reducing the quality of transactions between teacher and child by becoming a handing-out of packages. This can happen:

- by activities being so prescribed that they allow no space for learners to take them further

- by activities being insufficiently well linked, becoming just a series of subject-driven inputs with no natural relationship
- by taking away the responsibility for teachers to develop modules and activities
- by assuming that the quality of learning relates to a tightly-structured programme of assessable achievement. Learners do not all develop at the same speed in the same way. Learning achievement is, at least in part, unpredictable – and we must recognise its very close relation to (i) patience and persistence, (ii) insight and maturity, and (iii) personal motivation[6]
- by distracting the teachers from issues of the quality of delivery to administrative, bureaucratic issues, with priority given to meetings, form-filling and planning of a kind that fails to impact on the quality of the classroom.

We must remain wary. There is the possibility that behaviourist principles will define the programmes of work and assessment targets even more closely. We could emerge with the hugely over-developed curriculum of (say) the State of Missouri, which the format of the UK National Curriculum already so closely resembles.

It is critical at this stage, though, that the head conveys positive messages and takes up the opportunities on offer. The National Curriculum does not obviate the need for the head to develop a climate in the school which has its own sense of values and independence of mind. The old problems and challenges of leadership remain. The leader needs to encourage participation, to build on staff strengths, to help evolve a vision amongst staff – this remains the primary challenge of leadership, and the vision requires the building of quality in a participatory enterprise[7]. This is often extraordinarily hard to achieve, but remains at the heart of a successful school[8].

The National Curriculum offers an opportunity for a school to engage in critical thinking about practice. The debate must focus on the key issue of what good practice means in this school. And the focus needs to be, above all, on what happens in the classroom[9]. The head needs to give priority to the close analysis of practice, exploring the different kinds of learning going on in classrooms, reflecting it back to staff, assessing, estimating, reflecting and asking others to do the same. The action-research model is useful here, setting up procedures and observation procedures for deciding what makes for quality in learning experiences, and how best to observe, analyse and describe. The key questions are:

- What is actually happening in this classroom?
- What is this child actually learning?
- What does the learner make of it all?

- Where is it all leading?

All this has implications for the head's style of management. There is no substitute for a planned management style. How then do we best plan our approach? Certainly heads need to move (and read) fast in shaping, changing, directing, writing. There is the need for Napoleonic efficiency with time. The pressure is on to agitate the system, to put bite into it, to become more managerial. But there is a danger in the head mirroring this energising, anxiety-making delivery. LMS, appraisal systems and governing body involvements compound the demands of heads to remove themselves from the classrooms, and to dictate instructions down the line.

Implicit throughout is that close intelligent analysis of practice, leading – potentially – in all kinds of ways to new insight, is the key to progress. It means more time in classrooms. It means less rigid structures in planning. It means more on-the-job dialogue with staff. It means more imaginative deployment of staff. It means preparedness to experiment with new and possibly riskier arrangements. It means greater consciousness of the quality of pupil experience. It means tougher evaluation and assessment. It means increasingly precise understanding of high-quality delivery. It means higher quality corporate interaction of staff with staff, staff with head, and all adults with children.

The head has a clear dilemma: it is possible to lead staff in developing a curriculum in quite different directions. To survive successfully the head will need a clear sense of priorities, and the self-confidence and intellectual astuteness to maintain a chosen path. The staff will appreciate a head's professional confidence and patience in these turbulent times, who addresses dilemmas without panic, develops procedures with care and good humour, and who maintains a radical determination to use the National Curriculum to do the best possible, on the evidence, for the children in our care.

References

1 For an interesting discussion of cyclical and linear modes of learning cf. Young M *The Metronomic Society*.
2 cf. Neave G *New Challenges for Teachers and their Education* Council of Europe, May 1987.
3 For an interesting discussion of choices in the teaching of music, cf. Lawrence I *Composers and the Nature of Music Education*, Scolar Press, London, 1978, pp 111–135.
4 For further useful discussion, cf. *An Introduction to the National Curriculum*, Secondary Mathematics, National Curriculum Council, 1989, p 4.

5   For further discussion of the relationship between theory and practice, cf. Munby H *et al*, *Seeing Curriculum in a New Light: Essays from Science Education*, OISE Press, 1980.

6   For a powerful statement of the importance of such factors, cf. a recent article by the headmaster of Eton College, Anderson W E K, Responsibility of the Educator, Green College Lecture, *British Journal of Medicine*, Vol 298, 24th June 1989, pp 1699–1701.

7   cf. Winkley D R 'An Analytical View of Primary School Leadership', in *School Organisation*, Vol 3, No 1, 1983, pp 15–25.

8   cf. for example, recent research by Nias J *et al*, *Primary School Staff Relationships*, ESRC Research Project, Cambridge Institute of Education, 1985–7.

9   cf. the list of suggestions developed by one school in 'Practical Issues in Primary Education', No 2, *Consultation*, National Primary Centre, 1989, p 7.

7 Fitting the National Curriculum to one's own principles

Mark Hewlett, Principal, Quorn Rawlins Community College

Two weeks after the publication of proposals for the National Curriculum in September 1987, the *Times Educational Supplement* invited 13 curriculum pundits to give their views. Prognoses were gloomy.

Under the heading 'Defective Vision', subtitled 'Ill-informed or plain dishonest', Peter Cornall argued that 'the focal depth is too shallow. Has anyone asked what will be the fundamental concerns of people in the 21st century?' He quoted Bruner:'A curriculum ought to be built around great issues, principles and values that a society deems worthy of the continued concern of its members.' More specifically, Cornall noted; 'cross–curricular themes may be all right but they cannot adequately be taught through foundation subjects. Economic, environmental, political and social education must not be ignored.'

'Fundamentally flawed' was the heading for Denis Lawton's article:

> The document ignores the debate on curriculum which has been taking place for 20 years. The draft is subject-based in its thinking. There is nothing wrong with subjects provided they are treated as means not ends and as long as everyone is clear about what is to be achieved through them. But no justification is put forward for the selection of

subjects. Important areas of human experience are almost completely neglected. Little mention has been given to moral education, social and personal development, political understanding and economic awareness (much beloved of Keith Joseph). Simply to hope that such things will be taught through other subjects is not satisfactory for a planning document even at the discussion stage.

The heading for my own contribution, 'Can we complain?', seemed to strike a note of resignation, not inappropriately I suppose: after all we in schools are paid to get on with it regardless. But I was referring to a broader issue:

If politicians came to the conclusion that education was too important to be left to the educators, bear in mind the massive input of public resources, education's failure to demonstrate significant improvement of standards, poor marketing, uncertain professional leadership and the fact that every year youngsters leave school ignorant of much they might reasonably be expected to know and lacking skills that could have been acquired in 11 years of schooling. Simply complaining won't do.

Referring to testing I observed that, 'a reflex anti-testing reaction would be dismissed as naïve and the sort of soft headedness that hard-liners think is at the root of the problem', but observed that, 'effective, constructive, diagnostic testing is expensive and poor testing could distort the curriculum and demoralise learners.'

Accepting that politically it would be unrealistic to expect a National Curriculum to be couched in other than conventional terms, ie subjects, I questioned the absence of a rationale.

The National Curriculum's aims – to give pupils knowledge, understanding, skills and attitudes to equip them for the responsibilities and challenges of adult life and tommorrow's world – will be widely supported. But in order to achieve them you need to work out as precisely as possible what knowledge, concepts, skills and attitudes it is you want to develop. It isn't good enough to fall back on a somewhat arbitrary list of subjects without specific aims. This disconnection between aims and curricular plans seems to be an endemic disease of curricular planning and, unless amended, the National Curriculum will show that in the late twentieth century the policy makers still couldn't get out of the rut of traditional thinking that has dogged education throughout this century.

Of the other contributors, some expressed outrage, some were more optimistic, but I believe that these views of Cornall, Lawton and Hewlett typically reflected professional concerns of curriculum developers and teachers, especially those grappling with the persistent problems of how to implant enlightened ideas into a traditional subject-based curriculum.

Common themes included concern at failure to think through to an underlying purpose – the absence of any rationale. There was little sense of any forward-looking vision, of any sense of critical prioritisation. Where were the important elements: inventiveness, initiative, adaptability, intellectual curiosity, sensitivity, confidence, determination? There was disappointment that the best structure for our educational future was an unimaginative list of subjects, and fear that testing would turn the clock back even further. I think everyone felt it was stodgy; it was not a dynamic springboard from which we could leap into a new era of effective education.

How the National Curriculum looks now – remaining reservations and constraints

How do things look now? Superficially things look brighter. I need to say, lest this sounds too one-sided, that I leave more positive comments to the conclusion, in which I describe more specifically how we will be attempting to take advantage of those aspects of the National Curriculum which offer hope of progress.

I say, 'Superficially things look brighter.' Speaking at the 1989 BEMAS Annual Conference, Martin Davies, Director of NCC, referred back to the early gloom and outrage, but then went on to say: 'What is remarkable is how little dissent and how little opposition there is now the overwhelming majority have accepted the idea of a National Curriculum.' I recalled that Lawton had explicitly said that some kind of National Curriculum was not undesirable. Neither had Cornall and I condemned the notion out of hand. But perhaps, I wondered, had we not been a bit harsh, a bit premature? Of one thing I am certain: I am sure we all agree that what has emerged over the last two years has exceeded our expectations. In particular, much of HMI's enlightened thinking has permeated the National Curriculum. But let us keep a sense of proportion. Our original fears were so gloomy, our expectations so low, that almost anything would be better. While expressing relief that what is emerging could be worse, it is not the promised land; it is just about approaching the standard of some of the good practice which preceded it. And, as I say above, we are paid to adapt and to get on with what we've got; we are not going to waste energy on futile complaint.

How many of the criticisms and problems of the National Curriculum remain — or more accurately how many appear unlikely to be solved soon? It should be recognised that many of the problems that face us are not a result of the National Curriculum; they have existed in the curriculum for decades.

The overriding criticism of the National Curriculum proposals was that it was not designed to achieve significant fundamental aims: it did not obviously focus upon 'great issues, principles and values', or on the development of fundamentally important attitudes and skills, which educators, industrialists, and all those concerned with the welfare of society and the enrichment of the individual, would see as paramount. Having said that, it would be possible to extract from the rhetoric, and the general statements of the NCC and from the syllabuses so far produced, words which might suggest that the NCC executives agree.

But there are grounds for scepticism: there has not been produced a clear coherent overall plan which places significant values, skills and, characteristics at the forefront of the curriculum. There is a scepticism about the likely effectiveness of the cross curricular themes, which, if genuinely given prominence, would weld the curriculum together, giving it direction, coherence and purpose. The fact that the first components in the structure are syllabuses for four individual subjects which have been placed in position before the other components (subjects and cross-curricular themes) have even been sketched out, confirms that the approach is *ad hoc*. There is no evidence of their being part of any coherent overall design. Much rests on cross-curricular elements, but unless enmeshed as an integral part of the overall curriculum, assessment and testing systems which will give them parity of esteem with other elements, they are likely to be ignored, or to remain peripheral.

Omissions remain, of course. The preference for geography and history over other social sciences is pure inertia, unadulterated conservatism lacking rationale. From our own experience we know that sociology, psychology, political science and anthropology have proved much richer sources of theoretical models and general concepts with which to equip students for understanding the social environment they inhabit.

But aren't we asking for everything on a plate? If schools feel that the National Curriculum does not get to the heart of the matter, that it is a relatively superficial means to more important ends and has important omissions, then is it not up to the schools to work through the National Curriculum or *add* to it to secure their goals? Possibly so, but this brings us to two practical problems.

First, the curriculum appears seriously overcrowded. It is extremely difficult to provide a balanced education of core and foundation subjects and offer even standard additions like a second language, English literature, and a full careers and work experience programme. This we know already. We shall have even less time than before to enrich the curriculum with a range of imaginative exploratory activity.

Secondly, frequent testing and the enormous pressure of parents and pupils to succeed will almost certainly have the effect of focusing attention on assessment targets, at the expense of other activities

to an even greater degree than has occurred in the past. The safeguard for cross-curricular elements is, ironically, to ensure that they are fully incorporated into schemes of assessment.
We are thus constrained.

Rawlins' ideals and aims: education to serve people's needs

Having suggested that the National Curriculum is a constraint, what is it that we are being constrained from? The answer I have so far given that it is from achieving effectively and efficiently, fundamentally important aims such as developing inventiveness, initiative, adaptability, intellectual curiosity, sensitivity, confidence, and so on — general transferable skills and attitudes which will equip our students for their future lives.

There are some fundamental general principles to which we are committed, arising from our tradition as an active community college, including a long tradition of involvement in the arts; we have been involved in TVEI, whose emphasis coincided with our tradition of innovation in design, technology, IT and business studies and in our humanities, health education and fitness for life programmes, particularly our involvement with the local industrial community. This list reflects an acceptance of contrasting ideas and ideologies which does not allow us to be simplistically labelled ('progressive', or otherwise) and we don't want to be. This is best exemplified in our community education work where our idealism, our welcoming environment, our sensitive support for the handicapped and our intitiatives in integrating special-needs students into the college are underpinned by hard-nosed accountancy and entrepreneurial activity.

I present five extracts from the college's aims to give a flavour of our determined commitments, but we recognise that anyone can write rhetoric, so I hope they do not engender cynicism:

1. The short term sees the challenge of full entry into the European market bringing with it the prospect of intensive economic competition. The longer terms sees the continuing and growing challenge of educating people for an increasingly sophisticated technological world where business acumen and economic flair underpinned by management skills and intellectual flexibility are needed for survival. Academic success is no guarantee that a person is empowered to tackle challenges of modern society with confidence. We must ensure that our students leave school functionally literate for a complex competitive economy.
2. We need people who are not only economically literate, but politically and socially literate, well informed about and sensitive to crucial social and moral issues; we must be developing a society whose

members are aware and tolerant of others and manifest concern for their welfare.

3.   We want to lay emphasis on the concept of community education: it represents a whole attitude to education which makes science, maths and all the other subjects students learn, meaningful by relating them to the real experiences of life outside school. We should hope that all our students have opportunities to engage actively in and experience the personal satisfaction of working with and for others in the community.

4.   Giving students skills, information and conceptual abstractions is worthwhile but only if it is usable in the various circumstances of their future lives.

5.   If there is a danger that we have fallen into the trap of vocationalising education let me emphasise that we must actively encourage the development of intellectual curiosity and imagination by exploration in fields, however theoretically abstract – in science, maths, humanities, the arts or any sphere that captures students' interests; education has suffered as much from failure to excite interest in the world of ideas as failure to prepare for practicalities of daily living. It has fallen too often into a dull middle ground.

But the major problem with the curriculum has not so much been lack of vision or aims, as a failure to translate aims in a clear and logical way into a curriculum to achieve them.

A curricular structure to achieve our aims: the regions of application model

The conceptual hotch-potch of the traditional curriculum, based on subjects which are a random assortment of content-based, concept-based, skill-based and moral-based collections of ideas (whose confusing absurdity is in part exemplified by the NCC's cross-curricular skills which are exactly the same as the curricular subjects) has never been designed from first principles to do the basic job of a curriculum, which is to help achieve aims in the most effective and efficient way.

Our starting point of curriculum design was a carefully worded summary of aims (acceptable to the DES, TVEI, the governors, to a community college, indeed to any educational establishment). The curriculum should help learners acquire and develop (i) knowledge and conceptual understanding, (ii) skills, (iii) personal qualities and attitudes, so that they will be able (iv) to take advantage of opportunities and cope with challenges in the various circumstances of their present and future lives – to enable and encourage them to contribute responsibly and constructively to society (in its various facets) and so that their personal lives may be enriched.

Note that, roughly speaking, (i) (ii) and (iii) are *means* to (iv) *ends* which reflect the real purposes of the college; and it is the ends, the most important elements which tend to get lost or blurred in the confusion of the standard, over-crowded subject-based curriculum.

The above summary of aims reflects ideals given in the five extracts of the college's general aims given in the previous section. The essential idea is that the purpose of learning is to illuminate people's understanding of the environments (sets of circumstances) they (will) experience. The learning of skills, knowledge and so on must be applicable in *some* form, or it is dead. It is no good saying your curriculum is to prepare people for life, and then ignoring what life's experiences will or might consist of. Figure 7.1 incorporates the four major elements of the curriculum, focusing on the circumstances in which learning will be applied.

This model reflects the philosophy and the priorities of the college. The notion of the overriding importance of applicability of learning is born of long immersion in community education. Daily contact with infants in the crèche (next to the sixth-form coffee bar), the elderly, the frail, the physically and mentally disabled, employed people who come to us for literacy support or computing courses, active retired people attending daytime A-level classes, members of the community using our library, students on the threshold of professional careers in music playing with non-too-gifted amateurs engaged in recreation, academically-gifted students about to enter university engaged in social work with our special-needs students, has perhaps given us an unusually clear insight into the different ways people need and want education and the different circumstances in which it enriches their lives.

So we know that we have to think carefully and critically through the general idea of 'preparation for work and adult life'. This can be a vacuous form of words, conveniently forgotten as students settle down in their maths, their physics, their geography lessons to acquire ideas which are, we acknowledge, of *potential* general application, but which are likely to be of little use if the connections between theory and practice are not made explicitly. The details of how the connections are made appear in 'Curriculum to serve society, how schools can work for people' which incorporates a case-study of how we in Rawlins have thought about this problem. It considers the way in which we might make a reality of the observation (by Keith Joseph) that 'the curriculum should be relevant to the real world and pupils' experience of it' by considering the range of challenges and opportunities which people face in, say, the domestic environment, often regarded as too trivial for 'academic' education, but where arguably most important economic, technical and social decisions are made and acted upon:

Figure 7.1

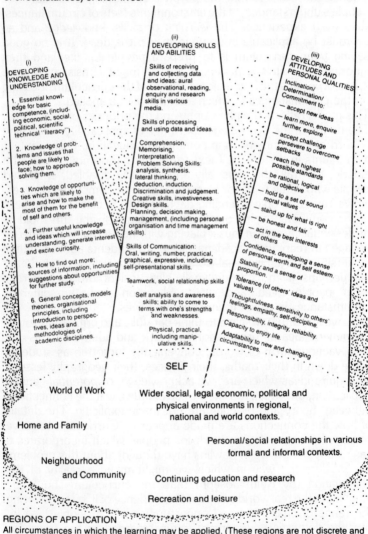

ELEMENTS OF A CURRICULUM IN WHICH THE LEARNING FOCUSES ON
REGIONS OF APPLICATION

This presentation emphasises the development of knowledge, skills and
attitudes to illuminate people's experiences, to enable them to apply their
learning effectively and to gain personal satisfaction in the various regions (sets
of circumstances) of their lives.

**(i)
DEVELOPING
KNOWLEDGE AND
UNDERSTANDING**

1. Essential knowledge for basic competence, (including economic, social, political, scientific technical "literacy").

2. Knowledge of problems and issues that people are likely to face; how to approach solving them.

3. Knowledge of opportunities which are likely to arise and how to make the most of them for the benefit of self and others.

4. Further useful knowledge and ideas which will increase understanding, generate interest and excite curiosity.

5. How to find out more; sources of information, including suggestions about opportunities for further study.

6. General concepts, models theories, organisational principles, including introduction to perspectives, ideas and methodologies of academic disciplines.

**(ii)
DEVELOPING SKILLS
AND ABILITIES**

Skills of receiving and collecting data and ideas: aural observational, reading, enquiry and research skills in various media.

Skills of processing and using data and ideas.

Comprehension, Memorising, Interpretation Problem Solving Skills: analysis, synthesis, lateral thinking, deduction, induction. Discrimination and judgement. Creative skills, investiveness. Design skills. Planning, decision making, management, (including personal organisation and time management skills).

Skills of Communication: Oral, writing, number, practical, graphical, expressive, including self-presentational skills.

Teamwork, social relationship skills

Self analysis and awareness skills; ability to come to terms with one's strengths and weaknesses.

Physical, practical, including manipulative skills.

**(iii)
DEVELOPING
ATTITUDES AND
PERSONAL QUALITIES**

Inclination/ Determination/ Commitment to:

— accept new ideas

— learn more, enquire further, explore

— accept challenge persevere to overcome setbacks

— reach the highest possible standards

— be rational, logical and objective

— hold to a set of sound moral values

— stand up for what is right

— be honest and fair

— act in the best interests of others

Confidence, developing a sense of personal worth and self esteem.

Stability, and a sense of proportion.

Tolerance (of others' ideas and values).

Thoughtfulness, sensitivity to others' feelings, empathy, self-discipline.

Responsibility, integrity, reliability.

Capacity to enjoy life.

Adaptability to new and changing circumstances.

SELF

World of Work

Wider social, legal economic, political and
physical environments in regional,
national and world contexts.

Home and Family

Personal/social relationships in various
formal and informal contexts.

Neighbourhood
and Community

Continuing education and research

Recreation and leisure

REGIONS OF APPLICATION

All circumstances in which the learning may be applied. (These regions are not discrete and
may be re-organized and sub-divided. This is just one categorization which seems to make
sense in terms of the different sets of experience that people have.)

in the community where a host of issues require an informed public to exercise judgment and active commitment to ensure that the quality of the social and physical environment is constantly improved, and so on in other contexts which will require people to make an active and hopefully informed response, underlain by conceptual understanding of general issues to which, *if taught effectively*, geography, history, physical sciences and design, indeed all academic disciplines, can make a powerful contribution.

In emphasising how theoretical study can be *applied*, in practice we are equally conscious of how the application of ideas in a wide range of specific context can contribute to the 'academic' pursuit of identifying *general* theories and models, traditionally taught and still to be taught through disciplines which often impose rather arbitrary boundaries of content. We hope we shall be educating future academics and researchers who will be much more effective and imaginative thinkers, who will perceive areas of conceptual exploration beyond the traditional boundaries of their disciplines.

This describes where we are in terms of an overall structure. We are equally concerned with the learning process. Recognising that while there is a place for carefully programmed input, we endeavour to emphasise active independent learning through direct experience: for example through business enterprise, designing products for and in local companies, work experience, residential experience, community experience, family placements, recreational activities, which we hope will be recreative in the fullest sense. We are equally concerned that backing this up is an organisation which (in addition to being efficient) ensures equal opportunity, and an adult ambience of personal care in which responsibility and individuality can flourish (not easy to achieve). There is, of course, nothing in this paragraph which might not appear in many schools' booklets. So what is the difference? Only that we would want all students to experience these things to the fullest, so that they *all* have varied and rich experiences in *all* these spheres, and that we make special efforts to provide the time and space for the students to explore and develop their abilities and inclinations to learn and develop personal qualities without being directed.

Although we acknowledge that the National Curriculum is presented in a conservative context, and probably has to be couched in conventional terms, we are conscious of its lack of a 'qualitative thrust', its inability to cater for all we want to offer all our students. And we are very doubtful about our ability to incorporate our ideas into a crowded programme in our ten-column curriculum with powerful constraints imposed by a heavy schedule of testing and assessment.

So we have a clearly articulated philosophy, and we have a curricular model which reflects it – a model which is superior we think to any off-the-shelf models, and we have looked at Bruner, White, Bloom, and at HMI's areas of experience, all of which lack the coherence and universality of the 'regions of application' model.

Adapting our ideas to National Curriculum requirements

But to present the 'regions of application' model as our only version of the curriculum in our prospectus would be to put us out of business.

So how are we going to manage with the National Curriculum? In a structural sense we have turned our model on its side. The focal points of the diagram are now arranged down the left-hand side of Figure 7.2 below. The regions of application have been amalgamated with the National Curriculum cross-curricular themes. How far this will work depends on how far we can inject into cross-curricular work the essence of our ideas and make them genuine focuses of our work (and not peripheral elements). We are assuming that the knowledge concepts and skills, also the development of attitudes and personal qualities, will be delivered through the foundation subjects, options, extra-curricular activities, tutorial and careers guidance programme, and our extensive individual staff–student consultations which are a major feature of the school's work, and perhaps more than anything else manifest our central concern for the academic and personal needs of each student.

The implications of the National Curriculum on our determination to enliven the learning process are not wholly discouraging. For example, subject guidelines encourage problem solving, exploratory, experimental activities. The effect on our ability to further enrich our work through a wide range of direct experiences or work and community involvement is arguable. Greater pressure on staff time significantly reduces our capacity. The solution to this problem lies elsewhere (in an increasingly aggressive fight for resources).

Figure 7.2

CURRICULUM FRAMEWORK

Nos of periods Subjects *Cross-curricular themes*	2 Maths	2 Science	2 Science	2 Design Technology (inc Business Education)	2 Arts	Hist/Gg Humanities	2 English	2 PE/RE	2 Foreign Language + Options	2 Options	2 Tutorial PSE Personal Consulta-tions	21 Total
PERSONAL AND SOCIAL EDUCATION (including *'self' family and other relationships;* moral and spiritual, multicultural and gender considerations)												
HEALTH EDUCATION (including mental as well as physical health, fitness and the development of *positive recreative activity.* Including *education for personal enrichment.*												
ECONOMIC AWARENESS/*WORLD OF WORK* (including business and consumer education *Careers* and opportunities in further and higher *education.*)												
CITIZENSHIP, POLITICAL and INTERNATIONAL UNDERSTANDING (as applicable in *local community, regional, national* as well as international contexts) to incorporate multicultural considerations												
ENVIRONMENT (in *domestic, local community, national and international contexts*)												

Positive opportunities offered by the National Curriculum

It sounds as if we are doing little more than making the best of a bad job. Compared with our ideal this is certainly true, and I shall await developments over the next decade with interest. But I should be more positive than this. I want to say that, given the political constraints, and the constraints of past practice which keep us within the old mould, it is a better-balanced mould than what preceded it.

Given the commitment to the arts which is a central feature of Rawlins, I welcome the inclusion of the arts as a foundation element: it strengthens our hand, though why just music and art are specified I do not know, but we can get around that *unless* SEAC imposes unrealistic demands and arbitrarily forces students into choosing just one specialism for GCSE certification: we *must* have flexible (eg modular type) arrangements to allow us to offer what is best for our students.

A specific element which has struck a chord with community educators is the encouragement to involve parents. Expand this to encourage involving other adults, and we should feel in tune with the NCC. But two features strike me as being particularly significant: cross-curricular themes and the planning of syllabuses from 5-16.

Cross-curricular themes were welcomed by Cornall, Lawton and Hewlett, but we were sceptical. For NCC to continue to reiterate the theme and amplify the idea of cross-curricular themes in official documentation is very encouraging: it is a definite step forward and one which I would want to secure. My fear is that the proposals of the relatively forward-looking NCC will come to naught in SEAC. In syllabuses produced to date, only perfunctory attention has been given to cross-curricular themes. But if SEAC can be persuaded to give parity of esteem to the assessment of cross-curricular themes within subjects, and better still, to revise syllabuses when an overall plan does eventually emerge, much will have been achieved – in fact, nothing less than the coherence and purpose educators seek.

The second feature which offers the possibility of overcoming the problem of how to incorporate the rich and exciting range of activities we would like, is the move to planning the curriculum as a progression of learning from 5–16 (hopefully eventually 3–21). If we can eliminate the wasteful duplication and discontinuity caused by *ad hoc* muddled planning in education, we in effect create space to fit in what we want. Our local family of schools is designing a business education/world of work/economic awareness curriculum 5-16 (which will incidentally identify the contributions of each subject). The immediate reaction was: 'just think what we can achieve given an 11-years span to work with. It gives us more than enough space and time to do what we want, even given the pressures of frequent assessment.' Planning over an 11-year period could, I believe, bring about a veritable revolution, especially if the whole curriculum (both subjects and cross-curricular themes) can be welded together, but I want to see some rapid practical progress if I am to be reassured.

Finally, I return to the introduction, in which the pervasive theme was failure to plan from first principles, and lack of vision. I am not wholly retracting that, but as Martin Davies said in the speech to which I refer, when questioned about the relationship between NCC and SEAC and our traditional disease. 'At least this time the assessment is curriculum led.' The fear that the assessors (SEAC) might ignore the curriculum developers remains. Educators must attempt to encourage NCC to accept their ideas and ideals, and to encourage NCC to insist as far as possible that SEAC follows their lead. This is one very powerful reason why I am writing this chapter. It would be tragic if teachers committed to achieving worthy and high ideals felt that idealism was dead, and if the innovatory drive which has characterised English schools ran out of energy.

Section Three: Issues for implementation

8 So what do parents expect?

Sheila Naybour, Governor Training Officer, Cumbria

Parents will find a new relationship with their children's school with the progressive implementation of the measures in the Education Reform Act. The context of that relationship is profoundly changed from that implicit since the previous great Act (1944) which was enacted at a time when there was an unusual degree of shared values in our society. Indeed one of its distinguishing features was an implicit assumed and understated partnership of agencies and people: Church and State; central and local government; ministers and locally elected councillors; civil servants and education officers; heads and governors and parents and teachers. The last 'partnership', was the most understated of all. That Act was the child of a more deferential and hierarchical age – partnership implied each being left to get on with their own role without daring to question the role of the other. And so it was.

Parents had a duty to secure education for their children. Although a few exercised their right to carry out that duty themselves without recourse to schools, most entrusted their children's education to the care of the school, and having done so for many years, had minimal contact or opportunity to consult with schools. They were not by right on governing bodies; there were few PTAs, and even parents' evenings were few and far between. The contact was often confined to terse reports on children's progress in the form of a letter, grade or form order. Progressively that has changed, with school-supported moves towards greater parental involvement and, in recent years, successive legislation (Education Acts of 1980, '81, '86, and '88) has highlighted parents' rights to be more closely involved in decisions relating to their children's education.

Parents can be school governors; or they can be in a parents' association – a captive support group prepared to give time to school duties or raise money, or a group of people who meet for social reasons because they happen to be connected by the attendance of their children with the school community. The 1986 Act in particular gave prominence to parents' role as governors; indeed in such a role the few who may be governors are likely to receive training alongside teachers and other governors, in the new programme of in-service training required of local education authorities. It would be a pity if the potential benefit of the partnership of parent and governor is not examined in such training. The potential of parents as a source of supplementary funds has often been the driving force of Parents' Associations and PTAs. Indeed the combination of increased school autonomy over the budgets as a result of local financial management, and the new rules on charging for extras is likely to highlight parents' role as fund-raisers. Once again, however, as with governors not all parents will be involved.

The 1988 Education Act will add pace to the rate of change, partly because explicitly and implicitly it underscores the role of the parent as a consumer of services. Consumerism, of course, is a theme common to many aspects of the provision of public services as they are being reformed, and one which the government argues will be a guarantee of quality and of stimulating beneficial competition among providers. The parent, in consequence, is to be provided with information about the performance not merely of their own children but of classes in schools in order to facilitate comparison. Some will argue that such a role will provide an opportunity for open and honest relationships between teachers and parents; others that it will lead to defensiveness on the part of teachers only too keenly aware of the increased emphasis on their school's performance in an increasingly volatile market place.

The consumer model usually emphasises rights rather than responsibilities, and it is perhaps significant that the first circular of 1989 sets out the requirements for each LEA's arrangements for parental complaints against either schools or the LEA, should they be thought to be failing in the delivery of the National Curriculum. It could be argued that there will be a clearer demarcation of the respective and distinctive roles of the teacher and the parent, as some commentators suggest is the case in France and elsewhere. Whatever the future holds for most parents, it will be influenced by their own recollections of school. It is there really that my story begins.

When my first child started school, after that unfamiliar walk up to the drive, the passing of the school gate, and through the highly polished school entrance, we found ourselves facing the headteacher over her desk. My apprehension was well-matched by my son's fear of the unknown.

During an interview which concentrated upon discipline, uniform and school dinners, I posed the question, 'Can I help in any way?' The response was: 'Are you a teacher?' – the inference being that if I wasn't, I couldn't; my place was outside the school gate and education was a teacher's job. School reports explained nothing, and our anxiety about the progress of our child at school was ignored repeatedly throughout the infants school. After some unexplained assessment procedure at 8+, we were told that his progress was unsatisfactory; he wasn't eleven plus material. At that point my diffidence and complacency were replaced by anger; we changed house, we changed school. My first-born now has a degree in physics.

It still remains difficult to demonstrate adequately our gratitude to his subsequent teachers, teachers who were committed to close co-operation between home and school and the concept of partnership. Both Bob (my husband) and I developed a closer understanding of our school, its aims and expectations. We shared a deep concern about the difficulties we faced as a school community, in ensuring that each and every child was valued equally and had the opportunity to reach his full potential at school.

I make no apology for this seemingly irrelevant story here. The hidden agenda to recent changes, like parents' involvement in the curriculum, the plus factor if you like, and the hope for future children, is surely that, armed with more knowledge and understanding of our schools and the serious under-funding of education, parent and public opinion will demand a larger slice of the national cake for our schools.

Understanding and partnership can only come about through leadership and guidance of headteachers and governing bodies. Although, my introductory anecdote is of an experience some twenty years ago, just last night I spent over half an hour on the telephone offering sympathy to a distressed parent whose concerns about her son and his progress at school were being dismissed as unimportant. The National Confederation of Parent-Teacher Associations (NCPTS) receives many letters from parents who are concerned that the only permitted item on their home school association's agenda is fund-raising. In many schools, parents are still thought to be interfering when they seek to know what happens at school. This is clearly totally unacceptable.

Few parents currently understand the intricacies of the National Curriculum. It sounds a good idea that all children should follow the same kind of curriculum, it might make moving about the country easier in this 'On your bike' era. Ask parents for the first word in their head at the mention of testing and assessment, and the list includes desk, pencils, ruler, silence, tables and spelling; eleven plus grammar success and failure. Ask if this is what they want for their child and the answer is an emphatic 'no'.

However, believe me, the first thought in any parent's mind is, 'how is my child progressing at school, and what can I do to help?' In order for parents to ask the question in the first place, they have to feel at ease; the school door has to be ajar. Many feel that Mr Baker may have removed the door altogether, thereby causing too great a wind of change through the 'secret garden'. The National Curriculum and its assessment procedures certainly give parents that right to ask and to know. For that right I and many shy and diffident parents are grateful.

The challenge to the teaching profession is to be pragmatic and accept the needed changes contained within the 1988 Education Act, to realise that the main threat is possible pressure from uninformed parents for a return to the classroom practice of yesteryear, to stop paying lip-service to partnership, stop raising the old chestnuts about parents' apathy or interference, examine the causes, and find the solutions.

Parents in power

The 1988 Education Reform Act has been flagged as the 'parents' charter', for it gives parents a much greater influence in their children's schooling. In addition to the right of their child to a National Curriculum entitlement, parents have a right to real dialogue with the school about their child's progress. They are entitled to discuss with the teachers the results of testing and assessment procedures.

The teeth are provided for this power base by a complaints procedure, organised and delivered by the local education authority. Added to this, parents have the right to choose a school for their child, so that the school that apparently fails to deliver the goods becomes vulnerable, especially as each child carries a funding allocation under the local management of schools.

The DES paper, *The National Curriculum – From Policy to Practice*[1] states that to increase the amount of information available to parents will help raise standards, for it will widen access to information about the school's objectives. It will give parents the information necessary to reinforce at home what happens at school.

It will enable a school to report the achievements of children in a way which not only the parents, but the whole community can appreciate. Schools will be able to evaluate their achievements by comparison with others.

It is envisaged that information about the curriculum will be contained within the school prospectus, and that this information will include details of how the school intends to deliver the National Curriculum. Parents are to have access, within the school, to a range of documents about the curriculum, including schemes of work. A parent who is dissatisfied about a child's education in relation to the National Curriculum will have access to a complaints procedure which will be handled by the local education authority.

These may be laudable aims. However, most schools would be well advised to undertake a full-scale review of the way they relate to parents, not only in written communication, but in and throughout their attitudes, their environment, and their willingness to allow parents to experience and share in their children's school life, in order to help ensure a successful outcome.

Too many parents, having been kept beyond the school gate, or having had a bad experience of school themselves, have scant understanding of the value of present-day classroom practice. Since all of us have spent many years at school, many rate themselves experts. Unfortunately, although around ninety per cent of parents are happy with their own children's education, public opinion and the popular press tell a different story.

On a recent journey to London, my attempts to work were thwarted by Mr Friendly Double Glazing Salesman. *He* didn't write reports – 'waste of time'; he didn't attend meetings, life was good, 'Spain last week, down to some big do in London today'; earned more money than he could spend. A few boisterous youngsters in the next compartment turned the conversation towards the failure of our schools today. Why were children so infuriatingly badly behaved? Why, oh why, couldn't they be seen and not heard! Why didn't schools do a good job? Why did he have to provide the wherewithal for the village football team? What had happened to school sports? Teachers were hopeless, kids were hopeless. Why not spelling tests and tables?. . .

I could have wrung his neck. Did he never think beyond the garbage of the tabloid that he rolled between his smooth fingers? Joe Public's view is entrenched and drip-fed by the poison of the popular press, but unfortunately it is based upon his unease of schools and all that pertains to them.

The Act certainly promotes powerful reasons for seeking to improve understanding and partnership between parent and teacher.

What a pity

Those who share my commitment to home–school co-operation feel saddened that there was so little voluntary progress towards real partnership. The messages about the value of parental involvement in education were clearly spelled out in the Plowden Report in 1967[2], and in much education research[3]. The value of parents having an understanding of what happens at school is recognised in many papers published by Her Majesty's Inspectorate, for example *Good Teachers Observed* [4], and in DES papers such as *Parental Influence at School* [5], and *Better Schools* [6].

. Nonetheless, a comparative study of parents' involvement in education across Europe by Alastair Macbeth[7] serves to illustrate a lack of commitment in the United Kingdom compared with our European neighbours. The Taylor Report of 1978[8], which sets out an agenda for parents' involvement in school management, was greeted as a 'busybody's charter' by one teacher union leader.

Sadly the effects of industrial action by some teachers during the mid-eighties upon relationships between home and school will have long-lasting implications, for some parents had no access to school or dialogue with teachers for three years. Similarly, low morale within the teaching profession, and the pace and pressure of change, is leading many good teachers to opt out, or to become disillusioned and depressed. As a committed 'professional parent' I feel for them, but worry about what the future holds. It will take more than hollow words from the Secretary of State to restore that high morale in our classrooms which is so essential to good home–school liaison and the implementation of the National Curriculum.

Implementing the National Curriculum

The successful implementation of the National Curriculum is dependent upon parents having an informed awareness of what happens in the classroom; the understanding and co-operation is necessary not only of school communities, but of employers and local industry.

If schools are not to be judged by a league of crude test results, local education authorities and schools, and indeed the whole education world, must undertake an enormous public relations and information exercise.

The Reform Act places many responsibilities upon the local education authority in relation to the National Curriculum, including the delivery of a complaints procedure.

The local education authority will be responsible for ensuring that the National Curriculum is in place. Surely, therefore, parents will have the right to assume the LEA advisors will have much greater authority to ensure that all children have access to best practice? This will involve the authority in genuine dialogue with teachers and parents, so that parents can appreciate good practice when they see it.

The local authority has a responsibility to train school governors and to clarify the interrelated roles of those involved in education of children.

In 44 local education authorities, NCPTA has developed Area Federations of home school groups. Such a forum needs to be available in all LEAs, where discussion can take place about the National Curriculum. Questions like valuing the professionalism of teachers and the contribution of parents and governors need to be addressed in a positive way.

Local education authorities have great responsibilities for our children, their teachers and our schools. Theirs is the task of raising public awareness about the good news, the progress of classroom technique in recent years, the ability to project the aims of the National Curriculum and its targets of achievement through topic work, the limitations of pen and paper tests. The local education authority surely has a responsibility to sing the praises of schools for children in difficult areas, and, to find a way of illustrating their achievement in real terms. Ways will need to be found by which those children, too, can experience that much vaunted improvement in standards.

Seven years ago in Bob Blackledge's paper[9] I read of the idea of 'high street education shops'. In the conclusion of this paper he wrote, 'There is a wealth of talent, goodwill and help, to be had from parents. They can act to interpret the school to the community, their advice can bring into school new ideas, observations and criticisms, all of which can improve its effectiveness.'

Recently some education authorities have taken classrooms right into large department stores, and a few have attempted to get positive messages across – but we need much more done in this area.

It is necessary to identify models of good practice, such as those developed in Oxfordshire where a combined health and social services and education authority approach has been developed. Warwickshire also has done pioneering work in appointing an advisor for home-school liaison. Both initial teacher training and INSET should be reviewed in order to relate to parents, thereby involving parents and helping them to understand. Much understanding can be fostered by the promotion of projects like the Social Curriculum Award and the RSA Education for Capability

Award, for such schemes raise morale by recognition of achievement and celebrate good practice.

There is an urgent need for every LEA to have a clearly defined
policy for home–school co-operation which is implemented and
regularly and effectively evaluated.

Within the school, 'easy there, please'

Many teachers say that developing good home–school relations
is difficult, and that repeated efforts have achieved little. However
it is surely self-evident that the successful delivery of a National
Curriculum which reflects the best of classroom practice and
therefore has the support of the teaching profession, needs the
understanding and co-operation of parents. It is therefore an
opportune time to take a careful look at the whole school
community and evaluate what could be done to improve
relationships.

'EASY' is my acronym for: Environment – Attitudes – Sharing
– and saying Yes. Yes! – *That is making a positive commitment
for the future.* Under these headings, I suggest that most schools
could successfully identify useful strategies for improving the
involvement not only of parents, but of whole school communities.
I have recently been involved in preparing a video for NCPTA,
entitled *Welcoming Parents into School*[10]. During its preparation
I visited many schools, seeking examples of good practice in home–
school cooperation. They were not difficult to find, but many
illustrated different aspects of getting it right, and all schools
involved could gain from good practice elsewhere. It would be
useful if a group of parents, teachers, and governors could be
formed to consider each of the following headings.

Environment

Take a careful look at the approach to the school. Is the car park
signposted? Is the school entrance obvious and welcoming, are
there comfortable seats and interesting displays in the foyer? Does
the school take this opportunity, as a parent enters school,
sometimes to wait a few moments, to make the welcome obvious,
so they may also see the messages of good news about the school?
Can anything be done to improve the environment of the school
by involving parent, pupils and older community members in
planting shrubs, trees, and plants? Could plants be used and cared
for in a similar way within the school, for these soften the
environment?

What about the Head's office? Could a comfortable seating
arrangement be planned for interviews with parents? Is there room

within the school for a 'parent corner' where they could feel at home, and where useful information, not only about the National Curriculum, but about other things like requests for help with child-minding or uniform exchange, could be placed upon a notice board?

Attitudes

In my search for video material, I discovered a notice above a school secretary's desk that read: 'Smiles will be returned'.

It is necessary to widen the circle of people who understand and support the ethos of the school, and yet it is human nature to talk only to those we know. Therefore it is helpful to consider the prevailing attitudes within the whole school community: can efforts be made to encourage the welcoming smile and greeting?

The staff need to discuss a strategy for involving parents in school life in a way which makes parents feel valued and welcome, but an essential precursor for such involvement has to be that the school has a policy with which the staff feel comfortable. A haphazard development where neither staff nor parent understand the nature of the partnership, or their complementary and mutually supportive roles, is fraught with potential for disaster, and so careful discussion is necessary between all concerned.

The support of the school caretaker is fundamental to creating goodwill amongst the school community. He or she needs a tolerant attitude towards 'trespassers' if we are to achieve our objectives.

Other questions to discuss include written communication between home and school and between school and home; please notice the two-way emphasis. Could parents help in the preparation of newsletters, thereby creating a sense of shared ownership? Contact with the local press could be an on-going relationship so that the good news is reported, and damage limitation facilitated at time of disaster. Could positive links be developed with local industry and shops so that future employers can appreciate that aforementioned excellent present-day classroom practice?

Mr Roy Sowden, the Head of Dukeries Complex in Nottingham, a community school serving a rural area, seemed to pitch it right in saying that it is not just about the paper messages that the school puts out, it is about the messages that the wider community carry to, from and within the school, and then promote, as a result of their interest and involvement with the school.

Sharing

Any gardener knows that the cultivation of a good tilth requires careful preparation of the soil, a good load of muck or fertilisers and a great deal of tender loving care: otherwise they will never grow that prize show of beautiful flowers.

Having created the right atmosphere within the school, the group could consider what they would like to grow. What do teachers want of parents, and equally what do parents want of teachers? Where are the perennial weeds that need to be eradicated?

The agenda here could be: 'Is it possible to restructure the Home–School Association?' (The title NCPTS refers to PTA since it is inclusive of the whole school community.) It is essential that parents form and run the Home-School Association, so that attitudes are promoted which ensure that it is seen that their contribution is valued and relied upon.

In many schools, each year has its own parents' group: this can be successful in that parents share similar interests as their children progress through the school and lasting friendships are formed. Year grouping could provide a useful forum for discussion about the National Curriculum and its assessment procedures.

An excellent way of increasing parents' understanding of the school's curricular aims is to encourage parents to take classes as pupils alongside the children. In other schools, parents' workshops have proved successful.

In the wake of local management of school, those responsible for school management may wish to review the involvement of parents within the school. Many parents can bring special skills and talents which could enrich the learning experience of our children, even if only by allowing them the experience to mix and communicate with adults.

Such a wider involvement of parents can have a positive spin-off, in that parents see for themselves what happens in class and can therefore come to understand and support good classroom practice.

Imaginative homework also has its place in fostering understanding; my own young son one evening had been set the task of measuring six round objects – 'I have to measure them around and across and divide one into another'! 'Has that school never heard of *pi r* squared?' was the immediate reaction of scientist father. 'Stick with it', I said: and we did. Son now knows that three and a bit diameters equals the circumference. I rote-learned about quarts, pints, pecks and bushels in days at school, and will never understand their comparative values. Other sharing activities, although not strictly related to the National Curriculum, can improve the general understanding of the school's aims and objectives.

Report to parents and the annual parents' meeting

The annual report from the governing body to the parent body and the annual parents' meeting are of great importance in that they provide a vehicle of accountability for the schools' governors. Attendance at meetings to date have been a great disappointment to those making efforts to arrange them. The greatest difficulty is the formality of the 'vibes' raised by the title 'Annual Parents Meeting'. What is needed is openness and truthfulness between governors and parent body; parents will understand if an answer to a question is genuinely not known. What parents find off-putting is the officialdom of the 'questions only in writing' syndrome, and the oft-quoted situations in primary schools where governors sit on big chairs and parents sit on small ones.

Nonetheless, the occasion is one which will grow in its relevance with the introduction of the National Curriculum and the greater accountability of schools. Displays and demonstrations involving the children are the best way of attracting parents to attend school; perhaps too in the future, some exhibition of assessment tasks which parents could experience for themselves would be possible and useful. Certainly an appeal to the parents by parent governors to attend, written in a friendly letter may help. For greater effectiveness this could be addressed to the parents by name, even if this were done by the pupil. I have seen examples of invitation cards to such meetings that have been designed and hand coloured by pupils.

The written annual report is perhaps of greater importance than the actual meeting. Its preparation by the governors ensures that they have that necessary close liaison with their school, which is so crucial to its well being. Essentially the report must give parents an outline of the curricular aims of the school; a good report will do much more and will be an interesting and readable account of the school year from a governing body which has an empathy with the school, its staff and pupils. Most governing bodies are arranging sub-committees to cover different areas of responsibility, and therefore possibly different governors could report on their own area of subcommittee work. Parents with a problem will sometimes turn to a governor rather than a teacher, and great sensitivity is needed on the part of the governor in handling such situations.

Since the role of governors is discussed elsewhere I will not develop this topic further: suffice it to say that the governors, and especially the parent governors, have a crucial role as catalysts in bringing about understanding between parents and teachers.

Say yes today

In conclusion therefore, without this essential all-encompassing whole-school approach to relationships between home and school, it is difficult to envisage how new powers vested in parents can lead to the raising of standards of education. If involvement of the many is not encouraged in these ways, one has fears about the effects of a vociferous minority group.

Possibly the very necessary antidote to the possibly corrosive effects of parent power has to be an urgent review of partnership policies, and the development of an era of school-wide parent participation and understanding. This is essential in order for there to be an appreciation of the progress of education throughout the last decade and the needs of our children in the future. The advantages of genuine partnership are well documented both in research and in practice.

The beneficial effect of the Education Reform Act has to be that governors, teachers and local education authorities are aware that the 'secret garden' era of education is over. There is a willingness to talk to parents and to develop partnership. More people are saying, 'How can we help parents to make a responsible and informed input into education?' – and that is good.

Education has nothing to hang its head about, except its inability to sound the trumpet of success. Let's therefore toast the post-gerbil era and be determined to get it right.

References

1   *The National Curriculum: From Policy to Practice*, DES 1989.
2   The Plowden Report, DES 1967.
3   Research findings –
     Much to do about education, Ann Corbett, Council for Educational Advance, (The Southern Publishing Co. Ltd, April 1972).
     Raising Standards. Parental Involvement Programmes, Paul Widlake and Flora Macleod, (Community Education Development Council, August 1984).
     Parents in Partnership. Involving Muslim Parents in their Children's Education, Flora Macleod (Community Education Development Council, August 1985).
     Belfield Reading Project, A Jackson and P Hanon (Belfield County Council).
     Parents, Teachers and Children, J Raven (Scottish Council for Research in Education, 1980).
     Parental Participation in Children's Developments and Education, Sheila Wolfendale, (Gordon & Breach, 1983).
4   *Good Teachers – Education Observed*, DES May 1985, p. 13.
5   *Parental Influence at School*, DES 1984.
6   *Better Schools*, DES 1985.
7   *The Child Between: A report on school-family relations in the countries of the European Community*, Alastair MacBeth *et.al*, (EEC 1984).
8   *The Taylor Report*, DES 1978.

9   *Reflections and Observations of Transitions from School to Working Life*, Bob Blackledge (EEC, 1981).
10   Video: 'Parents – Partners in a Shared Task – Welcoming Parents into School' (NCPTA 1989) (2 Ebbsfleet Industrial Estate, Stonebridge Road, Gravesend, Kent DA11 9DZ).

9 Governor responsibilities

Joan Sallis, Governor

Teachers who so passionately defend their professional territory against the incursions of too many busybodies are often surprised to learn that the territory has no sanctity in law or history. The teacher's last word in the classroom was never even laid claim to before the twentieth century, and even then it had no foundation in law, but was merely a convention which grew up because those who were supposed to decide what children learn had no equipment or taste for the task. This was indeed power by default.

> The introduction of a new branch of study, or the suppression of one already established, and the relative degree of weight to be assigned to different branches, are matters respecting which a better judgment is likely to be formed by such a body of governors as we have suggested . . . than by a single person, however able and accomplished . . . What should be taught, and what importance should be given to each subject are therefore questions for the Governing Body; how to teach is a question for the Head Master[1].

The sexist language of the concluding words gives the show away. Otherwise I might have been able to pretend that this was a fevered contemporary outpouring of a parent activist, a quotation from the Taylor Committee's report of 1977[2], or a rearguard action of a governors' lobby against the National Curriculum in 1988.

It is, of course a jewel of mid-Victorian history, culled from the Report of the Clarendon Commission in 1864, and it was not at all controversial at the time. Ever since people had tried to give institutional form to the principle that the content of education is the responsibility of society, it had been assumed that the territorial rights of the educator were concerned only with the 'how' of teaching. The 'what' was a matter for public debate and ultimately public policy.

The tortured history of government's attempts to enshrine this principle in law is no concern of this chapter, and I have in any case set it out in detail elsewhere[3]. Now we only need to remind ourselves that the imposition of a National Curriculum is not just an attempt to force schools to compete fiercely in the delivery of a more standard product. It is not just part of a programme in which you have to standardise so that you can test, test so that you can compare, compare so that the strong can segregate themselves, devolve so that that segregation can be made secure. It is not just a stage in what is planned to become a demand-driven service no different in essence from a voucher scheme. I believe it is all three, but that is a controversial statement which will be hotly contested – though not by many teachers. But it is also an expression of despair about the failure of other measures to induce educators and democratic institutions to co-operate in the devising of learning goals and programmes. Local authorities for many years failed to grasp firmly enough their responsibility for the curriculum, while school governors, who in relation to individual schools always had that responsibility – extraordinary that so much fuss had been made about spelling it out in the 1986 Act – either were not the right sort of people in the past to do the job, or found professional resistance too much for them. The Education (No.2) Act 1986 is in danger of being forgotten before it has even in all respects arrived. The education system, punch drunk with so much new law in such a short time, is aware that there has been a great deal of change, much of it in some sense threatening, most of it in their secret hearts unnecessary. At extremes they see the agenda as (i) to undermine local government; (ii) to deprofessionalise and devalue teachers; (iii) to jeopardise the free, fair and full entitlement of the child; (iv) to make a service meeting needs into one responding to demand; (v) force schools into cut-throat competition; and (vi) to these ends, to shift the balance of power away from teachers to confident representatives of the public, especially business.

I would not actually dissent from this cynical view of the agenda, nor would I doubt that there is an underlying drive to confine the full educational experience by these means to those who can identify it, positively choose it, fight for it and in the end perhaps pay for it, to the detriment of those unrepresented children who do not have confident adults to see that their needs are met. Where I part company with most teachers I meet is on not seeing this as an objective of the *1986* Education Act, which is not about taking power from local government, undermining teachers, threatening free education, forcing schools to compete. It is simply about how schools make their decisions, and as such it will stand in my judgment with the great Education Acts of 1870, 1902, and 1944. It is about sharing, about debate, about consensus, about partnership, about openness, and it is supported by all political parties and no more likely to go away than trial by jury. It is the *1988* Act which could be said to fulfil that much more political agenda, and it is tragic that so many educators confuse the two, see them as part of the same package, or think that the earlier Act, if they remember it at all, has been washed away.

The 1986 Act firmly restated the obligation of the LEA (pre-National Curriculum) to establish a curriculum for all the schools in their area and to publish it. This was then the subject of further refinement and adaptation to the individual school and a statement (published) by the governors. If there were variations from the LEA policy, it was the headteacher who in the end had to reconcile and choose. Although these provisions have been overlaid (I choose this word rather than 'overtaken') by the National Curriculum, there is one thing which we must never lose sight of. In so far as the school still has an individual character, a character determined by its values, by the choices it makes in meeting its National Curriculum obligations, by the way it uses what time is left after those obligations have been met, by the learning environment it creates and the messages it gives to children, it is the partnership between the governors and the headteacher and staff which shapes that character. I wish I were allowed to repeat that sentence or print it in red, for the quality and efficiency of the partnership are now paramount.

Under the 1988 Education Reform Act, the governors share with the LEA and the headteacher the responsibility for ensuring that the National Curriculum is delivered in the school. Since they will also in future have a right to share in the determination of the school's policies as expressed in its spending programme, and will be responsible for the choice of head and staff to deliver those policies, it is vital that school and governors communicate well about the learning process and that there is a genuine sharing of thought on every aspect of the curriculum. This is easy to say, very difficult to achieve, given the tradition that most governors have approached the curriculum like frail old ladies confronting a rotweiler or a doberman.

I believe we have indeed reached a very dangerous roundabout on the road to partnership. Shall I signpost some of the wrong turnings before I go on?

Firstly we could allow the power which the law intended to be transferred from LEAs to governors and parents to end up somewhere else. It could easily in effect revert to headteachers, with all concerned merely going through the motions of consultation. It could find its way to the already powerful Secretary of State. Or it could – and this is what schools themselves most fear – be hogged by unrepresentative minorities of all kinds in the school community, social, political, or simply selfish. The 'don't-let-my-child-be-held-back-by-slow-learners'-brigade, the 'back-to-basics'-army, the 'keep-the-riff-raff-out'-merchants, the 'caring-parents-will-always-find-the-money'-faction. In politics as in education, there is only one answer to extremist minorities, and that is the participation of very large numbers – and this is hard work.

Secondly there is the danger that primary schools in particular will lose confidence in what they have been doing so well for twenty-five years, twenty-five years which to this outsider have looked like old sepia photographs bursting into colour. If teachers are afraid to stray from the paths leading to tests, they will soon forget how many flowers grow well away from paths. They will forget how many children will never go on any voyage of discovery unless the school takes them there. An unnecessarily narrow curriculum will rob children very unequally, because the lucky homes will easily make good what the school no longer provides – as they did with the cuts – while the poor go without. Yet one must accept that in future parents will be understandably anxious about whether their children are going to make the grade, and they will need reassuring that the way the school approaches the goals is the right one. One must accept that all parents have a right to be so reassured, however old-fashioned and inappropriate their aspirations may seem to teachers.

There is plenty of evidence that child-centred methods, cross-curriculum approaches, social and personal education, investigative teaching, emphasis on the arts, all contribute to basic skills, but this is rarely shared with parents. Most parents, despite the greater openness of schools, still don't know what drawing round your feet, weighing, pouring, and sailing things, going to the churchyard, looking at the last census, recording what people buy in the supermarket, producing a newspaper, running a mock-election, or role-playing a family drama, have got to do with anything. These bridges have to be built, and I see governors as vital ambassadors for schools in making the connection. But if they are to spread the word, they must know it.

Thirdly, and again governors must receive and then spread the message, there is this fashionable word 'relevance'. Of course learning must be relevant, and of course we must not neglect the wealth-producing activities of society or give up the hard struggle to wipe out the false values which in times past have led the most able and ambitious to spurn such activities. If we fail, then we shan't be able to afford good schools or libraries, aid to the arts or care for the environment. It is worrying, however, that relevance is so often preached by people of great power and influence who have reached those positions through the great privilege of an irrelevant education, and are choosing it for their children, but who prescribe for others a programme of the most narowly conceived relevance.

Relevance must be for everybody, and not too narrowly defined. It must be special to every stage of education, too. So often the goals are handed down, ultimately from higher education and employers, like shoes in a large, poor family, fitting worse with each new owner, and the early stages of schooling are seen as having no value except as preparation for what is to come. If schools are to stand up for the right of children to their own shoes, and each stage of education to respond to the unreturning moment, they must share these visions with governors, particularly perhaps those who come from the business world. The business community can find involvement in schools so much more rewarding if it looks beyond the basic skills it expects from tomorrow's employees and values also their adaptability, curiosity, stability, and capacity to enjoy worthwhile things. Incidentally, the value in any workforce of people who have had the life-enhancing experience of being school governors should also be a part of the symbiosis of school and business.

Fourthly at this perilous roundabout comes the danger that schools will swallow whole the competitive ethic which is dangled daily before them. The best thing about schools used to be the way they shared good ideas. Our system, despite much more central interference than there was, is still second to none in the freedom it gives to individuals to be creative at every level, and to demonstrate their ideas in mechanisms to spread good practice, and this essential process has been left to people to organise for themselves. Tragic if that process were threatened by schools becoming jealous and isolationist, hiding their work like children doing a test, instead of sharing it. We may have to work rather harder, especially when the weakening of the framework of local government leaves the schools much more to their own devices, and when everything we hear is about competition, to keep the sharing process alive.

Fifthly, and perhaps the biggest concern within the service, is that the curriculum and policies of schools will be irresistably market-driven to the service of the strong. The delegation of budgets to schools, with only 7% allowed to be retained for central services and with 75% of the sum delegated having to be based only on numbers and ages, allows pathetically little to cater for all the differences between schools and children. Schools with many pupils with special needs and poor catchment areas will not have enough extra means to meet those needs and compensate for those disadvantages. If there is a drift of pupils without disadvantages away from schools with many (and this is what open enrolment will encourage), taking their average funding with them, poor schools will have even less to manage on. The poverty will be further increased by the new charging policies, which it is feared will lead to many schools having to give up enriching activities because none of their parents can contribute. Governors will have to understand these difficulties, and be encouraged to support all that the school can do to use its resources with care and humanity.

All this is about sharing of values, essentially, and it is an activity which will have to proceed apace if governors' new responsibility for the curriculum and policies of the school is to be exercised with humanity and wisdom. How well are we equipped for this development, and what are the obstacles?

Heads will say that many governors have neither the interest nor commitment to reach any real understanding of what underlies curriculum decisions, that they need training to enable them to grasp essential concepts, that at extremes their involvement is trivial, dubiously motivated or even destructive of those values I have been talking about. All this is true. What is wrong is the assumption that schools can do nothing about it.

Training is certainly important. Its provision by local authorities is still patchy, and much of what there is is very poor. Teaching adults of mixed ability, with a rapid turnover, the skills needed to operate confidently in a complex system and to do so quickly, given their relatively brief involvement, is a highly skilled business, and trainers who can do it are scarce. Much training is not active enough, does not use enough sound and realistic material (that's scarce too) and tends to adopt a linear or thematic approach, rather than a 'windows-on-the-school' approach. Governors can't hope to go through all the things they might ever have to do – they'd be out of office before they had got to the second chapter. They need insights, a feeling about how schools work, an understanding of the underlying concepts, so that their experience in the world and their common sense can be liberated to approach whatever comes up. They also need to be asured that it's their ordinariness schools want – it would all be pointless otherwise. And you can be certain that if not enough ordinary people are encouraged to participate, some very undesirable extraordinary people could fill the vacuum.

Nevertheless, the training outlook is improving. Many local authorities have now appointed governor training officers under various names, and some imaginative choices have been made.

A number of LEAs have devised good programmes with plenty of practice and participation, and some have produced materials of their own – case studies, video and audio cassettes, and informative literature about education. A number of colleges of further and higher education, university departments, adult colleges, the Open University, the WEA, voluntary organisations like the National Association of Governors and Managers, the Advisory Centre for Education, the National Confederation of PTAs, the Campaign for the Advancement of State Education and others have developed some expertise, got training programmes off the ground, and produced materials. The BBC have produced an excellent series of audio tapes with work books, and in many areas governor training bodies or groups of governing bodies can borrow materials and perhaps have the services of a tutor to organise their own training.

Here too, sharing experience is the great need, since it can so easily be wasteful for agencies to work in isolation. In 1987, after long preparation, an organisation was formed to meet this need. It called itself AGIT, Action for Governors' Information and Training[4], and aimed, not to supplant any agency which was providing training, but to provide a shop window for them all, encourage them to co-operate and share materials and strategies, and spread information about what was available and what was being done. It brings together local authorities and diocesan boards, training institutions and voluntary groups, and soon had a high enough proportion of these in membership to be able to set up an office with paid staff.

When all is said and done, the best training ground may still be the school. Without in any way belittling the need for organised training, I would still say that genuine access to the processes of a school is indispensible to those insights I mentioned earlier. If governors are to play their part in curriculum development, they must be enabled to come close to the learning process.

I would say that the greatest obstacle to improvement is the tendency of head teachers to see governors as external to the school. They will complain to each other about them if they are awful, boast about them if they are not too bad. But they see them as brought by the stork, or thrown at the school from a great distance like a custard pie, but not funny. They will say that they did not choose them. They did not choose the staff they inherited when they were appointed to headship either, but they nevertheless accepted responsibility for welding them into an effective team. In their view of management they would include the negotiation of objectives; the identification and orchestration of individual talent; the establishment of a climate of high expectation; the building of effective working structures; and the professional development of individuals. Yet they would not normally include governors in these expectations of themselves, or see the quality of governors' work as an index of the quality of their management skills. It is this which has to change. High expectations will not make perfect governors, but all human beings respond to expectations. High expectations will also help to squeeze out the hopeless cases. Good working structures are also essential, and it is a management responsibility to create them.

Governors need access to the process of education and educational decision making. This means something very concrete and visible. I stress this because so often on courses headteachers will write on their flip charts that they are going to build better partnerships with their governors, involve them more in the school, and similar abstractions. We need to spell out *how* we are going to convey those high expectations. We need to realise that governors can't just 'drop in any time', any more than a teacher could drop into a factory or an acquaintance into your home. They must have it constructed for them, know the occasion, the process, the purpose, and have a framework to sustain their will to be involved. They need to observe teaching (and heads have a task to convey to their staff if necessary that this is legitimate, necessary, expected of them, and is for the purpose of governors learning, not judging). Governors should attend some staff meeetings about the curriculum, share in the debate about change. They should see classes at work and take part in pupils' activities. They should be informed about and shown the connection between classroom activity and learning goals. And we should all work to create a climate in which school governors accept that some of their leisure time and annual leave should be used this way, and that they may have to be resourceful in making more time. We should also all try to create a climate in which employers accept the importance of service as school governors, and all do what the best now do, which is to allow time off with pay for school duties. It's no good just grumbling about bad practice. All can do a little to spread good.

It is vital that there should be a system of regular governor visiting in schools, something which supports their will to be involved, as I put it earlier, and makes best use of the time. Some schools have a duty governor of the month, whereby instead of the chair attending to all those matters which come up between meetings – nagging the office, planting the tree, interviewing for the new teacher, giving out the swimming badges, being there when they come back from the sponsored walk – the duty governor is called upon. S/he also visits for a day and looks at some aspect of the school's work. Other schools attach a governor to an aspect of school life – the arts, special needs, sport, dripping taps. Some attach a governor to a class or year group, and such personal involvement with pupils has much to commend it. A primary school where a governor was assigned to a class arranged things so that the governor 'went up' with the class and so followed children through four years of their school life. A secondary school, at the request of the staff, arranged for each governor to shadow a teacher for a whole day, a practice giving superb insights into the process of teaching, especially as it was so well structured, arranging for preparation for the visit and explanation of what went before and after each lesson, the part it played in the scheme of things, what it hoped to accomplish etc.

It is important that all teachers should attend governors' meetings in turn (and please don't forget deputies, who so often reach the hot seat themselves with no preparation) to talk to governors about their curriculum areas, using the opportunity to explain how classroom activity leads to skills, how different abilities are catered for, how children learn, what plans the teacher has for developing the subject area, what resources might be needed. This educates governors, encourages teachers, and is good practice in explaining educational concepts to lay persons. Sometimes a theme, rather than a subject, should be tackled — multi-cultural education, behaviour, special needs, health, truancy, school clubs. In future it will be particularly important to cover intercurricular themes, since it is here that many anxieties about the National Curriculum will be concentrated.

Schools should not assume that governors would never have a wise comment to make on a professional matter. Often points which jump at an outsider can be overlooked by those too close, and this applies particularly to discontinuities arising from responsibilities in schools being split. A simple example would be where no sex education was given at all in one year of a secondary school because of responsibility being with the science team in the early years and the social education team in the later ones. It was a parent governor who brought the house down by saying: 'What do they do in the third year? Practise?'

A major obstacle at present to a better working relationship with governors is the reluctance of professionals to share information or problems until they have made them their own. So much material is descending on schools in the wake of the new legislation that this particular form of defensiveness works against the proper use of governors. It is understandable: deep in the teacher's make-up is the desire to be a step ahead, to have the advantage, to have the answerbook. These days it isn't always possible, and when a new curriculum document, a budget statement, a set of plans arrives, it is so hard to spread them out straight from the envelope and look at them with all concerned, so tempting to say, 'I'll make a date to discuss this with you when I've digested it.' Yet infallibility makes few friends.

A related problem is the reluctance of many professionals to go public on any kind of school problem, a reluctance increased by the present competitive climate – the school must not appear with any warts showing. This arises in an acute form often when composing governors' annual reports to parents. Yet a school with no problems is hardly a great subject for a meeting, and people often respond well to sharing. Governors certainly do.

The need to break governors' workload into manageable bits will also prove to be helpful in gving individual governors more learning opportunities. No amount of information is a substitute for having to find out, and many more governors now will have to find out about a subject themselves. I do see some dangers in too much delegation to small groups, which if not properly controlled can frustrate debate; distort opinion patterns; exclude some governors unintentionally; obscure the fact at extremes that no consultation is taking place; fragment processes so that governors lose sight of the central purpose of it all; and create horrendous communication problems. Yet small groups are a uniquely valuable learning aid, and giving an individual the responsibility for coming to grips with some really terrible DES circular, then sharing the result, greatly enhances the quality of governors' discussion.

In the last resort, it is the will to share school decisions in a genuine way which makes everything easy. No collection of good ideas is a substitute for that will. I think we are quite a long way from being able to take it for granted, I'm afraid. That time will come only when the realisation dawns that a good LEA and a highly-skilled professional force cannot alone guarantee a fair and secure service any more. Perhaps they never could. Perhaps it was always true that the learning process depended for its health on parents and communities having a sense of commitment and ownership. Whether or not that is so, it seems now that many things vital to the delivery of a free, fair and broad education to children are in peril; that we have lacked in recent years sufficient public pressure to protect the service; and that in the climate of today it is essential to secure the understanding of many agencies outside the school if we are to replace the friends who are not so powerful any more. Unpowerful friends can in combination be even better sometimes.

References

1 · *Clarendon Commission Report*, 1864.

2   *A New Partnership for our Schools* (HMSO, 1977).
3   Joan Sallis (1988), *Schools Parents and Governors: a new approach to accountability* (Routledge), ch. 7.
4   Action for Governors' Information and Training. Lyng Hall, Blackberry Lane, Coventry, CV2 3JS.

10 Some special considerations

Mick Molloy, District Inspector, Manchester City Council

Let us start with three assumptions, the first two of which I hope are uncontentious. One is that good schooling is that which is good for *all* children and young people, and another is that the management and learning systems related to special educational needs should not be separate from other systems in a class, school or LEA.

The third, if contentious historically, is crucial: it is that difficulties in learning are socially constructed and essentially arise from a mismatch of what a learner, whether a child or adult, can do or is willing to do. It is this relationship which it is important to focus on, rather than taking a view which sees the term 'learning difficulty' as one that describes a group of people, as though some fixed set of characteristics or deficits existed. Whilst both the terms 'special educational needs' and 'learning difficulty' are used interchangeably in the 1981 Education Act, I prefer the latter term. It is a more accurate description, and leads the teacher into the critical question, 'How do I reduce the difficulty/ies in learning something for a particular child?'

It is well accepted now that all children make better progress when parents and teachers work together; parents play a critical part in how well their children learn, and have the potential to be especially helpful when they are the parents of children experiencing learning difficulty; it is vital that we unwrap the myth

159

and reality in the National Curriculum for them as well. They face difficulty enough with the blockages to learning which some youngsters present, without piling on yet more through ill-considered haste in the design of the new arrangements.

Just reflect, however, on what has happened, and wonder whether it can really be the best way of introducing a common learning entitlement for all children into our schools. I provide some (admittedly rhetorical) questions:

- Do some attainment targets across the foundation subjects cover the same ground because the complete model has not been fully thought through, eg those on data in mathematics, some science areas and what may appear in geography?
- What attempts have been made to link these attainment targets, or has it just been left to teachers in the hope that they will notice the links and take them into consideration when they plan their lessons?
- Do some of the attainment targets naturally cluster round the child because they answer the question, 'What's it like to be a successful learner?'
- Could a core of these attainment targets be built around the child in a learning profile to reinforce the importance of the process of learning, eg using and applying mathematics; exploring science; talking/writing; listening/reading; planning. making things and evaluating what's been done?
- Has the curriculum framework been well worked out for different sized schools?
- Are ideas really clear about how the National Curriculum will relate to all-age small establishments, which is a characteristic of many special schools?
- Is there an appreciation of the resource implications and is there a likelihood of their being met?
- Have teachers been given time to think through ideas and modify their curriculum and teaching methodologies accordingly?
- Is this the only major change that is taking place in the world of education at the moment?

The first radiogram my parents bought in the 50s was second-hand, and there were some records with it. After all those years the title or the first line of one suddenly comes to mind — 'Coming in on a wing and a prayer'. The rhetoric may be unkind but, if this is really a National Curriculum designed to raise standards to fit our educational system for the needs of the 21st century, surely we could reasonably have expected more systematic planning in its early stages and some sign of the necessary finance to back the introduction of a major innovation? Maybe when the dust settles on what actually happens in the classroom, we shall be seen to have been able to make proper sense of it, but for the moment we have to be content with what we can see, far too great a degree for comfort, to travel more in hope than expectation.

The advantages and disadvantages of the National Curriculum

Some, maybe many of us, resisted a National Curriculum, fearing it would restrict learning and could exclude at least some children and young people, as well as taking away from teachers the right to determine what is taught. Others welcomed the opportunities they felt such a curriculum would bring. Whatever our initial position then, it is now enshrined in educational legislation. The law which took away our responsibilities as educators to decide the broad terms of what to teach must now be used, along with other legislation to protect the individual right to a broad and balanced set of learning experiences in all our schools, whether these take place in mainstream or special schools.

The 1988 Education Act (England and Wales) states that in each maintained school there shall be a 'broad and balanced' curriculum, and that each school's basic curriculum will consist of at least the core and other foundation subjects of the National Curriculum, as well as religious education. These experiences, along with the rest of a particular school's curriculum, are intended to prepare children for adult life. The Act also clearly states that the school's basic curriculum will apply to each child between the ages of 5–16 in every maintained school. This is an entitlement curriculum and it must be seen to apply to all children, including those experiencing difficulties in learning.

It is now the right of each and every child to have access to the broad set of learning experiences in the school's basic curriculum. At first sight this strikes a blow for the principle of integration.

Ask what people understand by the word 'curriculum' and it's quickly clear that the word has many meanings. For me, curriculum consists of those experiences which adults value collectively and want to pass on to the younger members of the community for whom they have a responsibility. That there is now a 'national' view on this, rather than one's own class, school or local authority view, might be no bad thing. This could ensure that all children have the opportunity to become not only young mathematicians and writers and readers in the medium of English and/or Welsh, but also musicians, artists, technologists, historians, geographers, linguists as well as being healthy and fit. Who could deny any child such a guarantee? This is not to say that such an entitlement will not create difficulties for us as educators. The modern language requirement for instance in special schools will need particularly creative response if only because there are so few linguists at present working in these schools. A starting point for some special schools could be to explore the extent to which some of their children are bilingual or multilingual in non-European community languages such as Urdu, Bengali, Punjabi, Gujarati or Hindi, indeed any other languages, including those outside the National Curriculum. Clearly too it becomes essential that 'contracts' are formed between special and mainstream schools to ensure that the overall expertise of *all* staff is brought to bear to the benefit of all children wherever they are at school.

Some of the features of the common curriculum framework are also useful for those experiencing learning difficulties. For example:

- Attainment targets provide clearly defined aims for the teacher and the learner.
- Programmes of study are carefully defined ways of organising the broad content for learning so that experiences related to the attainment targets are given to all children.
- Assessment arangements will be the context for the evidence of learning and recording the achievements of children and young people.

There are opportunities, in respect of specificity and positive assessment, here which are especially of interest for children experiencing learning difficulties, not to mention the boost to continuity of experiences from class to class and between classes in parallel groups in all schools, at Year 2–3 and Year 6–7 transition points, and especially between special and mainstream schools when children transfer or share time as part of an integration programme. It has often been the bugbear of the best intentioned schemes of partial integration from special to mainstream schools that curricula haven't matched.

Whilst the National Curriculum will prescribe broadly what is taught, it will not dictate the detail of a school's curriculum. Neither can teachers be told how to teach; that is the art of the teacher and is safeguarded. It's true the National Curriculum is described in subject terms, and that requests from the Department of Education and Science for information from schools are likely to follow this pattern, but this does not mean it has to be the precise form of curriculum organisation adopted in a school. The National Curriculum comes alive in planning learning experiences that are reflected in the programmes of study. It is important that we all emphasise that it is a matter for teachers to decide in their schools whether they use thematic, integrated, cross-curricular or subject approaches. There is no single or correct answer.

How children learn, as any teacher of children experiencing learning difficulties will testify, is in any case more important than what they learn. All learners, whether child or adult, whatever their present status in terms of attainments or talents, want opportunities for:

- sheer pleasure, enjoyment and satisfaction in creating, accomplishing or achieving something on their own and with others;
- learning through content that is meaningful, interesting and applicable to them and based on what they do and will experience in their daily lives outside school;
- learning from observing others and explaining things and situations to others;
- understanding the importance of seeing all others as of equal value;
- practical experience of selecting and choosing, and solving real problems through exploring, experimenting and discovering;
- using their widening knowledge and skills, and communicating and expressing feelings, thoughts and ideas in a variety of ways.

It is of great benefit to us teachers, and to the children as well, that the legislators have left the process of teaching outside the 1988 Education Act. Had they not done so, then teaching would surely have moved away from a craft which has developed through time, to a position where it would now be relegated to mere instruction. This is not to suggest that all teaching is good teaching, but the answer to developing the art of teaching in teachers is not in restricting their practice. The history and inheritance of special education contains awful warnings of practitioners who 'cared' more than they thought 'critically': they have been the irritant too of more perceptive colleagues who constantly reflected on practice until they found the key to the child's mind. That struggle will be as great whatever the curriculum.

Since the summer of 1988 there has been a great deal of discussion in and between schools on what the curriculum consists of and the new demands that will be made by the National Curriculum. Many schools have also arranged meetings for parents to discuss the implications of the National Curriculum. Teachers, either from special schools or involved in special education needs teaching in mainstream school, are part of this debate in many local authorities. They are involved in working parties established to look at the reports produced by the various National Curriculum working parties. With their particular experience of a more behaviourally defined curriculum they have often helped to reduce panic among mainstream colleagues. It is important that they should for there are some matters of substance in the design of the National Curriculum which are unhelpful.

For example, on reading and re-reading the 1988 Education Act and the subsequent guidance, it is sometimes difficult to see where and how the child or young person fits. After all, children, (and adults as well, for that matter) do not live their lives in subject compartments, no matter how broad and balanced these might be. Anyone who has tracked a child or a group of children round a secondary school for a few days begins to see the disjointed world of schooling often presented to them, where experiences go uncoordinated and the child's life outside school is largely unrecognised as useful to the process of schooling. There is nothing in the National Curriculum to change this, although the opportunity to reconsider a school's curriculum could be used to create better continuity across a year group and from one year to the next. It is as though the National Curriculum has learnt the words but not the tune of how children learn.

There is a danger that these learning needs are seen as the same as those of children who experience learning difficulties which bring them under the 1981 Education Act. They are, of course, not the same. Bilingual children start from the position of being fluent in another language. Not only do the origins differ, but so do many of the strategies to reduce the difficulties in learning.

Of course, such a casual lack of attention is nothing new to those in special education.

From where the teachers of children and young people with special educational needs stand, whether in special or mainstream schools, education is usually experienced as a seperate rather than as an integrated part of a comprehensive system which educates all pupils. Wherever one turns in the system, nationally or locally, integration and the needs of those with special educational needs are, as it were, a forgotten aspiration, an inconvenient afterthought.

In 1983 when the Department of Education and Science requested all local education authorities to draw up their 5–16 Curriculum Statements, authorities were advised to leave out special schools until such time as the DES gave further advice. The advice never came.

Another example is the provision whereby children with a Statement of Special Educational Needs under Section 7 of the 1981 Education Act, whether in mainstream or special schools, are not included in the National Curriculum arrangements until September 1990. At first sight this is welcome, as it gives local education authorities time to write into each statement a description of how the National Curriculum should be modified, if at all, for that child. The writing of statements, after all, has been a vexed issue, with sometimes a thinly-veiled dispute between education officer, preoccupied with resources and often lacking direct experience of children with special educational needs, and the other specialist officers and advisors. The delay of course does nothing to clarify that. Moreover it could also signal that somehow special schools are less ready, and therefore require more time. It is better for both special and mainstream schools to work together on the National Curriculum since as I have already implied they have much to offer each other.

Finally circulars, guidelines and non-statutory advice refer largely to primary and secondary schools. Special schools are usually omitted. Circular 14/89 on the Education (School Curriculum and Related Information) Regulations 1989, for example, contains an annex relating to primary and secondary schools respectively, but there is no annex for special schools although they are covered by the regulation on which the circular is giving advice. Nor is the Department of Education and Science the only offending national agency. For example the very good booklet produced by the National Curriculum Council entitled *Framework No 1: Developing the primary curriculum* had lots of helpful advice about the organisation of the curriculum for young children of primary age. Yet neither the title nor the introduction refer to special schools, although on enquiry it is admitted that it is of course equally useful to them. Nor is it simply an oversight, for there is a more serious implication of exclusion which counters the integration movement of recent years and the last 1981 Education Act.

Consider the following three sections of the 1988 Education Act, which are about excluding children and young people from learning experiences in the National Curriculum:

- Under Section 17 the Secretary of State has the power to make regulations to specify cases and circumstances where the National Curriculum is not to apply, or is to be modified for groups of pupils.
- Under Section 18 the same process can be carried out for a particular pupil who has a Statement of Special Educational Needs under the 1981 Education Act.
- Under Section 19, Headteachers have powers to suspend or adapt the National Curriculum for a period intitially not exceeding six months.

The Secretary of State for Education has mammoth powers under Section 17 which could ultimately devastate the full curriculum entitlement for children attending special schools. In my opinion the first chips at the curriculum block would come from excluding children attending some special schools from the teaching requirement of modern languages.

It would have been better to have charged the education service with a legal duty vigorously to ensure the inclusion of all children in the National Curriculum. The advice from the Department of Education and Science to school governors in *A Guide to the Law* states that 'for example some or all of the requirements may not be appropriate for a pupil with a particular learning difficulty, who may need to concentrate for a while on catching up.' Is that a reason to be excluded? The very notion of 'catching up' assumes a convoy travelling at an average pace, which fits uneasily with the notion of stretching each individual child. Remember those children in first year secondary who were/are taken out of French to catch up with English, and then told in the second year that they had/have to follow 'funny' German because they do not 'know' any French? We cannot use our ignorance or lack of know-how as an excuse to exclude some children and young people. The challenge is that all should receive a broad, balanced and relevant education. Now there is a National Curriculum it is unthinkable to contemplate a child being excluded from it, for to do so would surely be to run the risk of seeing such children as being alarmingly close to the notion of 'ineducable', which of course had a particular meaning arising from Section 57 of the 1944 Education Act. Until 1970, indeed, children and people with a mental handicap were excluded from the education system on the grounds of their 'ineducability'. It would be unfortunate and indeed immoral to return to a situation where any individual is assigned a status analogous to 'ineducability' by being outside the scope of the National Curriculum.

There is ample evidence in schools for children and young people experiencing severe learning difficulties to show that this does not have to be the case. Modification should only be used to gain access to curriculum experiences, say for a child who is blind and uses braille, or a child who writes using a word processor because of a physical disability. These points are well covered in general terms in the National Curriculum Council document *A Curriculum for All*. The 1988 Education Act gives the Secretary of State power to make regulations so that schools have to inform parents/guardians of all children registered at the school of the child's individual curriculum plan. Part of me says this is good for all children and their parents, but the pragmatist says that most schools will not be able to move beyond what is already in a good school brochure, because of their limited administrative/ clerical support. However that may be, it is clearly essential that detailed personal curriculum plans are drawn up for those who are most at risk in school. The answer probably lies in spreading the best practice of 'teacher-parent briefings' on children's progress so that it is a right enjoyed by all.

Most of the things highlighted here could have been avoided with good strategies and a more thoroughly planned delivery of what constitutes the National Curriculum. Membership of future working groups for the foundation subjects should include people with experience in special education, and those who can put forward perspectives on education in multiracial and working class communities. Separate working groups are not enough. Even if this doesn't happen, since the detail of what is taught still lies with the school and the teacher, local working groups in LEAs must look at the programmes of study in order to turn them into detailed curriculum plans relevant to children experiencing learning difficulty. Local authorities and schools for example should not abandon moderation outside the GCSE and 'curriculum-led' summative assessments just because central government has done so. When the levels 'don't fit', a case will have to be made for change, and collective teacher/inspector evidence of what has been learnt will be important in supporting the case.

Indeed before turning to some practical next steps necessary to safeguard the interests of youngsters experiencing learning difficulties, it is sensible to reflect further on the assessment cart which is supposedly pulled by the curriculum horse.

The report of the Task Group on Assessment and Testing set down a framework for assessment, which appears at least initially to have commanded a general welcome and acceptance. This framework is interesting on three counts to those whose particular concern is the child experiencing learning difficulty.

First, it advanced the rather novel and unsubstantiated idea that all learning in the National Curriculum must be ten levels high. This is likely to create difficulties for many children experiencing difficulties in learning. Even now there is talk of level zero and pro-level 1, and grouping children of different ages together because they are all 'on the same level'. This last strategy has sometimes been used in primary schools with 'lumpy' numbers in Year 6. The children said to have the lowest attainments, usually in reading, are kept down in Year 5 and then expected to transfer with their age-cohort to high school. The social perspective of preparing to leave the primary school is lost for these children, and they can have transfer difficulties as a consequence.

Secondly, the report advanced the more contentious notion that progress in learning is linear; consolidation, breadth of understanding and better application could all be progress and be equally important for some children who do not conform to the 10 levels high model. What will be the effect of this failure on them? More than likely it is the assessment framework rather than the learning experiences in the National Curriculum which will make teachers, who work with the children and young people with profound mental handicap and complex physical disabilities, feel that National Curriculum is far removed from the learning experiences which they need to plan for their pupils.

Thirdly, there are more helpful ideas of formative assessment and teacher moderation supported by standard assessment tasks. It is in this area that most progress could be made in helping teachers to be clearer on what the evidence for learning is, establishing what children can do and using this to increase their attainments. Indeed, outside the old CSE and the new GCSE moderation arrangements it is a model found already in the best special schools.

As things stand now, the assessment framework is a set of guesstimates looking for further evidence, and should be seen as such. The danger is that formative assessment and teacher moderation will be dropped on the grounds of cost in teacher time. The emphasis will presumably then switch to externally-produced standard assessment tasks, delivered largely through pencil and paper tests. The effect of this would be to penalise children for whom this medium, for whatever reasons, is not suitable. And for many children experiencing learning difficulties in a literacy-dominated world, such an approach would be particularly unfortunate. Much more likely, on the grounds both of cost and complexity, is a move to abandon criterion referenced and formative assessment in favour of summative and norm-referenced assessment which will support a drift towards a 'skills-based' set of minimum learning experiences for all children, a large proportion of whom may be demotivated by the clear 'pecking order' which such a system implies. Schools which follow an assessment led rather than a curriculum-led model to develop the National Curriculum will quickly move to this minimalist position. The rest will be pushed towards it by having to complete something in the region of 900 assessment tasks at the end of the keystage. All this is far removed from what the writers of the TGAT report doubtless would have wished had their design requirements not been so circumscribed. Nevertheless it is hard to avoid the conclusion that the TGAT framework provides an assessment-led brief for the work of the subject curriculum working parties.

Finally there is the adequacy of resources, not merely for the whole tranche of changes, but especially for those children most at risk. Schools, as always, will look to secure additional resources, particularly for deserving cases such as children experiencing learning difficulties, but now this will be circumstances where the local management of schools and the effect on budgets of the community charge severely limits the ability of local education authorities to respond. There is likely to be pressure on them to carry out more formal assessments under the 1981 Education Act. Whether a Statement of Special Educational Needs is made as a result of these assessments is not the point. The number of formal assessments under Section 5 of the 1981 Education Act is likely to rise dramatically. If it does it will consume large amounts of educational psychologists' time and divert it away from more important preventive work. It will also place an additional burden on the school medical officers and hard pressed paramedical support staff in district health authorities. Moreover all will take place at a time when local education authorities' room to manoeuvre will be limited by the introduction of the community charge.

Some practical next steps

What else can we do? How do we control the juggernauts of change represented by the National Curriculum, LSM, open enrolment, the provision for charging, for collective worship and religious education, for grant-maintained schools, for governor training and the rest? We must avoid the change becoming a nightmare, as it so easily could, not only for many teachers but also for a large proportion of the school population and their parents.

Whether we are elected members, officers, governors, teachers, other school employees, or advisors, we are unlikely to achieve this unless we are clear about our principles – in particular those to do with equal opportunity and inclusive rather than exclusive practices – if we are to ensure that out everyday actions make the best of the opportunities presented by change while minimising the dangers.

At the LEA level it will be found in the care and attention given to the integrated approach to the organisation of the administration and advisory services, to the fine detail of the LSM formula and its operation, and to governor training and INSET for all teachers and heads.

It is at the school level, however, that I wish to elaborate in greater detail, and in particular on how all schools tackle the perennial and elusive issue of how they can be successful for all children.

The beginning of the answer to this riddle (and certainly a lifeline for children experiencing learning difficulty) may lie not so much in measurable outcomes, as in the atmosphere which is encouraged in schools which have given attention to certain processes. For example it may be sensible to ask whether a school has clear

statements of principle which are tested by matching them with
practice and whether it has a process of collective review that
leads to a school development plan which is then backed by its
approaches to staff development and the use of its finances. Is
there a sensitive understanding of the difference between
leadership, management and administration, and is attention given
to each? Has the school good relations with parents, the local
community and the partner primary schools, and what are their
practical manifestations? Does the school consider the subliminal
effects on children's confidence and learning of the environment and of its rewards, sanctions, marking and celebratory
practices?

Ideally, any organisation maintains a sensitivity for change, and
to the outcomes of such change, by involving itself in a continuous
process of planning, constructive action, and evaluation. In reality,
in the past schools have exhibited no mechanism to assess their
own requirements on a systematic and comprehensive basis. They
have relied too much on remaining in a steady state, unresponsive
to change save where it has been inevitable. In one sense the
National Curriculum, which has been accompanied by the
requirement that schools produce a plan to show how it will be
implemented, has unwittingly forced schools into the self-
questioning approach to change, adopted by successful schools
for some time. In my experience, successful schools, in coming
to such plans (or manifestos for action) have addressed five simple
questions:

(a) What are the strengths of the school and how can they be
     built on?
(b) What are the areas of weakness and how can they be
     improved?
(c) What does this mean for the governing body, head and
     deputy/ies, other school staff and the LEA, now and in the
     future?
(d) What changes can they make and how will the school as
     a whole respond to them?
(e) What steps can they take to implement these changes and
     how will they measure the outcomes?

In any process of review, each school should have measures against
which to judge its actions. If it wishes through its general review
to safeguard the interests of children experiencing learning
difficulties, it can do worse than consider three important measures:

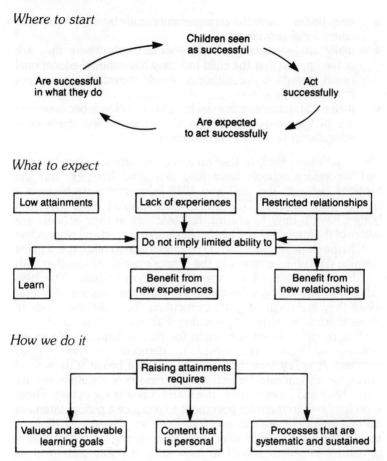

Where to start

Children seen
as successful

Are successful
in what they do

Act
successfully

Are expected
to act successfully

What to expect

| Low attainments | Lack of experiences | Restricted relationships |

Do not imply limited ability to

| Learn | Benefit from new experiences | Benefit from new relationships |

How we do it

Raising attainments
requires

| Valued and achievable learning goals | Content that is personal | Processes that are systematic and sustained |

There are also important features of the legislative system other than the 1988 Education Act that should be used to make certain that every child receives a full curriculum entitlement. The anti-discrimination legislation of the 1975 (Sex) and 1976 (Race) Equal Opportunities Acts makes it unlawful to treat anyone less favourably on the grounds of race or gender. Under the 1981 Education Act sections 2(1), (2), (4), 5(1), and 7(1), each LEA has duties to:

- secure that special educational provision is made for children who have special educational needs in primary and secondary schools;
- secure that, provided certain conditions are met, children with a Statement of Special Educational Needs are educated in a mainstream school;

- keep under review the arrangements made by them for special educational provision;
- make an assessment of educational needs where they are of the opinion that the child has/may have special educational needs for which the authority should determine the special educational provision;
- make a Statement of Special Educational Needs because they are of the opinion that they should determine the special educational provision for that child.

These duties are likely to take on a new importance when primary and secondary schools have fully delegated budgets, and the tensions between the 1981 and 1988 Education Acts become a reality. Under Section 2(5) of the Education Act 1981, governing bodies have a duty to ensure that teachers in their schools are aware of the importance of identifying learning need and responding to it. In the same Act, Section 2(7) requires that a child experiencing learning difficulties engages in the school's activities together with 'children who do not have special educational needs'. The 1986 Education Act charges headteachers with the responsibility that when they are organising the curriculum they take the needs of those children experiencing learning difficulties into account.

How do schools set the scene for this to happen? Many are drawing up 'policy statements' to demonstrate their shared concern. A policy statement can be either a broad statement of intent, or a manifesto for action. The best policy statements are clear, brief and have in them the starting points for action. There is no legal requirement for governors to produce a policy statement on reducing difficulties in learning. Even so, Circular 22/89 from the Department of Education and Science suggests one, and it is natural for every school to have such a policy statement as part of its overall equal opportunities commitment. At the time such a policy statement is made, the governing body should decide the date when it is to be reviewed. An example of one designed to help those with children who find learning difficult is set out below:

GOVERNING BODY POLICY STATEMENT
REDUCING LEARNING DIFFICULTIES WITHIN THE SCHOOL

This policy statement arises from the governing body's desire to ensure that the headteacher is clear on her/his own particular duties under the Education Act 1981. In this school we:

(a) Systematically review the curriculum to ensure its relevance and accessibility for all pupils;
(b) Provide education for children experiencing learning dificulties within a whole-school framework;

(c) Have systems of identification, analysis and action to lessen difficulties in learning, which accepts each teacher's responsibility to look at the tasks offered children in the light of their present competencies and to modify them accordingly;

(d) Work towards gaining the full involvement of parents and guardians in identifying and meeting the educational needs of their children;

(e) Provide regular opportunities for staff to discuss and plan for children experiencing difficulties in learning;

(f) Organise ourselves to make best use of the external support services and the school's community;

(g) Provide appropriate inservice training, especially school based for all staff.

Date ....   Review date ....

Clearly such a statement would only have real meaning when read alongside the school's curriculum statement: even so it would be used to ensure that development work is prioritised to create better practice.

Many policies fail or are ineffective because clear strategies are not devloped from them. One or two statements of action in each of the seven areas of the policy which the school intends to pursue over a set period of time would become the markers by which to judge its success. These 'performance areas' would relate to where each school was in relation to its statement of policy.

If children experiencing learning difficulties are to taste success their teachers must have good assessment strategies. These are founded on:

• a clear policy statement based on looking for evidence of learning in the 'taught' curriculum;

• whole school approaches with integrated systems for recording attainments and achievement;

• curriculum-led assessment where the intended outcomes of a piece of learning are articulated at the planning stage along with the likely evidence that the learning will have taken place;

• using what children can do with an emphasis on formative assessment;

• integrating assessment into the routines of teaching and learning and using existing classroom practice to arrive at judgments of children's performance against attainment targets;

• involving children in their own assessments;

• explaining children's progress in jargon-free language so that parents play their part in the child's learning;

• teachers discussing the evidence of learning with each other;

• obtaining significant results with the very limited time available.

This last point is vital for teacher survival. Teachers can be asked

to carry out time-consuming screening and identification programmes, often using standardised norm-referenced tests which
bear no resemblance to the 'taught' curriculum, and then have
little time left to respond to particular children's learning needs.
It is more practical to invest simply in teacher observation. Class
teachers are usually aware of those children at risk in the learning
situation, but it is unusual for a school to adopt a procedure for
the identification and monitoring of all children's attainments in
the curriculum as they move through school. Nevertheless a picture
of all children is important, and it cannot be left to the standard(ised)
assessment tasks alone. A simple school-made screening schedule,
used with each school class say in November and again in June,
might look like this:

SCREENING SCHEDULE
PUPILS EXPERIENCING DIFFICULTIES IN
LEARNING
CLASS   TEACHER

Note: If the class is a mixed age-group please
      put older age group first.

KEY:
1. Like most children
2. Very successful
3. Less successful
4. Disability hindering or preventing learning
5. Children who qualify for Section 11 support
6. Other difficulties hindering or preventing
   learning

		Please indicate with an * the descriptions which are most appropriate						Brief factual description of a child's difficulties in learning where appropriate
NAME	D.O.B.	1	2	3	4	5	6	

The description in the far right-hand column helps the teacher
focus on what the difficulty is. It is trying to move away from
labelling based on inferences, eg lazy, stupid, stubborn, to a brief
accurate description of the actual difficulty the child is experiencing.

The areas in which the teacher judgment is required can easily
be changed to suit the school: another school drew up this more
restricting schedule:

SCREENING SCHEDULE:

School _____

Class _____

Teacher _____

Key

1. Like most children
2. High attainments
3. Low attainments

NAME	D.O.B.	F	M	Please indicate with an * the description from the key which are most appropriate.												Please provide a brief factual description of the child's difficulties where appropriate
				READING			SPELLING			WRITING			COMPUTATION			
				1	2	3	1	2	3	1	2	3	1	2	3	

At this stage it is not some in-depth analysis that is taking place, but a sifting through quickly to establish the class learning profile as the class teacher sees it.

For those children whose attainments are a matter for concern, the teacher completes an additional needs profile to help gain more information about the child and to set the learning goals for the next week. At the end of the week the teacher reviews what has happened and plans the following week's work. The profile would look like this and would be part of the school's curriculum record for the child.

The whole school picture, essentially a management tool giving the headteacher an overall picture through collating the screening schedules, is achieved using a pro-forma similar to this one:

ADDITIONAL NEEDS PROFILE

Name of Child _____

1. Please highlight the child's strengths and the most effective ways of learning for this child.

   _____
   _____
   _____
   _____

2. Please indicate areas of the Curriculum where the child is experiencing difficulties.

   _____
   _____
   _____

3. What precisely is the child's performance and/or behaviour that concerns you.

   _____
   _____
   _____
   _____

4. Is the explanation of the difficulty to be found in characteristics of the child?

Vision ☐	Social Behaviour ☐
Hearing ☐	Emotional disposition ☐
Speech and Language ☐	Response to learning situations ☐
Physical co-operation ☐	Mastery of previous materials and contributory skills ☐

5. In what circumstances is this difficulty:
   a) most apparent _____
   b) least apparent _____

6. What particular measures have been taken to support the child? _____

7. What measures have been most successful? _____

8. What are the learning targets this week for the child? _____

ANALYSIS OF SCREENING SCHEDULE

SCHOOL	
DATE	
DATE NEXT SCREEN	

						ADDITIONAL SUPPORT						
						INTERNAL SUPPORT		EXTERNAL SUPPORT				
									1981 EDUCATION ACT			
Class	Teacher	Sire of Class	Additional Needs Profile used	Children to monitor	1981 EA	Home Office qualifying	SPCGS	HIST / VIS	Medical	Special School	110 Qual Staff	Trav service / Other
		Total / Girls / Boys	Girls / Boys	1981 EA: State-ment / Other · 110 Qual	Support Class Teacher Only / Other Support	Support Class Teacher Only / Support Soc II Staff	1981 Sec's / Other		Ph / Sp / N / O	Full / Part / Con		
1	2	3	4	5	6	7	8	9	10	11	12	13

KEY

Information on this pro-forma will provide

- a clearer picture of the number of children requiring and receiving additional support throughout the school;
- a check on the number of children in each class receiving support from staff funded under Section 1 of the Home Office Act 1966, if that support is necessary and available;
- a numerical summary of how the support available from outside agencies is being used, eg additional learning support to children who have received a broken education because their parents are travellers;
- a starting point for staff discussion on noticeable trends, eg more boys than girls identified, the different perceptions of staff.

It enters a school unobtrusively and is an inclusive rather than exclusive way of keeping a weather eye open for children's difficulties. The time given to schools from outside support services, such as educational psychologists, the school nurse, educational welfare officers, and visiting teachers, has always been scarce. As consumers, schools have to look more critically at what they receive. Under local management of schools some schools will be in a position where finance for support services has been delegated to them. All schools should be involved in:

- knowing the range of services and the remit of each;
- establishing a routine working pattern with each service that gives a regular input to the school;
- making sure that staff know which services are working in school, who they are working with and why;
- letting each service know the range of external support the school is receiving, especially where there are services with a similar remit working in school.

Some schools are now holding regular but infrequent meetings for all their support services so that they can share the school's development priorities with them. These support services, whether they are left as services to be bought by schools or retained as a central service, will need to be generally aware of the National Curriculum; there are considerable implications for their in-service training which LEAs, of course, rather than schools must attend if they are to be effective.

For children with special educational needs and experiencing learning difficulties, there is a real danger that the higher profile of market prices and competition will serve to reverse the painfully slow trend towards integration and an inclusive approach to the education of all children in a common curriculum in a local school. Our special schools may return to isolation, and the less fortunate in our society may once again quietly be forgotten. None of that has to happen if schools stick to some simple principles, forge policies that have an implication for action, and maintain an unsentimental but inclusive and responsible attitude for all children in their care.

LEAs can help with the small print of local management of schools schemes: they may or may not resource through their special school budgets and discretionary 10%–7% schemes which link support services and special schools to supporting work in the mainstream. They may or may not add to rather than rationalise, interpret and simplify the bewildering bureaucracy created in and by the Department of Education and Science following the 1988 Education Act. Time alone will tell: but if one were to extrapolate from the skills, devotion, commitment and optimistic energy in one northern city of those who deal with such children, the odds on making some sense of it look good.

11 So what does it do for teaching?

Leonard Marsh, Principal, Bishop Grosseteste College, Lincoln

A good deal of learning results from practical activity on the part of teachers and children in classrooms. It would seem necessary to remind ourselves that the introduction of a National Curriculum will not, in itself, lead to any improvement in the quality of teaching or the depth of our children's understanding. The National Curriculum is not a timetable device (though it may well become one) nor is it a contribution to teaching method. At a time when we have subjected our schools to an over-generation of theoretical and ideological schemes that have yet to prove their worth, the limitations implicit within the idea of a National Curriculum may well enable teachers to contribute a significant professional influence to the future development of primary education.

The main purpose of the National Curriculum is to provide a framework for the assessment of children's achievement and the means for the eventual assessment of teachers and the making of statements about the effectiveness of individual schools. Teachers have no ownership of contemporary planning at national level – whether in relation to curriculum development or schemes for assessment. But teachers will continue to make schools what they are, and the nation will continue to depend upon their professional commitment and their practical judgement in managing effectively children's learning. Children, in the company of teachers who know them well, come to understand themselves as people and as confident learners through their teachers' efforts to help them understand their world. Teachers will continue to be judged by parents for their ability to educate their children, rather than how they teach the National Curriculum. The focus for the parent will remain – What can my child do? What is my child like? Is he or she happy, confident, timid or uncertain? The teacher's first duty is not to innovate and implement change, but to ensure that they understand the children they teach and to ensure that they become effective learners.

The political focus and larger professional pre-occupation is upon the introduction of the National Curriculum for the five-year-old, and the mode of assessment for the seven-year-old. But for the teacher, the reality is that 62% of our four-year-olds are in infant classes and that for the foreseeable future a very large proportion (70%) of our primary classes will have a mixed age range.

The provision of a National Curriculum is akin to a driver being given a road atlas. It is useful in that it provides a broad perspective, but in the reality of the journey the effective driver is able to leave the atlas to one side in order to be free to 'read the road', adapt to the challenge of diversions and make judgements in relation to traffic flow and the behaviour of other motorists. With the walker, a pre-occupation with the map would merely serve to obscure the reality of the actual terrain.

Primary teachers face the professional task of assimilating within a few months the Byzantine complexity of an elaborate system of crude subject classifications related to programmes of study and a major emphasis on assessment. Schools will need to devise a means of re-ordering and grouping the subject content of the National Curriculum, in order to organise their teaching in ways that lead to children's ownership of ideas and competence in applying their understanding to a range of tasks. Teachers need a more practical and robust approach for the promotion and assessment of quality in children's learning, related to practical objectives that are the outcome of teachers' insights and judgements, than offered by the National Curriculum. The National Curriculum does not pose a threat to primary practice, but it does offer a professional challenge.

Teachers need to review and identify what it is that they do when they draw upon their deepest insights and most effective practice. They need to share their insights one with another, in order to bring their experience to bear upon the process of 'domesticating' or making functional the theoretical model incorporated in the National Curriculum documentation. The theoretical 'blue-print approach' of the National Curriculum has placed a heavy burden upon schools. Many teachers increasingly feel that there is an ever-widening gap between those who plan (and criticise) and those who have day-to-day responsibility for making things work. In recent years HMI have had an uneasy relationship with primary education. In contrast, HMI in the 1950s and 1960s were closely identified with development in primary education. *Primary Education* (HMSO, 1952) described the situation found by HMI within primary schools:

> What is now found in the schools has gradually evolved out of the free working and independent initiatives of teachers who have refused to discard the solid, the proven unassailable part of tradition in favour of what is bright and new and have preferred to base their practice on the foundations patiently accumulated.

The development of primary education in England has benefited from a deepening professional concern to relate teaching to a sound understanding of children and how they might best learn. This professional interest has been combined with an increasing concern for the intellectual worth of the curriculum content. How we are best to draw forward teachers' experience and insights in order to make the National Curriculum work provides the focus for the remainder of this chapter.

Teaching involves practical experience. A teacher's skill depends so much upon tacit, implicit knowledge. Primary education is the result of a slowly unfolding process whereby ideas about children's learning and teaching practices are established through a consensus achieved in practice. Practice has arisen from experience patiently accumulated over many years. Practice is best recognised in terms of a broad spectrum of strategies and methodologies, rather than 'theories' or 'models'.

In any description of a primary school curriculum there is a need for the teacher to establish some form of practical groupings. 'Humanities', clearly allied to a fundamental study of English, provides a primary teacher with a clear purpose beyond the confusion of individual programmes of study for a range of subjects. The study of the humanities offers the opportunity for children to widen their perception of, and sympathy with, the activities of the human race – the struggles and achievements of people in other times and in other countries – the conditions of life beyond the limits of locality, the ideas, aspirations and inventions of those who have contributed to our understanding. We need a framework that encourages the teacher to be concerned with more than mere accumulation of information as to whether children have 'done' this or that book or period. Any framework needs to contain a minimal but 'outstanding fact'.

In mathematics, teachers firstly seek to ensure that children have clear ideas about certain relations of number, time and space, and secondly to make the more useful of these ideas firm through practice in appropriate calculation, and thirdly to develop a confident application of ideas to problems. To this extent, the intention and the need has not changed from that identified in the 1930s by HMI in the *Handbook of Suggestions for Teachers* (Education Board of 1937). Then, as now, the full significance of the work was judged to be in the real use of understanding in practical problems.

The dangers of a limited viewpoint in curriculum planning have long been recognised. If teaching is restricted to, for example, the skills of reading, they often fade and lose their value when the learner is free to make their own choices. In English, there is first a need to ensure that children have the opportunity to develop an interest in the mastery of the language as a means of ordinary exchange. The teacher needs a curriculum approach that includes the use of English in everyday ordinary exchange through to an increasing perception of shades of meaning and an interest in its beauty. In this practical context, the teacher organises group class and individual activities that ensure that children speak English, listen and write it. And they also ensure that children have the chance to learn by heart and study how other people use English.

Similarly, the teacher needs a curriculum approach that makes a grouping for 'the arts', so as to inform a child's delight in colour, sound, pattern, movement, shape and texture. The two large groupings 'the arts' and 'the sciences' provide a framework for the selection of material that is fruitful and worthwhile. The inclusion of the sciences complements the developing interest of the young child in the ever-changing physical phenomena of the child's everyday world. Frost, dew, evaporation, hedgerows, the seasons, all provide a context for the essential purpose of science, a sharp observational focus on actual facts, the real natural growth, the sequence of actual events – the apparent phenomenon. Questions such as, What can be discovered? What do we already know? Comparing two facts, granting steps in the argument. What more can be found out? If this is done, what might happen and why are all interventions on the part of the teacher to support the child's interest in the process of discovery.

Such approaches to the setting out of a curriculum statement for the primary school support and strengthen the teachers' practical approach to the management of children's learning. Primary schools need to ensure that one or two of their members undertake a curriculum 'audit', cross-referencing from their established primary curriculum across to the National Curriculum documents. It has been the experience of those schools that have undertaken such audits that there is a considerable overlap and correspondence. Once the curriculum audit has been completed the school then needs to build up rapidly a new practical understanding of the school's curriculum (which will now include the National Curriculum) so as to provide the teacher with a working framework.

Within the primary school's own curriculum documentation it is possible to review the content in terms of themes and topics such as the study of a local stream or pond, the study through the year of a tree or section of hedgerow, the study of aspects of the environment in terms of physical phenomena such as dew, frost and evaporation, mathematical investigations and literary themes. Further, it is then possible to review the curriculum planning in the context of judgements about the value of the selected content.

The debate can be joined as to the worthwhileness, the fruitfulness of the content, whether it contributes to an understanding of the ways in which ideas are put together, modes of enquiry undertaken and the cultural context. The content can also be viewed in the light of our understanding of how best people learn. Herman Bondi in a speech to the Standing Conference on Schools Science and Technology (October 1980) suggested that schools give quite the wrong idea of what science and engineering are like. We give the idea that these are subjects consisting of well-defined problems, and to each such problem there is one right answer, preferably found at the back of the book. Rather than the self-contained exercise of the text book, somewhat dull in character and lacking integrity, Bondi suggested that all our work in technology, science and mathematics should be presented with a wealth of data, so that the problem involved in discerning what is relevant in a wealth of data is met in the classroom. A grouping of subject content also allows the teacher to select material that enables the teacher to maximise the intellectual dialogue between teacher and taught – choosing material that can be effectively managed within a classroom. Such an approach to the devising of an operational curriculum brings with it material that is 'for real' and has sufficient integrity to support a worthwhile evaluation of children's responses to the work.

The content of an operational curriculum that leads to practical action has to be clustered in ways that reflect the schools' understanding of how children best learn. Teachers breathe life into the planning, and the planning needs to be in a form that strengthens and enlarges the teachers' skill and draws deeply upon professional insights. If an intellectual dialogue is to take place between the teacher and the learner, the teacher must be a workmanlike manager. His or her classroom activity needs to include ways of making good use of work already done by children.

• Is work already done used by children as a prompt for new

work, or as a point of reference for continued investigations and experiment?

- Has the child a high level of self-awareness with regard to the forward planning and purposes of work being undertaken?
- Is the child involved in the evaluation of his or her work?
- Are group activities so arranged in terms of pace and balance that it is possible for a teacher to give a particular group five minutes of uninterrupted attention in order to judge the level of understanding reached and the best ways in which to prompt and guide the further development of the work?

Within the broad-based spectrum of a teacher's approach we recognise the teacher empirically bringing about a 'best practicable match'. With such an approach, time is managed so as to bring children into contact with the discipline exerted by the tools or materials and the exploration of the task. Any consideration of the National Curriculum in this reworked form should lead to a school concentrating upon the school's curriculum, organisation and management in terms of the provision of opportunities to observe and to work through sequences with groups and individuals. This approach, once established, can be carried over into the administering of Standard Assessment Tasks and overall teacher evaluation. Management of time, space, resources, questions to do with the pace and pattern of work over the school year, together with reviews of the nature of the planned activities, need to be incorporated in the initial planning of the school curriculum. The curriculum thus has the effect of focusing on the skills and insights of the teacher.

We need to strengthen the professional culture of the primary teacher (still neglected and subject to the pressures arising from the use in administration and planning of an essentially secondary model of curriculum development and implementation) so as to shift the focus to the skills and insights of teachers and the work actually done by children. The published statements of attainment need to be studied by teachers in relation to children known to the teacher, and teachers need the time to pool experience, to examine the evidence for their judgements and develop technique for sharing work with colleagues and moderating their judgements. The opportunity provided by the legislation for teachers to develop this aspect of their work is the most positive benefit for primary education. It is to be hoped that HMI and others will ensure that this aspect remains a central concern in the years ahead. The National Curriculum needs to be seen in relation to a developing and changing collection of samples of children's work.

In order to support the development of the teachers' professionalism, the school curriculum needs to be in a form that is almost concrete and physical in terms of the classroom it portrays. Work done by five-year-olds through the ages to aged twelve needs to be available for whole-school discussion. The sequence through the year produces a sense of familiar territory in the minds of teachers, and a sense of pattern, rhythm, and progression in the experience of children. 'The science of the potato patch', the through-the-year observation of a local habitat, is a commonplace and familiar vehicle for teachers' intervention and is judged by teachers to be apt response on their parts to children's interests arising from their commonplace experiences. Observational skills are thus developed and the process of identification and classification (for example of plants) is implicit in such work. The conversational gambit from, 'Have we seen anything like this before?', 'What do we already know?', 'What do we need to find out?', 'How might we do it?', through to the process of tentative explanations and the modification of hypotheses in the light of increasing evidence, takes forward a cross-disciplinary approach involving science, mathematics and languages. The teachers' professional, practical standpoint carries an awareness of children's experience and the practical ability to make use of it. The selection of material for the classroom involves a consideration of how we might best make use of the material and how we will best make judgements about the quality of children's responses to it. Our objective will remain how best to develop a child's interpretive powers. The curriculum has as its focus the influence and control of the teacher. The teacher, in turn, has the focus and responsibility for children's thinking, their capacities and attributes. It will require an imaginative and creative act on the part of teachers if we are to use The Education Reform Act and its associated national schemes for curriculum and assessment to bring about an improvement in our schools.

Firstly, the introduction of the National Curriculum makes it imperative that all our primary schools should develop an overall primary and school approach. In broad terms, a fortnightly meeting of all teachers will be needed to develop a greater shared awareness of children's development and the pattern of the focal points for curriculum activity needed to signpost teachers through the school's curriculum. Its development will have to be largely through working discussion and shared reflection. The programmes of study and, more importantly, the habits, insights and skills represented in attainment targets, will need to be assimilated in the practical vocabulary of the classroom teacher.

Secondly, the introduction of the National Curriculum requires all schools to consider ways by which the amount of well-managed learning can be increased. For some there will be the need to increase the actual hours of the week regarded as 'schooltime'.

For others, it will be the pioneering development of, say, summer schools, so that parents and children can share with the school assessment of progress and achievement from a deeper common understanding of how people actually learn. For all schools there is the need to tackle issues related to the introduction of a National Curriculum that cannot be delivered by a timetable devised in the context of a narrow subject classification. The problem can best be illustrated by reference to the fact that there will no longer be sufficient time available to teach reading as if it were a subject. It will be necessary to chart ways of using work that has a major scientific focus so as to ensure that appropriate use is made of them for the development of language and reading skills. It is in this reshaping and regrouping activity required to make the curriculum work that we find the greatest professional challenge. The challenge to the teacher is to achieve a greater command over the selection of worthwhile material so as to maximise the intellectual development of children.

The curriculum development required to make the National Curriculum operational will need to be related to a major opportunity for primary education provided by the Educational Reform Act. Though there is an unresolved tension between centralist planning and the devolution of authority to the governors of schools, there is a clear opportunity for the development of informed support for the work of the school. Headteachers with their governors will have to construct a 'neighbourhood raft' for their school, made up of a community well informed about the school's progress, and supportive of it. Within this larger grouping, schools will need to deliver to parents high quality information about their child's progress and achievement. It will also be necessary for the school to be confident enough about its knowledge of individual children to offer productive comments about a child's likely development. Teachers, when they plan for their operational curriculum, will need to test out the material included to ensure that it has the necessary integrity and depth to support assessment and evaluation intrinsic to the tasks, rather than as bolt-on extras.

The primary teachers, in considering 'What is in the National Curriculum for them', will see it largely as a tool for the analysis of children's work rather than as a direct contribution to the improvement of teaching. The National Curriculum demands a school approach, and can be used to develop the capacity of teachers to act as a team and to become more self-aware of the nature of their interventions and the experience of their children. As the process of curriculum adoption and adaptation takes place, the teacher will find the enduring, ever-present questions reappear. Well used, the National Curriculum may just be a contribution to knowing better how to answer the questions . . . but what can Jason do? The innovations demanded of the teachers in the contemporary moment will set a generation about the age-old task of building up ideas that have a practical import through the patient and careful development of a consensus of ideas about children's achievement and capacities in the practice of teaching.

12 Monitoring the effectiveness of the National Curriculum: receiving and interpreting feedback

Tom Christie, Centre for Formative Assessment Studies, School of Education, University of Manchester

The curriculum for elementary schools was strictly dictated by government until 1926, after which schools still had to follow central guidelines. The curriculum for secondary schools was controlled by regulations through to the 1944 Education Act. That Act dramatically reduced the power of civil servants to decide which subjects should be included at different stages of education and thus control the curriculum[1]. Now the 1988 Education Reform Act aims to ensure that schools teach a balanced range of subjects, set clear objectives, and formally assess each pupil's progress.

Education is again instrumental, and institutional change is to be imposed from the outside – the technocratic assumption[2].

The classic technocratic approach is the Research, Development and Diffusion model[3]. Research communities produce new knowledge which a team then develops into classroom materials and teacher handbooks. Trials are carried out in a number of LEAs and the materials are then mass produced as standard packages and made available to passive user systems (teachers) which will adopt them on their self-evident merits. The R, D and D model is firmly associated with the failure in the 1960s of the first phase of centralised curriculum innovation in Britain[4].

Dalin (1978)[5] provides an analysis of the failure. The R, D and D strategy assumes that people are reasonable and will respond to rational explanation and demonstration. As this is clearly not so, the R, D and D strategy will only work where the development team (the subject working parties) can use power to force compliance with their teacher materials 'and where diffusion patterns can be controlled'. That lesson has been taken to heart in the introduction of the 1988 National Curriculum. For not only is the curriculum centrally determined, it is policed by a centrally determined system of assessment designed to:

> show what a pupil has learnt and mastered, so as to enable teachers and parents to ensure that he or she is making adequate progress and to inform decisions about next steps[6].

The greatest weakness of the R, D and D model remains that the value of the change is taken to be self-evident. There is almost total neglect of strategies for adoption and implementation: the schemes of work remain the responsibility of the school, and the Secretary of State will not interfere in the work of classrooms. But arrangements for activity change[7] are in place. Activity change calls for changes in teacher and parent preference and these can only be brought about by communication.

> I attach considerable importance to improving communication and understanding at various levels about educational objectives and performance; and information derived from assessment and testing will play a key part in that . . .. I should be grateful for the Group 's views on cost-effective and practical arrangements for securing 'quality control' of school-based assessments, so as to secure credibility and confidence within the education service and with the public at large[8].

The design of that communication system was the remit of the Task Group on Assessment and Testing (TGAT). Its reports (DES/Welsh Office, 1988a[9], 1988b)[10] addressed as a central issue the major concern of this chapter, the receipt and interpretation of feedback. To whom is national assessment addressed and to what purposes should it be put? TGAT identified a range of purposes:

The terms of reference and the letter of guidance from the Secretary of State require that information derived from assessments (including tests) shall be capable of serving several purposes:

- formative, so that the positive achievements of a pupil may be recognised and discussed and the appropriate next steps may be planned;
- diagnostic, through which learning difficulties may be scrutinised and classified so that appropriate remedial help and guidance can be provided;
- summative, for the recording of the overall achievement of a pupil in a systematic way;
- evaluative, by means of which some aspects of the work of a school, an LEA or other discrete part of the educational service can be assessed and/or reported upon[11].

A key consideration in the design of any assessment or test is its fitness for purpose, but to introduce four sets of instruments, each serving a different purpose, would overload both teachers and pupils to an insupportable degree. TGAT proposed that one basic assessment procedure, teachers monitoring pupils' progress in terms of nationally agreed Attainment Targets (ATs) and their associated Statements of Attainment (SoA), should meet all needs, through the creation from these classroom judgements of aggregates of increasing generality.

Through the process of aggregation – combining the SoA into levels of ATs and the levels of ATs into levels of Profile Components (PCs) and the levels of PCs into levels of subjects using predetermined rules – the process would inform. Assessments of Statements of Attainment would give children a sense of making progress, and inform teachers' decisions about ways forward. Aggregates of SoA defining levels of Attainment Targets would inform teachers' and headteachers' plans for continuity and progression in the curriculum of the school as a whole, and give governors better access to curriculum plans and objectives. Aggregates of levels of ATs into levels of Profile Components would inform schools' decisions about the optimum deployment of time and resources, and provide parents with the information necessary to support an informed dialogue with the school and with the children themselves about their achievements, progress and future work. Aggregates of PCs to subjects would enable a school to report on the overall achievements of its pupils in ways that not only parents, but also the wider community, could appreciate, and inform national decisions about the specification of the National Curriculum itself and how standards might be improved.

That contention, that aggregation rather than a proliferation of assessment systems designed for specific purposes will meet the needs of all stakeholders in education, is open to challenge. This chapter seeks to elucidate both the rationale of the system and the interpretations it will bear.

The challenge to formative assessment

The essence of the challenge is that the formative and diagnostic purposes of assessment are irreconcilable with the summative and evaluative purposes of assessment.

In Nuttall's view, TGAT 'nearly reconciled the irreconcilable, that is the various conflicting purposes of assessment, the formative, the summative and the evaluative'[12]. He recognises that 'low stakes' (formative) assessment has positive educational effects, but in the final analysis he feels the evaluative pressure on schools through local financial management will increase the stakes till the summative and evaluative demands drive out the formative. Nuttall would prefer two distinct systems of assessment with a quick test of reading, of mathematics and perhaps of science got out of the way so that formative assessment may bloom. Goldstein and Cuttance (1988) are more direct. They charge TGAT with a failure to produce straight evaluative data which will promote the study of school effectiveness, not accepting, it appears, any threat to the interpretation of their regression techniques[13].

Neither addresses the problem of establishing formative assessment in classrooms. A record of the many competencies acquired in education – most forgotten as such, but living on as things to know with (Broudy, 1977)[14] – is generally seen as an onerous administrative adjunct to the process of teaching, rather than an integral and enabling support. And yet informing the child as to the nature of the activity in which it is engaged holds out strong promise (Feuerstein, 1979[15], 1980[16]; Pramling, 1988[17]) of making schools effective. Going so far as to record the information was one of the twelve indicators of more effective junior schools in the ILEA study[18].

The essence of the TGAT proposal is that all summative and evaluative data should be derived from formative assessment. This is not to say that the same data are simply put to different uses: the distinction goes deeper than that. Formative assessment is the assessment of movement, rate of progress. Summative assessment is about status, being located. Even measurement in advanced science cannot cope with both of these purposes at once. Heisenberg's uncertainty principle can be taken to imply that the location of a moving gas particle can only be established at the cost of uncertainty as to its momentum, while its momentum can be assessed but only at the expense of knowing precisely where it is. In the less advanced science of educational measurement, formative and summative assessments will have different design features.

Formative assessment is designed to be acted upon. If it is to improve learning it must be focused, detailed, precise, ie criterion-referenced[19]. If it is to be acted upon, it must be immediately available and must convince the actors: it is therefore interactive[20], suggesting next steps for both pupil and teacher. And if it is acted upon it will inevitably be rendered out of date. It is short-term, ephemeral and thus of no immediate economic consequence.

In contrast, summative assessment of the GCSE type is descriptive and in its reporting relatively indifferent to the precise achievements measured[21]. As a description it must convince third parties, and it is therefore objective: statistical and judgemental definitions of comparability do not share a common theory and, since they do not coincide[22], statistical methods are recommended. Above all to justify its economic consequence it must imply future performance. This it does by assuming stable differences in relative performance over time: 'it is suggested that grades can be defined as comparable if they are reached by the same proportion of a given group of candidates'[23].

The problem for educational measurement as conceived in the TGAT report does not lie in making proficiency visible to pupils and teachers through task setting, nor in the interpretation of performance, but in reporting to a wider constituency. Teachers' formative assessments of pupils do not have the accustomed, or at least assumed, generalisability of external tests or examinations. In the classic model of mental measurement the test and the child meet in a vacuum. The child is not changed by the test: nothing is learned during the test period. The test is not changed by the child: any such change is a rubric error and carries an increased risk of failure. The outcome is then taken to be an attribute of the child – the teacher does not get a certificate. Little wonder that school accountability studies using this model typically show little or no effect[24]. On the other hand, when assessments are classroom-based and informally made by the teacher, the teacher becomes part of the test and the quality of teacher/pupil interaction affects the outcome. Technically, there is no independent estimate of the pupil's achievements. The outcome is a record of the pupil's performance confounded with the quality of pupil/teacher interaction (p(t), pupil within teacher, in Cronbach *et al*'s, 1972[25] terminology). No amount of aggregation will get rid of the teacher effect, unless the aggregation is over teachers, logistically infeasible at Keystages 1 and 2.

This is the central dilemma in the distinction between formative (classroom-based) and summative (external) assessment. In these circumstances, TGAT chose to base the system on formative assessment.

The central function of assessment is to guide next steps for the child. There is little point in aggregating many Statements of Attainment for an individual child to guide classroom progress. As next steps are taken by both pupil and teacher, the teacher involvement in the assessment renders subsequent decisions based on that assessment more valid. There is point in aggregating over SoA for the individual child in a summative report to the pupil's parents. That report can be read as an account of the child's progress as transmuted by the teacher: the quality of pupil/teacher relations is an immediate concern to parents. There is considerable value in aggregating Statements of Attainment over many children for evaluative purposes (Newtonian physics work rather well with large aggregates of gas particles). The resulting data will avoid one of the major criticisms of the Coleman (1966)[26] approach to school effectiveness: 'it seems odd to measure what is admittedly a "side-effect" of education (standardised achievement tests) while at the same time ignoring the direct effects of particular curricula or courses[27], and, of course, teachers. These school aggregates are an account of the quality of pupil's attainments arising from the work of both pupils and teachers. They are informative as such. The problem they pose the professional evaluator is that the contribution of the pupil and the interaction of pupil and teacher during the assessment process are confounded. Without additional and independent information about the pupils' attainments the contribution of pupil and of teacher to the outcome cannot be separated. The latter can, however, be minimised by the process of standardisation discussed below.

TGAT recognised in advocating a hierarchical system of aggregated reports based upon formative assessment incidents, that there are many shareholders in the education system. If teacher appraisal is any guide[28], each has competing desires when it is proposed to increase the specificity of evaluation procedures, especially documentation. Headteachers on the whole want a system which is objective, quick and feasible; teachers want a system which respects the complexity of their work and encourages self-improvement; LEAs are interested in the relation of resources to outcomes and children and parents are interested in the future, in progression, in opportunity.

One form of record and report cannot possibly meet the needs of these diverse constituencies. The subject as the traditional means of communication becomes extremely important in a National Curriculum strongly influenced by manpower planning: 'a curriculum to meet the needs of children *and of society*'[29].

Such a report, however, is of little use to headteachers if they are seriously concerned with the curriculum. At the moment only the child knows what the curriculum is, thanks to the heavily subject-segmented nature of secondary education. TGAT advocated a system of profile components in which each subject would acknowedge its borrowings from the rest of the curriculum, its contribution to the rest of the curriculum and its own substantive concerns. A minimum of two, a maximum of five components was the TGAT ideal. In that way headteachers could look at how their timetable provision contributed to the progress of the child.

The formative interpretation of profile components was rejected by the then Secretary of State, in favour of a simplified summative picture. In science just two profile components have been accepted; exploration, smacking of content-free problem solving, and knowledge about science which is so disparate, 15 different attainment targets rolled into one, that any report in terms of science profile component two is essentially uninterpretable. It certainly cannot give a clear indication of what the child may in fact be able to do or what the child knows. For curriculum planning and reports to parents the Attainment Targets will have to take the strain.

Finally the most important consideration is the feedback to the child. Statements of Attainment are a direct borrowing from Records of Achievement: they are manageable goals. These are the fundamental unit of assessment of progress in the National Curriculum and to ensure their formative use the entire system of reporting has been based upon the progression they are intended to promote.

The progressive intent

In education it is not present position that is the professional concern, but momentum – change, growth and development. Nothing less than a paradigm shift in educational measurement is required if this concern is to be supported.

For too long, educational measurement has shown a slavish dependence on the procedures of mental measurement initiated by Binet[30], whose work grew out of an educational problem, to identify those Parisian children who would benefit from remedial education. His assessment started as any summative assessment might,with a detailed catalogue of what the ordinary child knows, understands and can do, the selfsame objectives as GCSE[31]. Binet's immediate objective was clear – to assess children's instructional needs. But those needs had an economic dimension, they called upon scarce resources, and he had to go beyond the assessment of need to the selection of the most deserving of help. He therefore set about dropping from consideration all those attainments which did not differentiate among children and from those remaining selected attainments which were most strongly related to an external criterion, chronological age. He was in Miles'[32] terms using the manifestations of a dispositional property, undefined other than through its age-related development, to establish a weak form of causality. Absence of the dispositional property, which he nominated as intelligence, might explain failure.

The parallel work of Spearman (1904)[33] reduced dependency on the external criterion by developing the statistics of a single general factor. These live on in mental testing as 'internal consistency'. Finally, the solution of the reporting problem through the normative device of the intelligence quotient[34] cleared the way for the abilities construct. It became possible to produce a single score which descibed[35] a set of almost unrelated performances: a 60-item test with an internal consistency of .94 has an average correlation between any two items of .2, ie not visible to the naked eye. The application of age norms to the score 'corrects' for the effect of experience on performance, and gives the resulting designation an apparent longevity.

These standard psychometric procedures make the two simplifying assumptions about pupil test behaviour mentioned above: that the attribute measured is fixed rather than changing, and that one task has no influence on another (the assumption of local independence which underlies reliability theory). But precisely the opposite conditions pertain in education: it is in the nature of the enterprise that competence should change through experience of educational tasks, and the tasks themselves should be chosen to ease the transition from one to the other.

Mental tests discount the efforts of teachers and learners as noise (error) or, if particularly effective, as noisesome (teaching to the test) and yet the basic psychometric techniques which enshrine the abilities construct have been adopted throughout educational measurement at all levels from initial reading tests to A level grades. Many schools give a grade for ability and a grade for effort in their reports, on the assumption that ability and effort together predict achievement. TGAT rejected the abilities construct in favour of the direct assessment of achievement.

> There has been some misunderstanding about the assessment of 'ability', to which our main report may inadvertently have contributed by occasionally using that term. We had intended to confine our proposals to the assessment of 'performance' or 'attainment' and were NOT recommending any attempt to assess separately the problematic notion of underlying 'ability'[36].

What TGAT in fact proposed is that the assessment of the National Curriculum should be the assessment of the observable, not of some hypothetical construct which through its very generality leaves teachers with a sense of impotence in the face of a task too ill-defined. The balance between the specification of a large number of performance outcomes and a proper respect for the professionalism of teachers is nevertheless difficult to strike. Aronowitz and Giroux[37], point out that the skills of American teachers are being undermined through dictated procedures and externally determined curriculum packages. They argue for teachers as directing rather than directed, actively responsible for their own teaching and engaged in self-critical analysis of their endeavour. Such analysis depends upon feedback. The TGAT solution is to put the collection and use of feedback firmly in the hands of teachers with the proviso that the feedback is intended to promote progression, not labelling.

In the United States, Bunderston (1988) has signalled precisely the same change of direction in response to the same impetus. He claims that America is faced with an economic crisis in its manufacturing base, and a realisation that it is through ready access to a large supply of competent and flexible trained manpower that economic prosperity is achieved. A curriculum which introduces design and technology and science into infants schools is concerned with the economic prerequisites for future prosperity. Bunderston recognises that 'measurement constructs, like aptitudes, abilities and generalised traits, have not proven useful in guiding instructional activities.[38]' He looks to 'Continuous Measurement', an approach to measuring the growth of competence as it develops over time as a result of learning, to redress the balance. Continuous measurement

> is integrated into an instructional system to provide continuing feedback for use by both learners and instructors. It is designed to guide and facilitate growth on several underlying mastery scales . . .. [These] are anchored by demonstrable performance on reference tasks along the way to mastery, so that context and specificity can be given to positions on the scale, rather than simply confronting the learner with a numerical score. Indeed, numbers do not have to be communicated to the learners and instructors – just the scales, the different types of tasks on each scale, and the complexities associated with mastering the constructs that lead to success on the tasks[39].

Unfortunately the abilities construct is deeply embedded, not only in measurement theory, but in the public consciousness. Ability tests (including reading and arithmetic tests) usually have all children respond to the same set of tasks, often in conditions of total secrecy. The responses are all added up so that information about task performance is lost, and all that is left is a very general impression of which children were more or less successful. Much classroom assessment mimics this norm-referenced technique. It has the advantage that performance can be reported as a single letter or number, the child's ability in the test.

When feedback to the child is based on a single letter or number, what is learned is not that progress has been made, but that one child has done better than another. Repeated exposure to common tasks results in an acute appreciation of 'position in class' as the outcome of five or six years of schooling[40]. In the absence of specific criteria of success, normative considerations hold sway and average performance is invoked as the only criterion. The problem is that as the child moves, so does the average, so that steady educational progress is seen by all concerned as statis.

TGAT sought to counteract this tendency by the introduction of a series of criterion-referenced ten-levelled scales which the child would move through. Statements of Attainment were the criteria and each successive set defined the threshold (Christie and Forrest, 1980)[41] for the next stage of development. Characteristic implementations of such assessment schemes are GAIM in mathematics (see Noss *et al*, 1989[42] Brown[43], 1989) and SAIL in English (Christie *et al*, 1989)[44].

Nevertheless the tension between formative and summative interpretations remains. Each of the subject working parties developing the National Curriculum has identified ten sets of Statements of Attainment for each Attainment Target. Treated as criteria of successful completion of a stage these cutting points define 11 levels, not ten. In effect the subject working parties must have had grade descriptors in mind, not criteria.

Grade descriptors are summative labels to be attached to the outcome, rather than objectives for pupils to attain. They belong, in Troman's useful contrast, to the field of 'market' rather than 'professional' accountability[45]. Market accountability[46], is concerned only with the product, and tends to move to the apparently best buy: public examination systems with their summative intent have always supported such consumer choice. Professional accountability is concerned with the quality of the educational process itself[47]: it has received growing support in the Records of Achievement movement, with its emphasis on negotiation and formative assessment[48].

The interpretation of Statements of Attainment by children, teachers and parents will eventually resolve the tension, but for the moment the interpretation as criteria holds. The School Examinations and Assessment Council has introduced a notional level, 'working towards level one', as the eleventh level. The decision to place an additional burden on the weak, rather than to dismiss the strong with 'completed the National Curriculum', is in itself problematic, but at least the formative intent of criteria continues to receive official backing.

The communicative force of criteria

The teacher is central to the decisions on the learning opportunities that will be provided for pupils, and this is as it has always been.

TGAT proposed that teachers should only assess the observable. Teachers have always based their teaching decisions, especially the decision to move on to the next topic, on an assessment, no matter how informal, of the children's responses to the current activity. That decision is often based on normative assumptions. Dahllof[49] suggests that many teachers have a target child somewhere around the 80th percentile in the class, who has an educational career of continuous confusion: the moment that child shows a glimmer of comprehension, it is time for the class to move on. In national assessment, it is the assessment of the current achievement of the individual child, not the class, which is the basic building block. The child's competence should change through tackling attainment tasks, and the tasks should be chosen to help the child to change. The upshot is information about many achievements based on current performance, not future potential.

That picture has to be expressed in terms of the Statements of Attainment in the various subjects. Here a problem arises. The Statements of Attainment are only words on a paper: they are open to interpretation by the teacher, who is in effect making a whole series of grade awards. The Statements of Attainment are criteria and the system is criterion-referenced.

Much lip-service is paid to criterion-referencing, not least in GCSE. The more recent manifestations of the idea, conceived in reaction to the worst excesses of norm-referencing, seek to produce 'measurements that are directly interpretable in terms of specified performance standards[50]. The essential problem is that in a decentralised decision-making structure, where teachers make direct judgements about standards, there could be as many interpretations as there are teachers, but these differences in interpretation will be attributed to differences in pupil's performance between classrooms. As noted above, teacher assessment is coloured by the teacher's as well as the pupil's interpretation of the task.

In public examinations or standardised tests there is a variety of complex statistical approaches to estimating the quality of criterion-referenced judgements based on multiple item tests (Huynh[51] 1976: Subkoviak[52], 1976, 1984[53], Kane, 1986[54]) but these are not suitable for classroom use. Moreover, given the scale of the national assessment operation, any *post hoc* procedure is almost ruled out. Without such quality control, teachers' success in interpreting standards can be limited[55]: the problem becomes one of communicating standards in advance, and in the context of national assessment it is the 'configuration or pattern of performance, taken over a series of testing episodes and assessment tasks, which takes precedence[56]. Sadler refers to this circumstance as standards-referenced assessment, an approach intended to guide the assessor's behaviour.

In promulgating standards, he rejects numerical cut-offs since the standards reside, essentially in unarticulated form, inside the heads of assessors, and the only means of communicating them is through 'sitting with Nellie' – joint participation of expert and novice in evaluative activity. Given the dearth of experts in the interpretation of Statements of Attainment this approach is not practicable.

He rejects exemplars where many or a variable number of criteria are involved, since the number of exemplars required to indicate the relative acceptability of the different patterns of performance exemplified is impossibly large in any aggregate of even moderate size. Science Attainment Target 1 would exceed the bounds for such exemplification, and yet the English Working Party have advocated general impression decisions for even larger aggregates[57]: it is not surprising that they have neither sought to exemplify them, nor to suggest combination rules. Unless the strands of English Attainment Targets are unravelled, performance in the subject is virtually uninterpretable by any user other than the teacher who has had the unenviable task of making the initial interpretation. Broadfoot[58] distinguishes a report, which is a judgement that outsiders can take as evidence, from a record, which is evidence on which outsiders can base judgements. English teachers will issue reports which can be taken as evidence that a judgement has been made.

On the other hand, where exemplars relate to single criteria they have proved their worth in many established scales. Exemplars and verbal descriptions (SoA) are 'complementary and constitute a promising basis for a standards-referenced assessment system'[59]. To which one might add task-definition as a further refinement of exemplification.[60/61]

The exemplification will be communicated by attainment in action, Standard Assessment Tasks (SATs). Each of the tasks is to be explicitly related to Attainment Targets. When teachers see their children working on these tasks they will get a very clear idea of how SoA are interpreted nationally. In this way the SATs will standardise interpretations of the SoA across the country, and training will support teachers in coming to a recognition of the appropriate interpretation.

The role of moderation

Moderation has traditionally been seen as a control on failures of interpretation by teachers[62/63], and there has been much debate about the appropriateness of various statistical adjustments especially in relation to small samples[64]. None of this literature takes account of criterion-referencing. Marks can be adjusted, but how can one adjust an interpretation after the event and, given that the interpretations are of Statements of Attainment, what are the logistics of doing so? Conventional notions of moderation have to be abandoned in national assessment.

What is emerging is a sequential decision-making strategy. Teachers will make their assessments. Teachers will then administer standard assessment material over a period of time in their own classrooms. If that material is explicit, task-oriented, well-formulated and persuasive, the process of SAT administration will itself lead teachers to adjust their standards, and the SAT outcomes will take priority over the Teacher Assessment, the burden of the controversial advice from SEAC to the Secretary of State in July, 1989. The caveat is that SATs must be first and foremost communicative devices and teachers as well as pupils must have time to learn from them.

Nor is the TGAT recommendation for group moderation meetings rendered otiose. TGAT valued communication much more highly than control. Group moderation is an opportunity for teachers to criticise SATs and to establish that the beam in the SAT is not perhaps a mote in their own eye. The staff development function is obvious. So too is the curriculum development. The National Curriculum is a legislated hypothesis. It needs to be tested in the fire of professional judgement, and no arrangement other than group moderation has been suggested for garnering the usuable feedback which can inform its development. The system should be formative at all levels.

Reporting

TGAT proposed a system which is formative, progressive, criterion-referenced and moderated. The government has decided how it should be reported. The various uses of reports have been referred to in passing, save the most contentious, that there should be an aggregated report of the performance of the year group at the end of each Keystage. Taken along with local financial management of schools and open enrolment this requirement is causing much concern about 'league tables'.

The concern about league tables is a concern about norm-referenced assessment in which the many and varied achievements of a school are reduced to a single number which is compared to the single numbers generated by other schools. It is instructive to consider how painful this form of report is; for many years it has been the main method of communicating the many and various achievements of children.

Just as schools and teachers have to learn how to create and to interpret alternative forms of criterion-referenced report, so does the wider community. In the longer run, and it may take several years, prospective parents will no longer be satisfied with a league table.

That will only come about if schools produce assessment information about themselves that can be used formatively, and take the trouble to educate prospective parents in its use. To the extent that the full complexity of the work of the school is represented, parents will feel more informed – access to information is often all that is required for reassurance.

TGAT did something to point towards the formative rather than the summative use of such reports in advocating the publication of distributions. Distributions are very informative. Some schools create considerable differentiation amongst their pupils, leading to a long flat distribution. Other schools seek to homogenise pupil progress, with everyone moving forward at much the same rate. This leads to a peaked distribution with a fairly narrow base. Yet other schools cater to special interest groups, perhaps ensuring that slow learners make the maximum amount of progress available to them, or alternatively deploying their resources for the benefit of gifted children. If such special provision is effective, it will produce a skewed distribution, either with no bottom tail, or with an exaggerated tail at the top[65].

This kind of information is very highly developed in American universities, where students select a college which caters to their rate of progress and where they expect to find a relatively narrow range of attainments in which they can comfortably work. Whether this tendency is to the benefit or to the detriment of students is not known, but it has arisen quite naturally, not through policy, but through student choice and the availability of information. Whether British schools at Keystages 1 and 2 will become similarly specialised in their provision is very doubtful given the almost total lack of mobility of young children but some such tendencies may emerge in urban areas.

It is unlikely that parents will have an immediate appreciation of distributions, but they will eventually learn to interpret how their child might fare. LEAs can assist in that respect, not by adjusting schools' results, but by contextualising them. In some areas of Holland, schools' distributions are accompanied by three or four aggregated school distributions, each representing different types of catchment area. There is no accompanying text to suggest to which distribution the school belongs: that is for parent and headteacher to negotiate.

That would seem entirely appropriate to national assessment. In a formative system the burden of interpretation lies firmly with the user.

References

1   Proctor, N (1988), 'Government control of the curriculum: some archive and recent evidence', *British Educational Research Journal*, 14, 2; pp 155–166.
2   Becher, T & Maclure, S (eds.) (1978) *Accountability in Education* (Windsor: NFER).
3   Havelock, R G (1971), *Planning for innovation through dissemination and utilization of knowledge* (Ann Arbour: Michigan University).
4   Stenhouse, L (1975), *An introduction to curriculum research and development* (London: Heinemann).
5   Dalin, P (1978), *Limits to Educational Change* (London: Macmillan).
6   DES/Welsh Office, Task Group on Assessment and Testing (1988a), *A Report*, (London: DES/Welsh Office), Appendix B.
7   Meyer, M W (ed) (1978), *Environments and Organizations*, (San Francisco: Josey-Bass).
8   DES/Welsh Office Task Group on Assessment and Testing (1988a), *A Report* (London: DES/Welsh Office): Appendix B.
9   Ibid.
10   DES/Welsh Office, Task Group on Assessment and Testing (1988b), *Three Supplementary Reports* (London: DES/Welsh Office).
11   Ibid.
12   Nuttall, D (1989), 'National Assessment – will reality match aspirations?', *BPS Education Section Review*, 13, 1–2; 7–19.
13   Goldstein, H & Cuttance, P (1988), 'A note on national assessment and school comparisons', *Journal of Educational Policy*, Paper 37116.
14   Broudy, H S (1977), 'Types of knowledge and purposes of education', in R C Anderson, R J Spiro & W E Montague (eds.) *Schooling and the Acquisition of Knowledge* (Hillsdale, NJ: Lawrence Erlbaum).
15   Feuerstein, R with Rand, Y & Hoffman, M B (1979), *The dynamic assessment of retarded performers: the Learning Potential Assessment Device, theory, instruments and techniques* (Baltimore: University Park Press).
16   Feuerstein, R with Rand Y & Hoffman M B & Miller R (1980), *Instrumental Enrichment: an intervention programme for cognitive modification* (Baltimore: University Park Press).
17   Pramling, I (1988) 'Developing children's thinking about their own learning', *British Journal of Psychology*, 58, 3: pp 266–278.
18   Mortimore P, Sammons, P, Stoll, L, Lewis, D & Ecobn, R (1988), *School matters: The junior years* (Wells: Open Books).

19   Black, H D, & Dockrell, W B (1984), *Criterion-referenced Assessment in the Classroom* (Edinburgh: Scottish Council for Research in Education).

20   Harrison, A (1983), 'Communicative testing: jam tomorrow?', in A Hughes & D Porter (eds.) *Current developments in language testing* (London: Academic Press).

21   Good, F & Cresswell, M (1988), *Grading the GCSE* (London: Secondary Examinations Council): p 25.

22   Ibid: p 27.

23   Ibid: p vii.

24   Preece, P F W (1989), 'Regression to the mean in the measurement of school effects', *Research in Education*, 41: pp 49–51.

25   Cronbach, L J, Gleser, G C. Nanda, M & Rajaratnam, N (1972), *The dependability of behavioural measurements: Theory of generalisability for scores and profiles* (New York: Wiley).

26   Coleman, J S, Campbell, E, Hobson, C, McPartland, J, Mood, A, Weinfeld, F & York, R (1966), *Equality of Educational Opportunity* (Washington: National Centre for Educational Statistics).

27   Madaus, G F, Kellagham, T, Rakow, E A & King, D J (1989), 'The sensitivity of measures of school effectiveness', *Harvard Educational Review*. Vol 49, 2: pp 207–230.

28   Munnelly, R 1979, 'Dealing with teacher incompetence: supervision and evaluation in a due process framework', *Journal of Contemporary Education* 50: pp 221–225.

29   Department of Education and Science (1989), *National Curriculum: Policy to practice* (London: DES): p 2.

30   Binet, A and Simon, T (1905), 'Upon the necessity of establishing a scientific diagnosis of inferior states of intelligence,' *L'Année Psychologique*, 11: pp 163–191.

31   Secondary Examinations Council (1984), *General Certificate of Secondary Education: general criteria* (London: SEC): Criterion 16.

32   Miles, T R (1988), 'Comments on Howe's paper', *British Journal of Psychology*, 79; pp 535–538.

33   Spearman, C E (1904), 'General Intelligence' objectively determined and measured', *American Journal of Psychology*, 15: pp 201–292.

34   Stern, W (1949), 'The psychological methods of intelligence', translated from German by G M Whipple, *Educational Psychology Monograph* No 13 (Baltimore: Warwick & York).

35   Howe, M J A (1988), 'Intelligence as an explanation', *British Journal of Psychology*, 79: pp 349–360.

36   DES/Welsh Office, (1987b); paragraph 3.

37   Aronowitz, S & Giroux, H A (1987), *Education under Siege* (London: Routledge & Kegan Paul).

38   Bunderston, C V (1988) 'Measurement science and training', *Educational Testing Service Research Report*, RR-88-63 (Princeton NJ: ETS): 1.55.

39   Ibid: pp 21–22.

40   Nicholls, J (1978), 'The development of the concepts of effort and ability, perception of academic attainment and the understanding that difficult tasks require more ability', *Child Development*, 49; pp 800–814.

41 Christie, T & Forrest, G (1980), *Standards at GCE A-level: 1963 and 1973* (Schools Council Research Study) (London: Macmillan Education).

42 Noss, R Goldstein, H & Hoyles, C (1989), 'Graded Assessment and Learning Hierarchies in Mathematics', *British Educational Research Journal*, 15, 2; pp 109–120.

43 Brown, M (1989), 'Graded assessment and learning hierarchies in mathematics – an alternative view', *British Educational Research Journal*, 15, 2; pp 121–128.

44 Christie, T *et al* (1989), 'A cross-curricular approach to language achievement: the JMBs Staged Assessments in Literacy', *Head Teachers' Review* Spring: pp 6–11.

45 Troman G (1989) 'Testing tensions: the politics of educational assessment, *British Educational Research Journal*, 15, 3; pp 279–296.

46 Ranson, S, Gray, J, Jesson, D & Jones, B (1986), 'Exams in context: values and power in educational accountability', in D Nuttall (ed) *Assessing Educational Achievement* (Lewes: Falmer Press).

47 Macdonald, B (1977), 'Accountability, standards and the process of schooling', in T Becher & S Maclure (eds.) *Accountability in Education* (Windsor: NFER).

48 DES/Welsh Office, Records of Achievement National Steering Committee (1989a), *Records of Achievement* (London: DES/Welsh Office).

49 Dahllof, U (1971), *Ability Grouping, Content Validity and Curriculum Process Analysis* (New York: Teachers College Press).

50 Glaser, R & Nitko A J (1971), 'Measurement in Learning and Instruction, in R L Thorndike (ed) *Educational Measurement* 2nd edn (Washington DC: American Council on Education): p 653.

51 Huynh, H (1976), 'On the reliability of decisions in domain-referenced testing', *Journal of Educational Measurement*, 13: pp 253–264.

52 Subkoviak M J (1976), 'Estimating reliability from a single administration of a mastery test', *Journal of Educational Measurement*, 13: pp 265–276.

53 Subkoviak, M J (1984), 'Estimating the reliability of mastery-nonmastery classifications', in R A Berk (ed) *A Guide to Criterion Referenced Test Construction*.

54 Kane, M T (1987), 'The role of reliability in criterion-referenced tests', *Journal of Educational Measurement*, 23, 3; pp 221–224.

55 Hubbard, J I & Seddon, G M (1989), 'Changes in the marking standard and reliability of successive assessments of practical skills in science', *British Educational Research Journal*, 15, 1: pp 53–60.

56 Sadler, D R (1987), 'Specifying and promulgating achievement standards', *Oxford Review of Education*, 13: pp 191–209.

57 DES/Welsh Office (1989b), *English in the National Curriculum* (London: HMSO).

58 Broadfoot, P (1988) *Introducing Profiling: a practical manual* (London: Macmillan Education).

59 Sadler, D R (1987) *op cit*: p 207.

60 Bormuth, J R (1970), *On the Theory of Achievement Test Items* (Chicago: University of Chicago Press).

61 Pollitt A, Hutchinson C, Entwistle N & DeLuce C (1985), 'What makes

exam questions difficult?' (Research Reports for Teachers: Godfrey Thomson Unit for Educational Research) (Scottish Academic Press).

62   Hale, D E (1974), 'Moderation', in H G Macintosh, *Techniques and Problems of Assessment* (London: Edward Arnold).

63   Smith, G A (1978) *JMB Experience of the Moderation of Internal Assessments* (Manchester: Joint Matriculation Board).

64   Walker, D A (1979), 'Scaling Small Groups at the O Grade Stage', *British Journal of Educational Psychology*, 49, 3: pp 316–318.

65   Cuttance, P (1988), 'Modelling Variation in the effectiveness of schooling', (Edinburgh: Centre for Educational Sociology, University of Edinburgh).

Section Four:
Policies for a local
education authority

13   Introduction

Tim Brighouse

The future and changed role of Local Education Authorities has been subject to much speculation and prediction as the overall thrust of the new legislation became clearer during the passage of the Bill through Parliament.

To some extent the removal of powers, both to the Secretary of State on the one hand and to schools and colleges on the other, has led some to speculate on the prospective and possibly imminent demise of local education authorities. After all, so the argument runs, unless absolutely new powers and responsibilities have been created which the LEAs are to exercise, they might soon be seen as an irritating and unnecessary extra cog in a world where all schools have more autonomy within, of course, the carefully constructed and constrained national guidelines of the curriculum. The same argument concedes that LEAs may be very busy in introducing the new dispensations required by the 1988 Education Act, but once in place there will be little work for LEAs to do. On the other hand, some counter such arguments by claiming that the LEA, especially its advisory/inspectorate force, will have a vital role in the new scheme of things as they monitor and inspect, ensuring that every school is carrying out the last detail of the National Curriculum. Moreover, so this school of thought maintains, the LEA will provide a budget for each school for which that school will have to give a clear account: in short the school will need to justify to the LEA its actions, even if the detail decisions about spending on staff, materials, and so on, are entirely at the discretion of the school in question.

Others counter such claims for an LEA role by pointing out that, unless the school is actually proving fraudulent or is grossly mismanaging the money, and providing it continues to attract pupils, it will be able to call any LEA's bluff just, as it has to be admitted, some schools in some LEAs have done in the past. What is more, claim the pessimists, the LEA will be wise to remember that any school which grows fretful with unnecessarily nit-picking local interference will have a route open to grant-maintained status. Once the schools have mastered the massive agenda of change implicit in local management of schools, the National Curriculum and the many other changes, they may feel in sufficiently calmer waters, and therefore more ready to take on the apparently attractive independence which opting out is claimed to provide.

However that may be – and there is clearly force in both points of view – the LEAs, or some local administrative and managerial bodies, seem to be required for at least three purposes, apart from those of inspection/monitoring and in-service development of teachers. First there are the many schools with fewer than 200 pupils which will require managerial assistance to an extent far greater than before. After all, the formula of LMS will apply to all such schools, as will the full rigour of the National Curriculum, and nobody familiar with the sheer volume of tasks, the busy round of daily crises and the unremitting demand on the few teachers in small primary schools, seriously believes that they can cope without continuing managerial assistance from the LEA. Secondly there are the many other managerial tasks of the creative LEA, ranging from managing special schools and units and support services on a system maintenance basis, through to a strategy for provision for those from birth to five and for post-16 on the more developmental side of their duties. Indeed there are signs already that LEAs, seeing their creativity curtailed by LMS and the National Curriculum in the age range 5–16, are calling for reports and plans on these two vital issues which were largely ignored by the 1988 Act.

There is too a third role for the LEAs. Once markets are created, as we have seen in America, there is a need for regulatory bodies which are charged with or assume for themselves the role of highlighting and calling for the correction of the grosser inequities which markets may from time to time accidentally create when they operate in the provision of public goods. Indeed the role of the LEA, as a regulatory body, is a new power, which may be exploited to the embarrassment of national government as the responsibilities for the continuing and perhaps growing inequity of provision becomes clearer. That it will grow seems inevitable as the new community charge diminishes the ability of individual local authorities to create new services or put right anything other than the grosser incidences of social injustice which seem bound to arise from such an unfettered application of market forces to the provision of education.

Most of that, however, falls outside the role of the LEA in the curriculum. Perhaps the greatest shift of thinking by the Government between the 1986 Education Act and the 1988 Education Act is a loss of faith in local education authorities as bodies capable of imposing and implementing any national agreement on what could be agreed to be necessary as a common entitlement within the curriculum. The Circulars of 1977, 1981 and 1983 admittedly revealed a growing commitment by an increasing number of LEAs to taking an active role in supervising the curriculum of their schools. For many LEAs, even the Inner London Education Authority, however, the completion of the first questionnaire in 1977 had required an inventiveness and imagination which confused reality with wishful thinking. For some moreover, the 1977 Circular itself was an unacceptable intrusion into matters which were best left to schools and therefore an occasion for a blunt refusal to complete the government's request. By 1988 all that had changed.

There was hardly a single LEA which had not been actively involved, at least in curriculum development, even if some had stopped short of formulating an explicit curriculum policy. The 1986 Education Act required LEAs to have a curriculum policy, and although the 1988 Act did not remove that LEA obligation, it made its influence subordinate to the new legislated National Curriculum. Given the considerable detail of the form of the National Curriculum, and the influence and power of the National Curriculum Council, it seems doubtful that any LEA, at least in the immediate future, will be able to do much more than support and interpret the National Curriculum and assessment arrangements for its teachers. The words 'much more', however, mislead, for that task in itself is hugely influential. Moreover the climate which LEAs will inevitably create will affect the daily lives of headteachers and teachers as they meet the challenge of the new curricular disposition. Their largest challenge will come in how they seek to add to and thereby change the reporting requirements of the tests and assessments, both of individual children's results to parents and of class-by-class and school-by-school collective results, to parents in particular and the local community in general. Will they encourage a minimalist, simplistic, league table mentality – however sophisticated for differing socio-economic background and/or added value? Or will they on the other hand require the larger, more generous picture based on the assumptions of success across the full range of human talent for every child and every school?

In the longer run it will be interesting to see how creative and influential LEAs will be in avoiding schools being too isolated and independent, and encouraging an interdependent approach to subsequent curriculum development and change. Perhaps too they will promote applications by schools to test that section of the Act which permits curricular innovations to be approved by the Secretary of State.

In this section, all that is in the future. What we sought was the general views on the LEAs' role in managing the National Curriculum of three Education Officers. Anne Sofer is CEO of Tower Hamlets, where the pressures of today, and in particular the need to secure sufficient teachers, must test to the utmost any resolve to take a longer view. It is clear from her contribution that she is combining heroically to achieve both. Chris Seville wrote his piece while Director in Wolverhampton, but will read it on his appearance as Education Officer in Avon, and Mike Raleigh in co-operation with Keith Hedger sees the task from the vantage point of the Deputy with the responsibility for implementing it in the rural county of Shropshire. So we have an inner London borough, a midlands metropolitan district, and a rural county and three education officers (and one advisor) with unusual backgrounds, since none has risen through the typical educational and administrative hierarchy. In a sense, however, they are representative of the new LEA world: the old conventions and habits have largely and suddenly disappeared and the role has been transformed. It says much for the resilience and adaptability of the LEA institution that such sudden change is possible and that new directions can be firmly, optimistically, and confidently essayed at a time of unparalleled and multifaceted change.

The annex presents six LEA case studies. One is struck not so much by their similarity, as the subtlety of tone, *which may be no more than the chance* of which officer completed the form. Whatever the reason, however, it illustrates, if illustration were really needed, that whatever the national dispositions are, the reality of the experience of the National Curriculum will depend on the interpretation of countless different people, in each of 116 LEAs and beyond that in 27,500 schools.

14 A view from Tower Hamlets

Anne Sofer, Chief Education Officer

The head of a Tower Hamlets Infants School phoned a colleague early in June 1989 and wailed 'How am I supposed to plan the introduction of the National Curriculum when five out of my six teachers won't be here next term?' On bad days, that is rather how all of us feel. The need to recruit enough teachers and find enough school places overshadows everything else. The National Curriculum? . . . Well, yes, of course, there's that as well, but first things first. And anyway, aren't most of them doing it already, sort of . . .?

But that is only the bad days, which – fortunately – are few. Most of the time we realise that, despite the horrendous logistical problems and the break-neck speed at which we are being required to operate, there are enormous advantages in setting up a new education department and implementing the various measures in the Education Reform Act at the same time. The structures needed to fulfil the statutory duties of a local education authority post-ERA seem significantly different from what went before.

An early confirmation of this came when we invited CIPFA to compare the staffing complements of our proposed administrative and inspectorate structure with those of other comparable authorities. The administrative numbers came out considerably lower than the comparators, the inspectorate numbers higher. Arriving at these figures through our own analysis of what we needed, rather than through any initial knowledge of what might be regarded as a norm, we were not surprised.

This needs spelling out a little more. Within the proposed Tower Hamlets education administration there are only three sections where our numbers seem relatively high. One is Personnel, where the transfer of 11,000 personnel records from the ILEA (the majority being hourly-paid staff) and the need for a huge teacher recruitment exercise seem justification enough. Another is Development, where the projected increase in our school population by 40% over the next decade, and the need for at least eight new schools, again indicates an unusual situation. And the third is support for governors, about which more later.

Apart from these three areas – all 'special case' and possibly transient phenomena – we hope to operate with a slim administrative structure. We do not even have an 'AEO Schools'. We did not intend to have an 'AEO FE' until our elected members embarked on an ambitious (and, I am sure it will prove, far-sighted) development of policy in the training area as well, which clearly then needed our involvement at a senior level.

In the Inspectorate, on the other hand, it became clear that more intensive and detailed support to the schools, rather than less, was what was needed. This has to do partly with the high proportion of newly qualified and inexperienced teachers, partly with the additional educational needs of Tower Hamlets (notably bi-lingualism), and partly with the introduction of the National Curriculum and assessment. But overarching every part of this rationale is the very explicit target we have set ourselves of raising levels of achievement.

This runs counter to some received wisdom. One fairly common prediction about the ERA is that it will remove culpability for poor school performance from the local education authority. The finger will be pointed – so this argument runs – either at government (which controls the curriculum and overall resources) or at the school (which manages). The local authority, with its monitoring function, merely reports on what is happening. Some local education authorities have followed this logic through to the splitting of the inspectorate into two autonomous groups of equal status: the advisers, on the one hand, advising the schools on how to implement the curriculum (but not being accountable for what happens after that) and the inspectors, on the other, judging performance (but having nothing to say about how it might be improved).

We do not accept this analysis. The Act requires the local education authority to

> exercise its functions with a view to securing . . . a balanced and broadly based curriculum which promotes the spiritual, moral, cultural, mental and physical development of pupils . . . and prepares [them] for the opportunities, responsibilities and experiences of adult life

– a sufficiently sweeping remit, one might think. The LMS Circular (7/88) further spells this out as 'monitoring the performance of schools and giving advice or taking corrective action if necessary'. It is quite true that the 'corrective action' within the power of the LEA is far more circumscribed than it was, and that the odd maverick school and governing body may defy all reasonable attempts to help them. Many exciting legal chapters remain to be written on all of that. But the reality of the situation is that – at least for the foreseeable future – the great majority of governors, heads, local education authority members and the community charge-paying public will all want an *accountable* education administration; that is, one which goes beyond planning, distributing resources and monitoring, to take responsibility for the quality of the system as a whole and is prepared not only to identify weaknesses, but to roll up its sleeves and help put them right. This means an inspectorate large enough to spend time in the schools, working alongside teachers.

Surprisingly, perhaps, in view of my earlier comments, we too are planning to have both inspectors and advisors – but not as two separate functions. Our 'advisors' will work to the inspectors, extending their range and coverage. This role will replace the previous one of the 'advisory teachers', which in our view was always unsatisfactory and is now inappropriate. Advisory teachers, if permanently appointed, have tended to become more and more distant from the classroom, and find themselves in a career blind alley. Secondments, which were a solution in the past, are increasingly problematical with the sort of teacher vacancy situation Tower Hamlets is in: heads and governors, under LMS, are not likely to let people go – except for the worst possible reasons. To solve the dilemma, our new advisors will be on three-year contracts, paid on the Soulbury scale: attractive salaries aimed at high flyers on the way to a deputy headship or headship. Between them, inspectors and advisors will add up to almost one for every two schools. With such ratios we expect results.

The way the Inspectorate will operate is heavily influenced both by the National Curriculum and by particular Tower Hamlets factors. We have advertised for inspectors 'to cover all subjects in the National Curriculum'. We are aware of the subjects this leaves out and have built in a budget to enable us to 'buy in' expertise. We are also aware of the historic and unresolved tension between the subject-based approach and the more holistic philosophy of primary specialists, who fear that hard-won gains of recent years will be eroded.

This is not easy. The solution seems to lie in combining subject expertise with two other factors: a 'whole-school' philosophy, and a deployment of the Inspectorate across phases.

To explain: advisors or inspectors in the past have tended, when appointed for subject expertise as they usually have been, to 'fight for their corner'. They couch their advice in terms of the time, resources, and status 'their' subject should have. Heads are battered by competitive demands from the inspectorate which mirror those within their schools. There is no way in which the local education authority can play its part in delivering the National Curriculum unless the Inspectorate leads the way in adopting a 'whole-school' approach: with subject specialists sharing their expertise with colleagues, and showing how it can be used across the curriculum, rather than hugging it to themselves.

On the other hand, the National Curriculum dictates that subject expertise will be important – and that it must be cross-phase. If pupils are transferring from primary to secondary school with attainments in the various subjects at anything between Level One and Level Seven (and this is probably the range in most local education authorities) it makes no sense at all to keep the primary curriculum and the secondary curriculum in separate enclosed boxes.

Primary specialists fear that this subject emphasis will mean the ascendency of a 'secondary culture'. It seems to me more likely, especially in an authority where achievement levels are depressed as they are in Tower Hamlets, that the reverse will be the case. This is a real risk. And yet with co-operation and discussion between primary and secondary specialists, it could turn out otherwise. Consider the following developments that have evolved gradually over the last decade. First, primary teachers, while remaining all-round class teachers, have increasingly developed specialist subject expertise. (I never go round a primary school nowadays without being told 'Miss X is our science specialist, Mr Y has the language post', and so on). Secondly, secondary subject teachers have increasingly participated in 'integrated' courses: integrated humanities, integrated science, a plethora of TVEI initiatives to name a few; all of these have involved thousands of individual secondary teachers having to step outside their subject bases and both teach and learn from colleagues. Third, the demands of the National Curriculum are forcing secondary subject specialists to explore areas of overlap with specialists in other subjects ('Look, could you cope with soil erosion and weather in geography? Science is just so overloaded . . .'). Fourth, the range of ability of children transferring to secondary school will be explicit once assessment is fully implemented; within a local education authority the range is likely to be between Level One and Level Seven. It seems to me likely that secondary teachers will turn to their primary colleagues for advice in this situation in a way they never have had to before ('What do you do to get them up to Level Three in history?')

In other words, I believe that, properly handled, the National Curriculum could be an agent for bringing primary and secondary practice closer together – on terms which strengthen rather than undermine the best primary practice.

In this primary/secondary debate, the particular administrative arrangements of Tower Hamlets council have provided a formula. In 1986, Tower Hamlets transformed itself into the most radically decentralised local authority in the country: it is divided into seven Neighbourhoods, each with its own Chief Executive and Standing Committee and with considerable autonomy and budgetary discretion in relation to housing, planning, social services and other matters. After considerable debate, the council decided not to decentralise the newly acquired education service – if for no other reason than that it is already due to be decentralised in another way under LMS. But everyone recognises that it still makes a lot of sense to align localised education delivery with the Neighbourhoods.

As far as the Inspectorate is concerned, this means giving one Inspector 'patch' responsibility – that is overall pastoral responsibility – for all the schools in a Neighbourhood; something between 12 and 15 schools. However, we will contrive to 'twin' contiguous Neighbourhoods so that a primary and a secondary Inspector can provide curricular oversight and support in their respective phases across the two Neighbourhoods, as well as working as a team on all the cross-phase issues.

The Neighbourhood structure has also suggested a way forward for supporting governors. The state of governing bodies in Tower Hamlets at present is not healthy. ILEA has had difficulties in recruiting in most categories – turn-out for parent governor elections is not high – but the greatest problems are in getting the LEA places filled. Many meetings are repeatedly inquorate. Of those governors who do turn up, many badly need training, but for a whole host of reasons find it difficult to attend the ILEA-organised training sessions.

Our response has been to increase the numbers of clerks to governors and to enlarge their role. One 'Neighbourhood Schools Officer' is to be appointed to each of the seven neighbourhoods and to be made responsible not only for clerking, but for organising locally-based training, innovating with approaches that will suit the particular population. We are even toying with the idea of commissioning bi-lingual training material from the local Theatre in Education team!

We are well aware that by 1994 at the latest the costs of clerking will have to be borne by the schools themselves under LMS. That

H

is all the more reason to make sure that we use the intervening years to build up effective governing bodies and a base of popular understanding of the National Curriculum that will, we hope, spread beyond governors to other parents. With a school population, the majority of which come from homes where English is not the first language and where experience of the English education system is minimal, the challenge is obviously huge.

So much for structures and the distribution of responsibilities. On the nature, content and effects of the National Curriculum itself, we have three overriding pre-occupations. These are: first, how to use the National Curriculum to raise levels of achievement; second, how to give access to it to our large proportion of children from non-English-speaking homes; and third, how to use the assessment processes in a way that will improve teachers' effectiveness and facilitate fair comparison between schools.

On all of these issues, probably in common with most LEAs, we still have more questions than answers. On the first – using the National Curriculum to raise levels of achievement – these are our questions. Will we be able to recruit enough specialists in secondary schools to make all children's entitlement to science and technology and modern languages a reality? Will there be enough time and resources in primary schools to cope with the programmes of study? More fundamentally, will the climate of learning generated by the demands of the National Curriculum help to improve pupil motivation? How we plan the timing and content of our INSET programme will be crucial here.

On the needs of our children from non-English-speaking homes, the statements of the NCC and SEAC leave us in something of a quandary. All of the three 'core subject' curriculum documents give a nod in the direction of bi-lingualism – (to be fair, somewhat more than that in the case of the English report). 'Pupils with a poor command of English may need to be tested in their mother tongue if their mathematical attainment is to be fairly assessed' says the Mathematics Working Group. The Science Working Group explains that 'a child who has difficulties with the language of instruction will experience problems . . . which may affect her or his receptiveness to science and other areas of the curriculum', and enjoins that teachers 'seek to be sensitive to the children's understanding of language . . . perhaps in consultation with a language specialist'. The English Working Party admits that 'there may be a need for bilingual teaching support and for books and other written material to be available in the pupils' mother tongue until such time as they are competent in English' . . ..

But are we to be funded to provide such bi-lingual support? SEAC has stated that no child should be debarred from assessment in any of the National Curriculum subjects because of difficulty with English. The resource implications of this for a borough like Tower Hamlets, with school pupils of all ages arriving from Bangladesh, Somalia, Vietnam and Turkey, with varying amounts of schooling in their own languages behind them, are mind-boggling.

In an attempt to devise some priorities pending a Government decision to fund a bi-lingual programme seriously, we are concentrating on two things. First, we need to be sure that our strategies for teaching English are as effective as possible. We are not satisfied they have been and are commissioning research into this area. And second, we need a programme to increase the numbers of bi-lingual teachers and other staff in schools as rapidly as possible, particularly for younger children, and particularly for first stage learners. In terms of the detailed clauses of the 1988 Act, their main function must be to give children access to the National Curriculum during the period that they are adapting to English as the medium of instruction. In terms of the ' . . . moral and cultural development of pupils . . . and of society' which the preamble to the Act enjoins us to devote ourselves to, they serve a wider purpose: to be role models for all pupils growing up in a multi-cultural society.

The decision to include Bengali and many of the other non-European languages spoken in our borough as permitted foreign languages under the National Curriculum has been welcomed, but this is a relatively minor aspect of the language needs of Tower Hamlets. These needs, it has to be said, remain to be addressed.

Finally I turn to the questions surrounding assessment. Can we use it to help teachers become more effective? Can we ensure that fair comparisons between schools are made?

Tower Hamlets schools, when their aggregated scores are presented in the ILEA tabulations, do poorly. In particular their 'Band Ones' – that is the top 25% assessed across ILEA at 11 – do poorly. And there are few enough of them. One third of primary school leavers still need help with reading. The high proportion of immigrant and ESL pupils is profferred as an explanation – to the fury of community leaders who regard this under-expectation as racist. The image of under-achievement clings to the system as a whole.

But for those privileged few officers and inspectors who get access to the individual figures for every school, the picture becomes very different. Secondary school A, with a 90% Bangladeshi intake is doing about three times better in terms of exam results than secondary school B, which is largely white working class. Primary school C, high on the index of deprivation, has reading scores which one judges to be predictably low until one sees those of primary school D down the road which is even higher on the index but has reading scores at the ILEA average . . ..

These figures are resounding confirmation of the judgment in Sally Tomlinson and David Smith's recent study of multi-racial comprehensive schools that 'if schools were improved only within the current range of performance, this would be enough to transform standards'. They have convinced me that it is of the utmost importance that schools themselves – governors, heads, and above all classroom teachers – should have access to this sort of comparative data. Without knowing what is possible, teachers will not raise their expectations. The challenge will be to present results fairly and comprehensibly, and to do so in a way that does not undermine either individuals or institutions. Can we do it?

The answer lies in how the whole process of assessment is devised, and this – at the time of writing – is another as yet unanswered question. Will teachers be spending their entire time ticking boxes? Will they regard the SATs as fair? Will 'teaching to the test' undermine the healthy developments that have taken place as a result of TVEI and GCSE? Will the overall presentation of results be comprehensible to parents?

All of us engaged in the process of setting up the new Tower Hamlets Education Authority have had the strange experience during the summer months of 1989 of seeing day after day in the media a picture of our own future responsibilities that would seem enough to make anyone despair. The public prediction is repeatedly made that 'they cannot possibly cope!' Our reaction – as would that of anyone embarking on such an enterprise – is to square the chin and resolve to prove them wrong. We are helped in this attitude whenever we visit schools, where those teachers (the majority) who are staying look remarkably cheerful despite it all; or the teachers' centre where earnest discussions on the National Curriculum, an exhibition of primary science, a Special Educational Needs fair, follow each other in rapid succession. The area, despite its deprivation, is one of rapid economic growth. It buzzes with the excitement of its own particular history. Defying logic, we are filled with optimism.

15 A view from a metropolitan district

Chris Saville, Ex-Director of Education, Wolverhampton

Perhaps the place to start is with a definition of what we mean by the term 'curriculum'. Maybe the simplest definition for the curriculum in school is, that it is 'the sum of all that a child experiences whilst at school'. The adoption of this definition, although undoubtedly flawed in the eyes of some educational philosophers, does enable a more holistic view of a child's life and development in school than what appears to be the rather simplistic construct of the National Curriculum. This definition also helps us to look at the curriculum in terms of processes, values and methodologies as well as content.

There seems to be a general consensus that schools should empower children through the development of knowledge, skills, concepts and the ability to raise hypotheses and manipulate ideas. Some authorities have gone further than this, in their curriculum statements, to claim, on behalf of learners, educational entitlements. The National Curriculum, in essence, sets out a series of performance targets for pupils, and *ipso facto* teachers, leaving unsaid both the broader qualitative aspects of the curriculum and the processes of teaching and learning. LEAs and governors now have statutory obligations in respect of the National Curriculum which will need to be managed, but to do so without recognising the other curriculum processes at work will ill serve the needs of children and their teachers. Therefore, whilst the theme of this essay focuses on the curriculum management role of local education authorities in the post-Reform Act era, it is based upon the above assumptions about the curriculum.

Perhaps as we begin to establish plans and structures for the next few years we should use the opportunity to study and question some of our previous practice. In adopting this approach we can use the same action research sequence that would appear to be the most effective approach to curriculum change. In this sequence we can look at our practice, raise some hypotheses, and replan our approach.

The first of these hypotheses relates to the issue of the ownership of curriculum management and change. Is it an occupational hazard for those who operate from outside classrooms to cast themselves (or be cast) in the role of experts upon what does or should go on inside the classroom or school? Have LEAs ever managed the curriculum? It can be argued that all that LEAs have ever done is to create a framework of expectation and influence the curriculum through the provision of support services and some other resources. Some LEAs have exercised more influence than others. The extent to which schools and colleges manage the curriculum is questionable, for when the teacher closes the classroom door it is there that the 'secret garden' blooms. This has long been regarded by many as one of the strengths of the British education system, for it has freed the curriculum from political control or influence. The extent to which the National Curriculum is able to remain free of political influence remains to be seen, although the Secretary of State now has power in this respect undreamed of by his predecessors.

Where local authorities have been more active is in the field of curriculum and professional development. Slowly at first after the War, and then with greater impetus, curriculum development and in-service training began to grow. Although often underfunded, and one of the first areas to take cuts, LEAs became very active partners with bodies such as Schools Council, HMI and institutions of higher education. However, the history of curriculum development since the early sixties is littered with examples of externally-inspired curriculum projects and packages which had all the persuasiveness of the alchemist's formula, but the extent to which they actually enhanced the quality of either teaching or learning is questionable. Many of those projects are long forgotten but there were examples of sustained classroom change and it is from these that we in local authorities could learn. Of particular value are those programmes that recognised the importance of development being both site-based and concerned for the legitimate professional role of teachers. If the aim is to enhance teachers's skills and understanding, then we need to question the expectation and practice of staff involved in support and advisory roles.

Put most crudely, advisory staff whose practice has been directive instead of enabling change may find their work less effective, particularly as no longer will they have the promotional carrot to dangle in front of the reluctant teacher. We also need to question the traditional role of identifying good practice and arranging its dissemination. Has this concept ever actually worked in practice? For example, what happens if the support role of staff is confused with making judgements about teachers? Or, to what extent is the teacher conditioned by the need to satisfy some ill-defined criteria of good practice? It could be argued that this is a quite legitimate thing to happen, since advisers and advisory teachers have been recruited on the basis of someone else's view of excellence. On the other hand one should ask if this represents a deficiency view of teachers, or is an attempt to promulgate a monopoly of wisdom about approaches to teaching and learning. Furthermore, does the act of external direction of curriculum development take the ownership away from teachers? In some ways the Education Act 1988 answers some of these questions for us. For example, whilst the LEAs will hold some of the purse strings for curriculum and professional development, it is the governors with the headteacher who will have the power to determine the enabling conditions for change in the schools. The LEA will have the important role of creating a framework of leadership in which both support for curriculum change and the monitoring of performance will have their place. A central principle that under-pins this paper is that this concept of leadership embraces a belief in the importance of empowering teachers to take ownership and responsibility for development and change.

The advent of TRIST and then GRIST and ESGs spawned whole new sections in education departments, whilst TVEI established new ground rules and demanded new management structures. Assuming that the system of specific funding continues, LEAs will have a role in managing these programmes. The key task will be to determine the interface between the criteria of the funding body, the LEAs own curriculum policies and the schools. Some of the criteria established by government agencies have caused LEAs to develop a whole new practice, loosely described as the submission game. Each year as more and more grant money became available and as the rate-borne expenditure became less, LEAs off-set proportions of staff costs against the grants. In some cases this has come back to haunt them as the projects ended, the funding ceased and staff who had been seconded had to join the redeployment queue or go to new grant-aided projects. The speed at which these specific grants emerged and the short submission times has caused problems for those LEAs wanting to take a holistic and planned approach to curriculum and professional renewal. For example, different groups of staff can be working simultaneously on ESGs, LEATGS, TVEI, COMPACT etc, often involving different schools. To bring some managerial consistency within a strategy and policy for curriculum and professional development is undoubtedly necessary but extremely difficult, and there is a shortage of staff with the necessary skills.

The second hypothesis and related questions focus on the sequence in which individuals change their practice. It is proposed that education practitioners move through the following sequence or stages of change as it affects aspects of their work or their perceptions of new demands:

> From unconscious incompetence;
> To conscious incompetence;
> To conscious competence;
> To unconscious competence.

If it is seen as desirable to support this process of change, then there are implications for managers of support staff and the support staff themselves. Firstly, this approach assumes that the central (LEA) management function is about management for change, as opposed to the management of change, which is manifestly a concern of each institution.

In addressing this issue it may be helpful to ask whether the existing pattern of organisation, the values expressed through the actions of staff, and the skills for support for change are congruent with the concept of site-based ownership. This review of structures and practice is necessary, for although we may think we are operating a benign supportive role, it may be perceived quite differently by teachers in the classroom. For example, if the advisory service has the dual responsibility for curriculum and professional development plus a monitoring role, might not the teacher ask which agenda the adviser is using at any one time? For the teacher there will inevitably be the suspicion that the adviser is judging competence, or preparing to write a reference. Does this not create a situation whereby:

- advisers are in effect monitoring their own work;
- support is confused with monitoring;
- monitoring is used as a vehicle for promulgating their constructs of practice;
- monitoring is used as a management control device;
- teachers' capacity to develop is conditioned by the biased orthodoxy of others;
- that monitoring is the LEAs hidden vehicle for curricular change?

It may be that LEAs actually want their advisers to undertake this dual role. If this is the objective, then it is essential that managers in those authorities raise the following question:

• to what extent is there an inconsistency between promoting the concept of the empowered professional teacher and using support staff as management's appraisers or control mechanism?

Few would deny that there is a need to have some form of systematic monitoring of performance. The LEA has a right and responsibility to know what is happening in the schools and colleges. It is equally irresponsible not to address the issue of competence, whilst recognising that teachers and others have a right to informed and objective feedback about their practice. This role has been variously undertaken by HMI and, in many cases, local authority inspectors and advisors. LEAs may like to consider whether or not the time has come for there to be a greater clarity about the role of their advisory services. In order to achieve this some LEAs have separated the monitoring and inspectorial functions from the developmental support roles. There is merit in this approach, even for the small authority, for advisors have suffered for years from the job collection syndrome, to the point, in some cases, where the time they spend in classrooms takes second place to a variety of field officer tasks. This has had the effect of actually de-skilling advisers from the very skills that warranted their appointment in the first place. At the same time advisory teachers and other support staff have lacked the status, organisation and management responsibility for their own highly skilled and important role.

Curriculum development and in-service training has often been an *ad hoc* response to ill-conceived notions of need or, worse, the shop window for the providers. Furthermore, much in-service work, traditionally expressed in the form of courses, has given support to the individual but has done little to address the institutional needs of the school or college. The advent of 'Baker Days' is at least a step in the right direction, for it meets the requirement of being site-based and within the control, if they care to exercise it, of the teachers. LEAs need to manage the support they bring to this opportunity, for there are still schools with little or no experience in designing development events. Headteachers and other staff with responsibility for curriculum and professional development need training and support programmes.

Given the delegated powers and the strictures of devolved budgets, LEAs are going to have to consider the deployment of advisory teachers and other support staff and their relationship with the schools and colleges. A move to a more clearly negotiated form of support would recognise the change in the relationship.

This process of clarification of the relationship between the LEA's support staff and the schools can be helped significantly if the LEA encourages schools to adopt a development planning approach. Already in some authorities the school/college development plan is the trigger for the release of resources for development and the basis upon which support staff 'contract' their services to the individual institution. Of course there are support staff whose work is primarily with individual pupils on a peripatetic basis. These staff too require support and a management framework within which they can operate.

The final hypothesis relates to the issue of teacher appraisal and is concerned to explore the relationship between appraisal and development. To what extent is, or should, teacher appraisal be linked to site-based curriculum and professional development strategies?

The National Steering Committee final report puts to rest the approach to teacher appraisal which has at its starting point the identification of bad practice. Properly developed teacher appraisal should enable a more systematic approach to needs-identification for teachers. A more appropriate term would be teacher *apprisal*, for this suggests the importance of informing practice, rather than the dictionary definition of appraisal – 'finding value in that being appraised'. If the purpose of teacher appraisal is the improvement in quality and standards, then it follows that the processes of appraisal should be linked to changes in teachers' practice. In order to enable changes in individual teacher practice, the school has an obligation to create the enabling conditions of confidence, trust and openness within a similar framework created by the LEA. Therefore, appraisal should be seen both by schools/colleges and the LEA as an inextricable part of curriculum, professional and institutional development.

The cynics may well be inclined to argue that this approach is 'soft centred' and sidesteps the issue of teacher competence. Not so, the issue of competence has to be addressed but the process of identification of incompetence must have at its starting point the aim of restoring competence.

The LEA has the following important roles to play in the appraisal process:

- the validation of site-based appraisal systems;
- the training of staff in appraisal techniques, including observation and feedback;
- supporting schools and colleges in collating the institutional implications arising from the outcomes of appraisal;
- supporting and enabling development action as a result of appraisals;

- the training and informing of governors of their role in appraisal systems.

In summary, the LEA has a significant management role to play in the development of teachers and the curriculum. However, it is also apparent that in some cases there will have to be significant changes in the methods of working. There will have to be a shift from the practice of control and direction to one of enabling and facilitating change. The need to clarify the role of advisers, inspectors and support staff would appear to be crucial, whilst the advent of a national scheme for teacher appraisal could be deployed to give effect to a more finely-tuned method of identifying development needs.

Many LEAs have already gone through the pain barrier of reorganising their departments, and some still have that task to face. Of greater importance still in any reorganisation is the development of attitudes and the renewal and development of skills. Undoubtedly there is a management task to be done, but departments will need to recognise that they will be operating in a new and as yet untried context. What we can be sure of is that those officers and inspectors who have carried with them a belief that they have a monopoly of wisdom, or see teachers as deficient, will find little comfort in the future. Conversely, for those who see their task as one of support, challenge and enablement, the future holds opportunities and excitement, as it always has done.

16 A county perspective

Mike Raleigh, Deputy Education Officer, Shrewsbury and Keith Hedger, Senior Advisor

Clothing the emperor

It is 4th September and it's started. On an early visit to one class of five-year-olds the first words heard from the teacher, governed now in her work by a framework of Statutory Orders, are: 'James, can you please take your hand out of the fish tank?'

Life goes on. In the August mails: a few more circulars; copies from the NCC, SEAC and the DES of various correspondence among themselves on this and that; a bill for the use of forklift trucks to shift last summer's load of non-statutory guidance; the interim report on history (where Babylon and the Tudors make a comeback); a letter from a local group of Exclusive Brethren asking for relief for their children from any requirement to use information technology. There is also a call from the father of an 11-year-old who will be in hospital for at least four weeks, asking what she will miss and can she catch up.

Apart from sending on the post, hiring forklift trucks and making comforting noises on the phone, what can an LEA do to help schools with the introduction of the National Curriculum?

* * * *

Shropshire has 270 schools, serving areas which range from the expanding parts of new town Telford to the sparsely populated Welsh borders, with Shrewsbury, the county town, and a number of smaller towns in between. From Shrewsbury it is 30 or 40 miles to schools on the border of Cheshire to the north, and Hereford and Worcester to the south. Forty per cent of Shropshire's primary schools have two or three teachers. Forty per cent of its secondary schools have four forms of entry or below, and most of them are 11–16.

This is an account of what Shropshire LEA is doing about the introduction of the National Curriculum. It is, quite obviously, an account of work in progress, and while the nature of that work in part reflects local circumstances, the main features we will describe are probably to be found in work going on in most LEAs in the country.

First, a digression.

*   *   *   *

Diddlebury is a village back from the Wenlock Edge which you would like if you could find it. It used to have a school of its own until it was shut in 1967 and, along with three others, replaced by a new school at Corvedale. To mark Diddlebury's passing, the Shropshire CEO was presented with the school's curriculum plan for 1927. The document, held together with tape still adhesive after all these years, records the subjects taught and the amount of time spent on them by different age groups. The plan was drawn in accordance with the national curriculum of the day, governed by the Education Act 1921 and the associated Code.

Both classes had much the same programme:

R.E.	175 mins
English Language –	
Reading	245 mins
Recitation	30 mins
Composition	180 mins
Arithmetic	245 mins
Geography	65 mins
History	60 mins
Music	60 mins
Physical Tr'ng	85 mins
Organised Games	30 mins
Practical Instruction:	
(Girls): Needlework	
(Boys): Handwork: cane weaving etc	210 mins
Recreation (Art 44.(e))	125 mins
Story Telling	30 mins

| Elem Science | 60 mins |
| Assembly/Registration | 50 mins |

There must have been options under the Code as, in this school, no time was given as it could have been, to such studies as to Beekeeping, Combined Dom. Subj. or Conversation Lessons.

The document was signed by the head and, six months later, by a visiting HMI who, coming presumably to do the testing, found the curriculum plan satisfactory and reflected in the reality of children's achievement. The space for the signature of the Chairman of the School Managers stands blank.

Things come and go, you understand.

* * * *

Given intelligence in its design and resourcing, the implementation of a national curriculum would be merely a daunting exercise. Unfortunately, since the decision was made to work it out backwards, in bits and on the hoof, the task has been made rather more difficult. It must have seemed a good idea at the time. Speculating too closely at this stage on how it will be when the whole thing is in place, assessments, records and all, tends to produce bouts of giddiness. Enough to remember that should it all happen as currently imagined, we will be, like Babylon, in another millennium, when the five-year-olds starting it this year take their hands out of the fish tank for the last time. In the meantime, best to avoid vertigo.

Certainly it could come a cropper sooner. A contemporary Diddlebury (a remote, two-class school with a full-time teaching head) could turn to a muddle fairly early if panic, induced by a feeling of overload and apparent incompetence, drives out good sense. The outcome then, at best, could be ironic detachment, minimum compliance and the fatalistic 'it's a fair cop' speech for the visiting inspector. Equally, the most earnest of secondary schools, trying hard to establish a rational pattern of curriculum delivery, could stumble into a maze of fine accounting and attainment target-hunting which cannot sustain the daily demand to make education make sense to children. That school too could end up faking it, with banks of individual worksheets, ability groups of mixed ages and practice SATS to do at home.

There wouldn't be any pleasure in being able to say in 2001: 'told you so . . . it didn't come off'. The job for an LEA must be to work optimistically and energetically with schools to make sure that it does, by:

• supporting the development and the spread of existing high

quality practice and exploiting the creative possibilities within
the framework with which schools are being provided;
- helping schools to plot a route for the process of implementation
which tries to keep the demands rational.

There is no alternative to being positive. We have to hope that,
in practice, the process of implementation will lead to greater clarity
in the design of learning activities, and a stronger emphasis on
progression. The task is one of encouraging schools to use the
National Curriculum to raise achievement by improving opportunities and making sure that all pupils have equal access to them.

We describe below four elements of the task that we have started
to work on in Shropshire.

Providing an intelligence service

There are no experts on the National Curriculum, only people
who had the latest document before you did. There isn't anything
like a complete picture and there won't be for some time.
Nevertheless it is necessary for the LEA and its schools to plan
ahead using the information available, while not second-guessing
what isn't known, if only to avoid making commitments which
will have to be unpicked. Like other LEAs, we have been looking
for arrangements which promote coherence planning and which
are flexible enough to accommodate shifts in the future.

This has meant reviewing the direction and priorities of a wide
range of existing curriculum projects, including local initiatives such
as in cross-curriculum technology, personal and social education,
integrated arts and lower secondary humanities. Clearly it is
important to make sure that specific developments like these are
not pursued in isolation.

In this respect a major concern has been planning in secondary
schools, particularly for the upper years: Keystage 4. The extension
of TVEI to all Shropshire schools and colleges began in 1989. It
requires a commitment to the enhancement of subject courses
and to cross-curricular planning, and brings with it the introduction
of a County Records of Achievement scheme for 11–18 year olds.
It is also accompanied in the Telford area by the setting up of
a Compact. In these circumstances, compatibility with National
Curriculum requirements is essential if schools are to avoid
discontinuities and dissipation of energies and momentum.

Anticipation of the implications of the National Curriculum has
also been critical at a time when the present system for the
management of schools and the provision of LEA services is being
dismantled and a new one set up. The implications include, for
example, those for:

- the number, recruitment, workloads and management of teaching staff;
- the employment of advisory and support teachers;
- the assessment of special needs;
- the collection and publication of information by schools and the LEA:
- the provision of materials and equipment;
- procedures for monitoring and evaluation.

Each of those areas involves critical decisions and detailed calculation within LMS funding arrangements – calculation which depends on estimates of likely needs drawn from an interpretation of the impact of requirements not yet fully determined.

All this demands continued pooling of information and prediction of demands by LEA staff and by schools. Some of this is being done through existing networks or through seminars involving inputs on national developments. In addition, the LEA has set up a National Curriculum advisory group consisting of heads, teacher representatives, advisers, educational psychologists and advisory teachers, who meet in sub-groups to draw together information, to monitor developments and to consider responses to them. Sub-groups have been set up to look at, for example:

- current practices in teacher assessment;
- record-keeping and the transfer of information;
- the reporting of assessments;
- modification and disapplication;
- whole curriculum planning.

Organising co-operation

It could hardly be said that encouraging co-operation among schools is a major thrust of the Education Reform Act. Nevertheless we see this as very important in the successful implementation of the National Curriculum, particularly, but not only for primary schools.

Groups of neighbouring schools have worked together in Shropshire, as in other LEAs, for a long time and the potential of 'clusters' has recently been emphasised in the experience of other LEAs. New arrangements in Shropshire are intended to apply those benefits in particular to work on the National Curriculum. 'School development groups' with an average size of 15 primary and special schools will provide a natural forum for the planning and delivery of in-service, for the sharing and production of curriculum plans and materials, and for teacher exchanges and short-term secondments. Individual schools within the group will be able to provide distinctive service to others by taking on the role of a development centre for an aspect of the curriculum. In 1989–90, much of the development work on design and technology, PE and the arts have been organised in this way. In the future we hope that the groups can be used for cross-school moderation of National Curriculum assessments, drawing on growing familiarity among teachers of work done by different schools within the groups. The plan is also to involve heads and teachers from the groups in county and regional activities to provide broader perspectives on local work. Each group will have the service of an adviser and a small team of advisory teachers, including those concerned with learning support. (These advisory teams are themselves sub-sets of new LEA area teams comprising education officers, advisers, educational psychologists, and careers and youth service officers.) Building on existing patterns of primary/secondary liaison, it is hoped that an increasing range of representatives from secondary schools will be increasingly involved in the activities of the school development groups as their work covers different curriculum areas.

For secondary schools themselves, the establishment of TVEI consortia builds on the existing extensive co-operation between subject specialists and at 16+ transfer and moves into other areas of development in the 14–18 age range, such as personal and social education, Records of Achievement and education/industry links. Here the secondary area adviser, who has general responsibility for a group of schools, will work with the TVEI consortium co-ordinator on activities identified by the schools and colleges. Science and technology feature prominently in 1989–90, as schools move towards balanced science courses and the systematic delivery of technological education.

Arranging an in-service programme

This is easy at the start, when there are clear priority groups. We planned the programme for October 1988 – December 1989 with these groups in mind and on the assumption that understanding and expertise could not be expected to develop all at once. The programme initially provided sessions for:

- heads, officers and others;
- advisers and advisory teachers;
- core subject co-ordinators and heads of department.

The special two-day closures were employed in the middle of the programme, in the summer term- Teachers of five-year-olds met together around the county in sessions run by advisers and advisory teachers. These sessions were designed to provide a chance for teachers to consider how the programmes of study in the core subjects could be shaped to fit in with the best of existing practice and to discuss their perceptions and reservations. Responses to these sessions underlined the value of in-service which is set in a practical context and relies on interaction rather than transmission. Meanwhile other teachers in primary, secondary and special schools were involved in school-based or school group sessions run by heads and other staff. A prior session to discuss the use of these two days was run for primary heads, for secondary inset co-ordinators and for heads of maths and science. Further school-focused work for all teachers will take place during the Professional Development days around the Autumn 1989 half-term, with additional sessions for co-ordinators throughout the term.

Arranging a rational and effective programme of in-service training becomes progressively more complicated over the next two years as more subjects and more teachers become directly involved and as the first cohorts move towards unreported assessments. It is clear that the system we are using for the first stage of the programme will need to be modified if teachers and trainers are not to meet themselves coming back. While the position will be clearer when the history and geography final reports are published and when the basis of the assessment procedures is established, it is obvious now that the programme will need to be highly selective in its targets for direct training and rely heavily on materials for individual and group study for coverage of other areas.

The table over outlines the proposed plan of activities from January 1990 to July 1991.

Setting up an evaluation scheme

Around the country there has been a good deal of discussion – some enthusiastic, some anxious – about the exercise of the LEA's evaluative role in relation to both the National Curriculum and local management.

The Advisory Service in Shropshire has for some time carried out inspections of individual schools and of practice in a number of institutions. The reports have been published. We have also operated a schedule of visits and observations, culminating in a report to the head, known locally (and foolishly) as 'the debrief'. In reviewing the experience of these procedures to work out a system for the future we were struck by the need to:

Inset Target Groups

What follows is an outline of the Inset programme relating to that part of the LEATGS funding supporting the Implementation of the National Curriculum. It is, of course, a subset of the whole Inset programme.

Primary and Special School Heads

5 days @ Head

Staff in these schools are likely to bear the brunt of the immediate pressures. It follows that Heads require an on-going collaborative forum for the consideration of subject reports as they come "on stream". The meetings are therefore based on the SDGs, spread throughout the year and provide an opportunity for appropriate advisory staff to mediate information and promote discussion about effective management and dissemination issues.

These forums are supplemented by a range of occassional "twilight" and weekend events on NC issues and by a full National Curriculum conference in the Autumn term. It is essential they feel part of a coherent and collective enterprise which keeps them informed of current developments.

Curriculum Co-ordinators

2 days on each of the current subject areas
1 day on each subject coming on stream in Autumn 1991
(costed half against the LEATGS budget and half against the schools'
delegated budgets)

Given the large number of small schools, in many cases the co-ordinator will be the Head. However the need for a closely-focussed, centre-based opportunity for setting LEA-produced materials into a methodological framework remains. The management of effective school-based dissemination is a central feature of these courses and schools will be energetically encouraged to devote time, attention and resources to this. One day is therefore centre-based and the other based in school. The ESG project taught us that Inset related to idiosyncratic classroom requirements is the most effective.

Individual Primary Teachers

5 Professional Development days
Twilight courses
Rolling Subject Projects
Advisory teacher support
1 day for each teacher at 2nd year of KS1 (Assessment/Moderation)

The mounting of a two-day exercise in the Summer 1990 for the teachers beginning KS2 in September will complete the face-to-face training of staff at years 1, 2 and 3. It was felt essential to create intimate forums for this potentially over-stressed group. The use of Spring 1991 PD days for training in Assessment and Moderation for staff at KS1 was part of the LEATGS rubric.

Other staff will receive school-based training on the PD days when Co-ordinators and Heads have an opportunity to put materials and guidance into the context of the particular school.

Secondary and Special Heads

A range of meetings, conferences and seminars enabling Heads and Deputies to keep abreast of current developments. Minimal supply cover. The Area Adviser infrastructure monitors concerns and will dictate the need for particularly focussed additional events.

Successful "Area" Deputies meetings will continue if funded from the delegated schools budget. Secondary Heads also have the benefit of an annual residential conference which allows access to speakers who have made a contribution to the national debate on NC issues.

Heads of Department

2 days for each HOD representing subjects to come on stream in the 1990–'91 period (to include Learning Support Departments). One day is centre-based working with advisory staff to put materials into a methodological framework and allowing the consideration of effective implementation strategies. The other day will be costed against the schools' delegated budgets.

1 day of cover is allocated to enable this group of HODs to attend appropriate Primary SDG sessions. This recognises the paramount importance of establishing effective primary-secondary links and understanding.

"Area" HOD meetings in all subject areas will continue if supported under delegation.

Individual Secondary Teachers

5 PD days
Twilight courses
GCSE forums
Advisory teacher support

The ultimate irony is the necessity of recognising the inevitability of depending on the recommended but discredited "Cascade" Inset system for staff at this level. The normal pattern of 2 day closure has focussed on a school-relevant NC issue on the first day (whole-school assessment policies, RoA, cross-curricular themes/skills, TVEI etc). The second day is then devoted to setting this in a departmental context.

Advisory staff not involved with directed Inset delivery at the primary stage are available for a more direct involvement at this stage.

Closely-focussed advisory teacher support available in some subject areas to work within departments.

- bring the various demands for planning and evaluation together within a single framework;
- ensure that the Advisory Service works systematically and continuously with schools, rather than spasmodically;
- make the relationship between internal and external evaluation as close and as healthy as possible;
- keep the functions of development and evaluation together.

The result is a scheme for planning and evaluation which goes like this:

1 The school development plan
Each year schools will be asked to produce a development plan, arising from consultation among staff, which:

- reflects on progress in the preceding year;
- takes into account the implementation of the National Curriculum, TVEI and other developments;
- sets out intentions for the year ahead within the context of a broad three-year plan;
- includes proposals for staff development and in-service training;
- presents information on curriculum provision and associated staffing;
- outlines allocations within the school budget (whether delegated or formula).

The plan will be discussed with the school's area officer and adviser, who will provide information relevant to it arising from contacts by Advisors and other LEA staff in the preceding year. In particular the area advisor will record observations on the aspects of the school's arrangements, including:

- the recording of achievement;
- the professional development of staff;
- the management of the school

The development plans will inform the LEA's planning of in-service and other forms of support, including the use of Advisory Service time and the use of special grants.

2 The school review
A school review will be carried out on a cycle of four years, although a follow-up may take place within a shorter period in order to focus on specific issues. An essential part of the process will be the joint identification by the school and advisers of priorities for investigation and development. The review will also be carried out collaboratively and will be based on published criteria produced in consultation with schools. These criteria will recognise the range of ways in which effectiveness can be achieved. They will

incorporate indices of effectiveness designed to focus evaluation on sound evidence, but these will not be considered in isolation.

A report of the review will be produced, summarising the school's current state of development and making recommendations for the future. The report will be presented to the governing body.

3 Surveys and inspections
In addition to these regular arrangements, the Advisory Service will also continue to carry out surveys of practice across a number of schools and, on occasion, full or general inspections of single schools.

4 The annual summary report
An annual LEA summary report will be produced on aspects of work in all schools and colleges, drawing on development plans, review reports, records of visits and other forms of evidence. Sections of it will be devoted to:

- the implementation of the LEA curriculum policy, including the requirements of the National Curriculum;
- the evaluation of in-service training;
- assessment and examination results;
- pupil destinations.

The report will make recommendations to the Education Committee on specific developments which should be pursued and any financial implications which they involve.

One of the most problematic issues here is the analysis and presentation of the results of assessments – at 16 now in the form of GCSE and at 7, 11, 14 and 16 in the future. There is perturbing potential in the system for setting one school against another at a time when the need for co-operation and sharing of expertise is at its most urgent. The importance of contextualising results has been accepted by the DES. What is clear is that 'contextualising' will demand more than 'a statement authenticated by the LEA about the socio-economic context in which the school finds itself'. Regrettably, despite pioneering work in ILEA and elsewhere, the state of the art remains under-developed. Our own modest work towards a system which reports on the progress of cohorts (ie a 'value-added model') has started with an attempt to provide secondary schools with an analysis of GCSE results designed to enable them to consider factors in their curriculum organisation and delivery which promote or inhibit progress, both generally and in relation to particular subjects. While the legislation may leave us stuck with the presentation of raw scores, we hope to be able at least to offer an intelligible way of interpreting them.

* * * *

Meanwhile, back to the present, and the real work in which teachers teach and children make progress. This is part of a description by the LEA's Mathematics Adviser on his visit to the classroom where James had his hand in the fishtank.

I intended to spend the best part of a day with a class of five-year-olds embarking on their National Curriculum careers with a teacher new to both. I lasted the morning.

As the second teacher in a class of 31, I had the luxury of working with a small group. To cover this eventuality I had previously identified a basic number attainment target from the mathematics document I thought I might helpfully broach on behalf of the teacher. The group I had were the oldest and I anticipated reinforcement to be the order of the day.

We exchanged pleasantries and names. From the pile in the middle, I asked them to select 10 multilink cubes. Stuart remembered the need for an urgent chat with David in the corner but promised to be right back. He was gone before I could reach him. Vicky and Russell took some cubes and, presumably thinking I was taking them through a design and technology activity, began to construct and appraise an artefact. 'Your's looks like a horse', she told him. Gareth appeared to have accumulated some 25 cubes in front of him. My attention was diverted by a simultaneous, multi-directional tugging at my shirt. Two children sought my approval of the pictures they had drawn. I gave it and returned to the matter in hand. 'What shall we do next?' they persisted, then and again at regular five-minute intervals.

Detailed records indicated that they were hot stuff on number bonds in July but the sun had clearly cleansed their collective memory banks. I caught their attention for sufficiently long to place four cubes in front of me. 'How many cubes are there here?' I asked. 'Five', 'Three', 'Four', and two more plumped for 'Five'. We counted them together. Slowly. 'And how many now?' I asked. They all agreed on four. I pushed them towards Russell and asked him to count them and for the others to watch. 'One. Two. Three-Four. Five. There's five' he said.

'What's he done wrong?' I asked Vicky. 'Wrong?' she said, bemused.'

17 Some further case studies

Six local education authorities from the north, midlands and south, were asked to complete answers to five questions about their planning and approach to the management of the National Curriculum.

The LEAs (with a coded initial for each) may be described as follows:

Northern Metropolitan
Authority (NM1)   with over 500,000 population
                                   and 200+ schools

Midland Shire County (MS)   with over 1,000,000 population
                                   and 500 schools

Northern Metropolitan
Authority (NM2)   with over 200,000 population
                                   and 100+ schools

Southern Shire County (SS1)   with over 400,000 population
                                   and 275 schools

Southern Shire County (SS2)   with about 600,000 population
                                   and 300+ schools

Midlands Metropolitan
Authority (MM)   with over 300,000 population
                                   and 150 schools

Their replies are as follows:

1 Information and training for National Curriculum

NM1

The LEA has largely diverted its INSET effort towards the National Curriculum and from January 1989 the provision of training for the National Curriculum has been a priority for the advisory service and will continue to be so as long as national priorities for LEATGS direct training in this way.

The training has focused upon Keystages 1 and 3 of the National Curriculum. By December 1989 all primary school teachers and the vast majority of secondary school teachers will have taken part in at least one day's training.

School closure days have been organised so that all primary and secondary schools have spent one day using the National Curriculum Council briefing materials. The second closure day has been staggered so that primary school teachers (summer term) and secondary school teachers (autumn term) will have taken part in a day's training organised by the Advisory Service with workshops on all core subject areas and on assessment.

Information

The Advisory Service has produced a series of information booklets on the National Curriculum which have tried to give an LEA gloss to the basic information coming from the DES and the NCC.

Priorities

The main priority as far as the LEA is concerned is to present the National Curriculum within the context of the LEA's own curriculum policy and initiatives, and to ensure that no teacher stops doing anything which is currently deemed to be good practice.

MS

After consultation and negotiation with the professional associations, it was decided that the priority for the summer term 1989 would be the direct training of all teachers responsible for Y1 children. A conscious decision was taken that this training would not be of a cascade nature. It was with this in mind that every Y1 teacher was involved in three days' training. In total some 800 teachers have received support, approximately 25% of the primary teaching force. The objectives of this training were:

(a) Develop their understanding of the new language connected with the National Curriculum.
(b) Further their understanding of the principles connected with

assessment.
(c) Consider some of the issues connected with recording children's achievement.
(d) Become more familiar with the documents relating to the core subjects.
(e) Recognise that present classroom practice relates to the National Curriculum.

The training was undertaken by a group of advisory teachers.

Primary headteachers and secondary headteachers
Termly meetings/seminars/discussion days on training and joint planning.

Keystage 3
Subject specific training for secondary teachers – heads of department and subject specialists.

Work on curriculum development, Awareness raising and training for teachers on specific curriculum areas as the working reports and documents appear.

NM2

The LEA Advisory and Support Service has taken the lead in creating opportunities for teachers to reflect on the statutory curriculum as it emerges in primary and secondary legislation.

The LEA publishes its own information booklets to supplement DES and NCC documentation and act as a stimulus to debate. The training programme differentiates between the need for all teachers to develop and maintain a whole-curriculum perspective and the specific needs of individuals in relation to the tasks they are required to perform. For example, all staff will be spending four school closure days during 1989 considering whole-curriculum issues and, in this context, developing a basic awareness of the statutory orders in the core subjects. Further training is targetted at school managers, core subject co-ordinators and teachers of core subjects in Keystages 1 and 3. Similar targetting by subject and age group is likely to continue in parallel with the implementation timetable for the National Curriculum but with structured opportunities for all staff to explore cross-curricular and curriculum overlap issues.

SS1

Information about the National Curriculum was provided from a variety of sources, including NCC, SEAC, DES and the LEA itself. LEA material included reports from a number of County Working

Groups that were established to offer guidance and support in specific subject areas, on cross-curricular issues and on issues that impacted on whole-school policies. These sources provided supporting material for the training that was undertaken at this time, which was mainly during INSET days when staff from schools could be trained simultaneously. Teachers in primary schools were supported in this training by a group of 35 Primary Support and Advisory Teachers and the intention was to match as closely as possible the support available to the training needs identified and expressed by schools (mainly through the production of their school curriculum development plans). The approach for secondary schools was to train senior staff (usually heads and one or more deputy) who could then plan and lead the INSET day(s) for their own staff.

SS2

DES/NCC documents have been and will be circulated to schools and used as part of any centrally organised INSET. Curriculum advisers are responsible for subject specific INSET relating to Level 3 work with the secondary phase. In the primary phase, the Co-ordinating Adviser for Curriculum 0-14 has overall responsibility and the task team consists of general primary advisers and curriculum advisers. To date, the centrally organised INSET has been largely subject specific but plans are well underway to deliver fully integrated cross-curricular INSET in future although there will still be some subject specific work.

In 1988-89, seven thousand teacher days of centrally organised INSET were delivered. These included: headteacher awareness days, days for curriculum co-ordinators in the core subjects, and days for classroom teachers affected by Keystage 1 in the core subjects. Significant support for the Advisory Service has also been given to school-based developments on INSET days.

MM

The Advisory Service has organised a series of seminars for senior managers of schools. The seminars have included/will include; information update, planning the whole curriculum, schemes of work, assessment and information requirements. Further time has been allocated for central meetings of curriculum leaders in order to enable them to begin preparation of schemes of work, and to equip them to carry out school based INSET.

Advisory teachers are supporting developments at school and classroom level. Much of the planning for the INSET programme has been done only in outline to enable a flexible response to be made to national developments during the year.

2 National Curriculum plans and school development plans

NM1

The Authority has developed a National Curriculum development plan guide book which has been presented to headteachers in a series of one-day workshops and has been used as a 'workshop manual' for generating each school's own development plan within a format common to all schools within the LEA.

A separate manual has been produced for primary and secondary, and advisors have been working with management teams in schools to produce a development plan which will provide the baseline for future interaction between the LEA and the school in the realm of monitoring and evaluation.

The development plan will be kept in a 'customised' loose-leaf folder so that sections can be updated and amended as required. A copy will also be lodged with the LEA advisory service for information. All schools are expected to have a National Curriculum development plan in operation by the end of October 1989.

MS

For the last three years the Authority has been encouraging schools to produce school development plans. The requirement that institutions should produce National Curriculum plans was a natural extension of this work.

In the spring and summer terms, headteachers' meetings were solely concerned with providing a structure for the production of individual development plans. A detailed document of guidance was produced; this document followed the usual cycle of evaluation of present situation, comparison with national requirements leading to the production of an Action Plan. These plans will be collated in the Autumn Term to produce the LEA's programme of INSET which will form the basis of future LEATGS budgets and submissions.

NM2

As part of their training programme, headteachers have agreed that the planning framework should be the LEA Entitlement Curriculum Policy which was designed to meet the requirements of Section 1 of ERA. Guidelines and a sample format have been distributed to schools. The discussion of plans with governing bodies is being timetabled during the 1989/90 academic year and governor training is emphasising the school curriculum plan as the starting point for successful local management.

SS1

The LEA gave schools advice and support in developing curriculum development plans in the comprehensive reports of the County Whole School Working Groups (primary and secondary) and colleagues in primary schools were also provided with supplementary exemplar material. The emphasis was on the use of the plan as a strategic planning tool for heads and governors, which could lay out a clear framework for the future. It was also recommended that the plan should be reviewed and, if necessary, revised annually and the links with LSM and resource allocation and information requirements were also stressed. Training for all primary teachers in whole-school review, using the GRIDS approach, had preceded the information about curriculum development plans and provided a procedure that would contribute directly to the production of the plan.

SS2

The LEA has no written policy or common *pro forma* for schools to complete, but there has been a major training input. In relation to secondary and special schools, the training, via deputy headteacher groups, was for developing curriculum programmes and was linked to TVEI. For primary schools, headteachers in groups considered the issues arising out of whole school planning.

MM

All schools have asked to prepare school development plans, incorporating National Curriculum requirements. The Advisory Service has offered assistance in the construction of these plans. It is intended that the school development plan will be an instrument for:

(a) identifying resource requirements and priorities;
(b) contributing to a staff development plan;
(c) providing a baseline for periodic school review.

The Authority has recently revised its curriculum policy with a view to providing a framework for the whole curriculum.

3 Extra or diverted resources for introducing the National Curriculum

NM1

In the present financial situation of the LEA – the Education Committee is seeking to reduce expenditure this year by about £4m – it has not been possible to provide extra resources for National Curriculum. There has been a major diversion of the time of advisors, advisory teachers, and teachers to enable the thrust of the development programme to be realigned to take account of National Curriculum in the context of the Sheffield Curriculum Initiatives. Some of the subject advisers, especially those concerned with core subjects, have had to neglect much of their normal work to facilitate the introduction of core subjects at Keystages 1 and 3.

MS

The LEA found an extra 84 secondary teachers for the current year and ten for 1990/91, and an extra 40 primary teachers for 1990/91. It has also provided an extra £0.5m for primary books and materials over the five years 1990-1995. INSET money has been used to assist teachers. A large percentage of the 1989/90 LEATGS has been directed to providing a complete range of teacher support.

In addition, both ESG and county development programme finances will be used to supplement resources, but not on a large scale.

NM2

Maximum use has been made of the opportunities for specific grant funding to provide additional advisor, advisory teacher and technical support for schools. In a reducing budget situation, the LEA's contribution has been found by diverting resources. No budget flexibility exists to provide schools with additional staffing or capitation.

SS1

Extra funds for introducing the National Curriculum were allocated by the Education Committee and much of the money was devolved to primary, middle and special schools in the first instance. ESG funds were also secured, specifically for introducing the National Curriculum, and several advisory teacher appointments were made from this source. Substantial local funds within the LEATGS were also diverted for this purpose and used, for example, to fund the County Working Groups mentioned above and dissemination of the material they produced. Support for introducing the National Curriculum was seen as the highest LEA priority and the securing of additional funds and diverting existing ones reflected this priority.

SS2

Existing resources were re-allocated from LEATGS to give approximately £500,000 for curriculum, including NC training. In addition, there was some topping up with LEA money. Some ESG funds were re-allocated for English. In 1989-90, the County Council voted £250,000 to support primary schools (approximately £1,000 per school). For 1990-91 the support will be £1.25m.

MM

The Authority has taken the view that the National Curriculum represents a confirmation of good practice. It has been the Authority's practice to provide adequate resourcing for good curriculum practice and at this stage the only additional funding made available has been a one off allocation of £876 (the cash equivalent of a Grade A allowance). The aim of this allocation is to provide a resource to be used at the discretion of the school in the management of change. The Authority is currently considering the need for non-contact time in primary schools, and pump priming funds to equip schools to teach those areas of the curriculum which have not been widely developed in the past – eg primary science and technology.

A consultant head has been appointed to support school based management development.

4 Monitoring its introduction

NM1

The school's National Curriculum development plan will be the baseline from which monitoring and evaluation will start. It is intended that there will be a partnership in monitoring and evaluation between the school and the LEA but the priority at present is seen to be coping with the work of introduction. There are very little resources, if any, left for monitoring the introduction itself.

MS

Although the Authority has no specific plans to monitor the immediate effects of the National Curriculum on children and schools, the developing and changing role of the County Inspectorate will be addressing this issue. This group of LEA officers are preparing detailed planned programmes of visits to schools, this programme will ensure that over a reasonable period of time all institutions will have been evaluated. A key component of the evaluation will be an examination of the effect of the National Curriculum on children and their activities in classrooms.

NM2

The whole staff training at school level during 1989 is being formally monitored and evaluated by the Advisory Team on a sampling basis and an evaluation report will be issued. The implementation of the NC will be monitored during the 1989/90 school year in two ways: pastoral advisors will be making a timetabled visit to all their schools each term and their observations will be logged; a structured sample of schools will be receiving more extended visits by a team of advisors to look at whole-curriculum planning and the introduction of the core subjects. In the local management context the LEA will be assisting schools in developing their own self-monitoring and review procedures which would include the provision of the National Curriculum.

SS1

The scheme devised for monitoring and evaluating the introduction of the National Curriculum in secondary schools was based on departmental and team reviews. These are conducted externally (by advisors of the LEA) and internally on a programmed basis, which avoids 'bunching' of the reviews. The same instruments and similar procedures are used for internal and external reviews, with moderation provided through a whole-school framework with external reviews being under the guidance of a nominated LEA officer and internal reviews under the guidance of the appropriate deputy head. Advantages of this scheme included the fulfilment of the LEA obligation to conduct regular and formal reviews of the National Curriculum (and other aspects of the Education Reform Act), enhancement of the quality of teaching and learning, reinforcement of the important quality control role of middle tier post holders and an increased flow of valid and reliable information which contributes to better planning and management for both schools and the LEA. Procedures in primary schools were developed from the whole-school review approach to monitoring and evaluation, with a reduced LEA involvement in the procedure itself (because of the large number of schools involved), but with LEA advisors and officers reviewing a representative sample of schools each year.

SS2

The introduction of the National Curriculum will be monitored as an integral part of the LEA's Institutional Monitoring and Review Scheme, which is firmly based on institutional self-evaluation. Education department staff will increasingly act as consultants to institutions, looking with them at their work rather than just at them. Institutions will be responsible for generating their own evaluative documents and for providing data and reports which will be shared with their local community, members of the county council and the staff of the education department. The monitoring and evaluation of individual institutions, in partnership with the LEA, will aim to integrate the reporting process across the three broad fields of individual curriculum and progress; overall curriculum and deployment of resources; the community context and the management of public funds.

The need for the LEA to take over the evaluation process on behalf of an individual institution is expected to be minimal and would only be necessary when a significant anxiety about local processes or issues existed.

MM

The Advisory Service is working on instruments for curriculum analysis and classroom observation. Effective monitoring and evaluation of the introduction of the National Curriculum will become possible when:

(a) all subject and cross curricular arrangements are known;
(b) assessment, recording and reporting requirements are fully established; and
(c) information systems are in place.

At present, monitoring and evaluation are dependent on reports from teachers which suggest that the majority feel ill-prepared and are anxious about the future.

At a more general level we intend to introduce a service wide approach to performance review which will seek to establish coherent connections between the assessment of the pupil, the appraisal of the teacher, the review of the institution and the LEA.

5 Revised role of advisors/inspectors and officers

NM1

The LEA is currently engaged in consultation on the future of the education service and the plan of the education department in it. The draft proposals anticipate the creation of support teams whose members would have the range of generic skills you would expect to see in a good headteacher. The intention would be that such officers should work very closely with institutions in the process of development plan formulation, implementation, review, revised development and so on. It is proposed such teams should have available to them specialist support in curriculum domains. In time such support might be identified by the institutions themselves but in the early years we would expect to use some of those officers presently designated advisor/advisory teacher. We see no place for the Inspector role in the future of the service.

MS

Connected to 4; the Inspectorate is now programming and detailing more fully and in an expanded way, the arrangements for visiting schools and evaluating procedures. Linked to and extended from school self-evaluation, outside evaluation from teams of Inspectors will be designed to support and promote forward planning and targeting future developments. The Inspectorate team is being increased by use of ESG finance, and more care and thought is taking place for recruitment of an Advisory Teacher team as the main source of in-service.

NM2

The Advisory Team is being enlarged and restructured to provide specialist support in all areas of the curriculum and improved co-ordination and monitoring of the work of advisors to promote cross-curricular working and a whole-curriculum perspective. In particular, it is felt that a functional role in relation to the whole team is more important for senior advisors than a phase role, given the blurring of the distinction between primary and secondary in the concept of ten attainment levels. It is not planned to separate the evaluation and support role at advisor level but to retain the duality. However, a time plan for each advisor will shift the balance towards monitoring and evaluation with a compensatory enhanced support role for advisory teachers.

SS1

An internal restructuring of the education department was undertaken to facilitate a more effective framework for the operation of the Advisory Service as the roles of advisers and officers developed and changed in response to the requirement to monitor and evaluate the operation of the Education Reform Act. Their increasing involvement in monitoring, evaluating and inspecting schools will of necessity reduce the time available for other aspects of their work which they have undertaken hitherto (such as delivering INSET, for example). In the longer term it is possible that the roles of officers and advisors may become less distinct, with each undertaking aspects of both types of work (officers involved in monitoring and review, for example). Changes in designation will reflect changes in role, where this is appropriate and helpful in clarifying their function to schools and colleges.

SS2

The monitoring and evaluation work of the education department is not seen solely as the province of the advisory service but as a partnership between advisors and officers, harnessing expertise to particular needs. It is expected that there will be a change of emphasis in the role of general advisors, with more time being spent on providing monitoring and evaluation support and rather less on direct INSET delivery. There will be a greater emphasis on programming the time of the advisors and ways will need to be found for the systematic collection, retrieval and sharing of information. Some officers will increasingly be concerned with curriculum matters.

At the suggestion of the institutions concerned, an experimental scheme will be put into operation in part of the County during 1989-90 whereby an institution will link with one member of the Education Department staff. This person, either an officer or adviser, will provide first line whole school support which will embrace issues previously dealt with by advisors and officers acting separately. The Authority welcomes this initiative since it believes that in the future LEAs will not need to have separate education officer and advisory posts and that existing staff will need to broaden their skills to meet the new situation.

MM

In anticipation of the requirements of the legislation and in support of the Authority's own view of schools' needs the senior elements of the Advisory Service have been restructured to place an emphasis on support for the whole school rather than subject specialisms. This has involved a separation of the function of general and specialist support. It is intended the general advisors will take on whole-school/whole-curriculum responsibilities including monitoring, institutional review including support for self-review; management of staff development programmes; co-ordination of curriculum and institutional development programmes.

Specialist advisors/advisory teachers will be deployed to support needs identified in School Development Plans.

Index